16. SEP. 1996

HEREWARD COLLEGE OF FURTHER EDUCATION
BRAMSTON CRESCENT
COVENTRY
CV4 9SW

THE NEW CAMBRIDGE SHAKESPEARE

GENERAL EDITOR
Brian Gibbons, *University of Münster*

ASSOCIATE GENERAL EDITOR
A. R. Braunmuller, *University of California, Los Angeles*

From the publication of the first volumes in 1984 the General Editor of the New
Cambridge Shakespeare was Philip Brockbank and the Associate General Editors
were Brian Gibbons and Robin Hood. From 1990 to 1994 the General Editor
was Brian Gibbons and the Associate General Editors were A. R. Braunmuller
and Robin Hood.

MEASURE FOR MEASURE

Since the rediscovery of Elizabethan stage conditions early this century, admiration for
Measure for Measure has steadily risen. It is now a favourite with the critics and has attracted
widely different styles of performance. At one extreme, the play is seen as a religious
allegory; at the other, it has been interpreted as a comedy protesting against power and
privilege.

Brian Gibbons focuses on the unique tragi-comic experience of watching the play, the
intensity and excitement offered by its dramatic rhythm, the reversals and surprises which
shock the audience even to the end. The introduction describes the play's critical reception
and stage history and how these have varied according to prevailing social, moral and
religious issues, which were highly sensitive when *Measure for Measure* was written, and have
remained so to the present day.

THE NEW CAMBRIDGE SHAKESPEARE

All's Well That Ends Well, edited by Russell Fraser
Antony and Cleopatra, edited by David Bevington
The Comedy of Errors, edited by T. S. Dorsch
Hamlet, edited by Philip Edwards
Julius Caesar, edited by Marvin Spevack
The Second Part of King Henry IV, edited by Giorgio Melchiori
King Henry V, edited by Andrew Gurr
The First Part of King Henry VI, edited by Michael Hattaway
The Second Part of King Henry VI, edited by Michael Hattaway
The Third Part of King Henry VI, edited by Michael Hattaway
King Henry VIII, edited by John Margeson
King John, edited by L. A. Beaurline
King Lear, edited by Jay L. Halio
King Richard II, edited by Andrew Gurr
Measure for Measure, edited by Brian Gibbons
The Merchant of Venice, edited by M. M. Mahood
A Midsummer Night's Dream, edited by R. A. Foakes
Much Ado About Nothing, edited by F. H. Mares
Othello, edited by Norman Sanders
The Poems, edited by John Roe
Romeo and Juliet, edited by G. Blakemore Evans
The Taming of the Shrew, edited by Ann Thompson
Twelfth Night, edited by Elizabeth Story Donno
The Two Gentlemen of Verona, edited by Kurt Schlueter
Titus Andronicus, edited by Alan Hughes

THE EARLY QUARTOS
The First Quarto of King Lear, edited by Jay L. Halio

MEASURE FOR MEASURE

Edited by
BRIAN GIBBONS

Professor of English Literature
University of Zürich

CAMBRIDGE
UNIVERSITY PRESS

Published by the Press Syndicate of the University of Cambridge
The Pitt Building, Trumpington Street, Cambridge CB2 1RP
40 West 20th Street, New York, NY 10011–4211, USA
10 Stamford Road, Oakleigh, Melbourne 3166, Australia

First published 1991
Reprinted 1995

Printed in Great Britain at the University Press, Cambridge

British Library cataloguing in publication data

Shakespeare, William *1564–1616*
Measure for measure – (The New Cambridge Shakespeare).
I. Title.　II. Gibbons, Brian *1938* Oct 8–
822.3′3

Library of Congress cataloguing in publication data

Shakespeare, William. 1564–1616.
Measure for measure/edited by Brian Gibbons.
　p.　cm. – (The New Cambridge Shakespeare)
ISBN 0-521-22227-3. – ISBN 0-521-29401-0 (pbk.)
I. Gibbons, Brian, 1938–　　.　II. Title.　III. Series:
Shakespeare, William, 1564–1616. Works. 1984. Cambridge
University Press.
PR2824.A2G5　1990　822.3′3 – dc20　90-38361　CIP

ISBN 0 521 22227 3 hardback
ISBN 0 521 29401 0 paperback

THE NEW CAMBRIDGE SHAKESPEARE

The *New Cambridge Shakespeare* succeeds *The New Shakespeare* which began publication in 1921 under the general editorship of Sir Arthur Quiller-Couch and John Dover Wilson, and was completed in the 1960s, with the assistance of G.I. Duthie, Alice Walker, Peter Ure and J.C. Maxwell. *The New Shakespeare* itself followed upon *The Cambridge Shakespeare*, 1863–6, edited by W.G. Clark, J. Glover and W.A. Wright.

The New Shakespeare won high esteem both for its scholarship and for its design, but shifts of critical taste and insight, recent Shakespearean research, and a changing sense of what is important in our understanding of the plays, have made it necessary to re-edit and redesign, not merely to revise, the series.

The *New Cambridge Shakespeare* aims to be of value to a new generation of playgoers and readers who wish to enjoy fuller access to Shakespeare's poetic and dramatic art. While offering ample academic guidance, it reflects current critical interests and is more attentive than some earlier editions have been to the realisation of the plays on the stage, and to their social and cultural settings. The text of each play has been freshly edited, with textual data made available to those users who wish to know why and how one published text differs from another. Although modernised, the edition conserves forms that appear to be expressive and characteristically Shakespearean, and it does not attempt to disguise the fact that the plays were written in a language other than that of our own time.

Illustrations are usually integrated into the critical and historical discussion of the play and include some reconstructions of early performances by C. Walter Hodges. Some editors have also made use of the advice and experience of Maurice Daniels, for many years a member of the Royal Shakespeare Company.

Each volume is addressed to the needs and problems of a particular text, and each therefore differs in style and emphasis from others in the series.

PHILIP BROCKBANK
Founding General Editor

CONTENTS

ILLUSTRATIONS

Illustration 2 is reproduced by permission of the Master and Fellows of Magdalene College, Cambridge; illustration 6 by permission of the Henry E. Huntington Library and Art Gallery; illustration 7 by permission of the Trustees of the Tate Gallery; illustrations 8 and 9*b* by permission of the Shakespeare Birthplace Trust; illustrations 9*a*, 10*a*, 10*b* and 4*a* by permission of Angus McBean; and illustration 4*b* by permission of Sophie Baker.

ACKNOWLEDGEMENTS

The scholarship of the past as well as the present concerning *Measure for Measure* is extensive, and it is a pleasure to acknowledge it, particularly in the work of three recent editors: Mark Eccles in his New Variorum edition (1980), with its large bibliography, G. Blakemore Evans in his Riverside Shakespeare (1974), with its judicious decisions on textual and lineation problems, and J.W. Lever, whose Arden edition of 1965 presented new and stimulating material. For more particular assistance of various kinds, all in their way valuable, I am indebted to the late Philip Brockbank, to David Bevington, A.R. Braunmuller, Peter Blayney, Ben Daniel, Jude Davies, Dieter Mehl, Kurt Tetzeli von Rosador, Peter Thomson and the Northcott Theatre, Exeter, the Librarian of the Brotherton Library, University of Leeds, Marianne Kaempf, Annette Kreis, Marion Pringle.

I owe a special debt to Robin Hood for his general editorial work on this edition, for his stimulating criticism and eagle eye for detail. At Cambridge University Press I thank the copy-editor, Paul Chipchase, for his exemplary attention to the manuscript, and Sarah Stanton for her help with the illustrations and much else. The drawings of C. Walter Hodges were produced with his customary vitality and good humour, and patience in handling my suggestions. The errors and mis-judgements that remain I do acknowledge mine.

Fulford–Leeds–Zürich   B.C.G.

PREFACE

Between the closing of the theatres by the Puritans at the time of the English Civil War in 1642 and the rediscovery of Elizabethan stage conditions in the period near the beginning of the First World War in 1914, *Measure for Measure* was not one of Shakespeare's more popular plays, either with readers or on the stage. Its outspokenness on sex, crime and social divisions, topics which increasingly polite society preferred not to mention, would perhaps have been enough to secure unpopularity, but in addition the play's exploitation of the mixed dramatic mode of tragi-comedy was not understood, especially by readers familiar only with neo-classical dramatic rules for comedy and tragedy. Certainly the play deals with painful experience, and to read it or see it performed may be a troubling as well as a humorous and moving experience, although in recent times admiration for it has steadily risen and since the end of the Second World War the play has been more and more frequently performed in the theatre. It is now a favourite with the critics; at the moment of writing it attracts the two most significant new approaches to literature, deconstruction and new historicism.

The mixed genre of tragi-comedy involved the bringing together of seemingly incompatible narrative materials and deliberately contrasting dramatic styles, which the dramatist would strive to combine in a design offering a spectacularly surprising conclusion, just when this seemed least possible. Perhaps it is more true of this play than of other Shakespeare plays that each fresh production presents it in a different shape by making its own choice of tone, rhythm and emphasis among a number of different yet most important issues. Yet where a selective emphasis may be the key to theatrical interpretation (as the stage history on pp. 51–72 shows) it is one of the duties of an editor to try to give recognition to the sheer variety of elements – heterogeneous and volatile though they may be – which Shakespeare includes in *Measure for Measure*.

Shakespeare is inspired to exceptional and adventurous artistry in imposing an answerable style on such materials. The release of such conflicting energies within the chosen frame is daring, and it is important to recognise the newness and complexity of the challenge he sets himself: the play, in performance, speaks for itself, its robust form sturdy enough for a stage interpretation giving release to the darkest forces, or to a performance in which the comic elements achieve control of the tone. The play's design generates energies which may not be harmonised – though they may be, sometimes, and with conviction – in its formal conclusion. The Introduction which follows on pp. 1–72 develops this sense of the play by three related approaches: though they may be read separately, they are also a continuous argument.

ABBREVIATIONS AND CONVENTIONS

Shakespeare's plays, when cited in this edition, are abbreviated in a style modified slightly from that used in the *Harvard Concordance to Shakespeare*. Other editions of Shakespeare are abbreviated under the editor's surname (Rowe, Eccles) unless they are the work of more than one editor. In such cases, an abbreviated series title is used (Cam.). When more than one edition by the same editor is cited, later editions are discriminated with a raised figure (Collier[2]). All quotations from Shakespeare, except those from *Measure for Measure*, use the text and lineation of *The Riverside Shakespeare*, under the general editorship of G. Blakemore Evans.

1. Shakespeare's plays

Ado	*Much Ado About Nothing*
Ant.	*Antony and Cleopatra*
AWW	*All's Well That Ends Well*
AYLI	*As You Like It*
Cor.	*Coriolanus*
Cym.	*Cymbeline*
Err.	*The Comedy of Errors*
Ham.	*Hamlet*
1H4	*The First Part of King Henry the Fourth*
2H4	*The Second Part of King Henry the Fourth*
H5	*King Henry the Fifth*
1H6	*The First Part of King Henry the Sixth*
2H6	*The Second Part of King Henry the Sixth*
3H6	*The Third Part of King Henry the Sixth*
H8	*King Henry the Eighth*
JC	*Julius Caesar*
John	*King John*
LLL	*Love's Labour's Lost*
Lear	*King Lear*
Mac.	*Macbeth*
MM	*Measure for Measure*
MND	*A Midsummer Night's Dream*
MV	*The Merchant of Venice*
Oth.	*Othello*
Per.	*Pericles*
R2	*King Richard the Second*
R3	*King Richard the Third*
Rom.	*Romeo and Juliet*
Shr.	*The Taming of the Shrew*
STM	*Sir Thomas More*
Temp.	*The Tempest*
TGV	*The Two Gentlemen of Verona*

Tim.	*Timon of Athens*
Tit.	*Titus Andronicus*
TN	*Twelfth Night*
TNK	*The Two Noble Kinsmen*
Tro.	*Troilus and Cressida*
Wiv.	*The Merry Wives of Windsor*
WT	*The Winter's Tale*

2. Other works cited and general references

Abbott	E.A. Abbott, *A Shakespearian Grammar*, 3rd edn, 1870 (references are to numbered paragraphs)
Alexander	*Works*, ed. Peter Alexander, 1951
Bald	*Measure for Measure*, ed. R.C. Bald, 1956 (Pelican Shakespeare)
Basilikon Doron	James VI and I, *The Basilikon Doron of King James VI*, ed. James Craigie, 1944–50
Bevington	*Works*, ed. David Bevington, 1980
Bullough	*Narrative and Dramatic Sources of Shakespeare*, ed. Geoffrey Bullough, 8 vols., 1957–75, II, 399–524
Cam.	*Works*, ed. W.G. Clark, J. Glover and W.A. Wright, 1863–6 (Cambridge Shakespeare)
Capell	*Comedies, Histories, and Tragedies*, ed. Edward Capell, [1768]
Chambers	*Measure for Measure*, ed. E.K. Chambers, 1956 (Red Letter Shakespeare)
Chapman	George Chapman, *Comedies*, ed. Alan Holaday *et al.*, 1970; *Tragedies*, ed. T.M. Parrott, 1910
Chaucer	Geoffrey Chaucer, *Works*, ed. F.N. Robinson, 2nd edn, 1957
Collier	*Works*, ed. John Payne Collier, 1842–4
Collier[2]	*Plays*, ed. John Payne Collier, 1853
Collier[3]	*Comedies, Histories, Tragedies, and Poems*, ed. John Payne Collier, 1858
Collier[4]	*Plays and Poems*, ed. John Payne Collier, 1875–8
Colman	E.A.M. Colman, *The Dramatic Use of Bawdy in Shakespeare*, 1974
conj.	conjecture
Craig	*Works*, ed. W.J. Craig, 1891 (Oxford Shakespeare)
Davenant	*The Law Against Lovers*, in *Works*, Part 2, 1673
Delius	*Werke*, ed. Nicolaus Delius, 1854–60
Durham	*Measure for Measure*, ed. W.H. Durham, 1926 (Yale Shakespeare)
Dyce	*Works*, ed. Alexander Dyce, 1857
Dyce[2]	*Works*, ed. Alexander Dyce, 2nd edn, 1864–7
Eccles	*Measure for Measure*, ed. Mark Eccles, 1980 (New Variorum)
ELH	*ELH: A Journal of English Literary History*
Evans	*The Riverside Shakespeare*, ed. G. Blakemore Evans *et al.*, 1974
F	*Mr. William Shakespeares Comedies, Histories, and Tragedies*, 1623 (First Folio)
F2	*Mr. William Shakespeares Comedies, Histories and Tragedies*, 1632 (Second Folio)
F3	*Mr. William Shakespears Comedies, Histories and Tragedies*, 1663–4 (Third Folio)
F4	*Mr. William Shakespears Comedies, Histories and Tragedies*, 1685 (Fourth Folio)
Geneva	Geneva translation of the Bible (1560)
Globe	*Works*, ed. W.G. Clark and W.A. Wright, 1864

Greene	Robert Greene, *Works*, ed. A.B. Grosart, 15 vols., 1881–6
Halliwell	*Works*, ed. James O. Halliwell, 1854
Hanmer	*Works*, ed. Thomas Hanmer, 1743–4
Hart	H. Chichester Hart, '"Measure for Measure": some additional notes' *N&Q*, tenth ser., 10 (1908), 63–4
Hart (1905)	*Measure for Measure*, ed. H.C. Hart, 1905 (Arden Shakespeare)
Hudson	*Works*, ed. Henry Hudson, 1851–6
Johnson	*Works*, ed. Samuel Johnson, 1765
Jonson	Ben Jonson, *Works*, ed. C.H. Herford and Percy Simpson, 11 vols., 1925–52
Keightley	*Works*, ed. Thomas Keightley, 1864
Kittredge	*Works*, ed. G.L. Kittredge, 1936
Knight	*Works*, ed. Charles Knight, 1840
Knight[2]	*Works*, ed. Charles Knight, 1842
Lever	*Measure for Measure*, ed. J.W. Lever, 1965 (Arden Shakespeare)
Linthicum	M. Channing Linthicum, *Costume in the Drama of Shakespeare and his Contemporaries*, 1936
Lyly	John Lyly, *Works*, ed. R.W. Bond, 3 vols., 1902
Malone	*Works*, ed. Edmond Malone, 1790
Marlowe	Christopher Marlowe, *Works*, ed. Fredson Bowers, 2 vols., 1973
Mason	John Monck Mason, *Comments on the Last Edition of Shakespeare's Plays*, 1785
MLR	*Modern Language Review*
Munro	*Works*, ed. John Munro, 1958 (London Shakespeare)
N&Q	*Notes and Queries*
Nashe	Thomas Nashe, *Works*, ed. R.B. McKerrow, 5 vols., 1904–10, rev. F.P. Wilson, 1958
Neilson	*Works*, ed. W.A. Neilson, 1906
Noble	Richmond Noble, *Shakespeare's Biblical Knowledge and Use of the Book of Common Prayer*, 1935
Nosworthy	*Measure for Measure*, ed. J.M. Nosworthy, 1969 (New Penguin)
NS	*Measure for Measure*, ed. J. Dover Wilson and A. Quiller-Couch, 1922 (New Shakespeare)
OED	*The Oxford English Dictionary*, ed. James A.H. Murray *et al.*, 12 vols., and supplement, 1933
Onions	C.T. Onions, *A Shakespeare Glossary*, revised by Robert D. Eagleson, 1986
Partridge	Eric Partridge, *Shakespeare's Bawdy*, rev. edn, 1968
Pope	*Works*, ed. Alexander Pope, 1723–5
Pope[2]	*Works*, ed. Alexander Pope, 2nd edn, 1728
Promos and Cassandra	George Whetstone, *Promos and Cassandra*, 1578, in Eccles
Rann	*Dramatic Works*, ed. Joseph Rann, 1786–[94]
RES	*Review of English Studies*
Ridley	*Measure for Measure*, ed. M.R. Ridley, 1935 (New Temple Shakespeare)
Rolfe	*Measure for Measure*, ed. William J. Rolfe, 1882
Rollo Duke of Normandy	In Francis Beaumont and John Fletcher, *Dramatic Works*, ed. Fredson Bowers, 1966–
Rowe	*Works*, ed. Nicholas Rowe, 1709
R.S.C.	Royal Shakespeare Company

SB	*Studies in Bibliography*
Schmidt	Alexander Schmidt, *Shakespeare-Lexicon*, rev. Gregor Sarrazin, 2 vols., 1902
SD	stage direction
SH	speech heading
Singer	*Works*, ed. S.W. Singer, 1826
Sisson	*Works*, ed. C.J. Sisson, 1954
Spenser	Edmund Spenser, *Works*, ed. Edwin Greenlaw *et al.*, 8 vols., 1932–49 (Variorum)
SQ	*Shakespeare Quarterly*
S.St.	*Shakespeare Studies*
S.Sur.	*Shakespeare Survey*
Staunton	*Works*, ed. Howard Staunton, 1858–60
Steevens	*Works*, ed. Samuel Johnson and George Steevens, 1773
Steevens[2]	*Works*, ed. Samuel Johnson and George Steevens, 1778
Steevens[3]	*Works*, ed. George Steevens and Isaac Reed, 1793
subst.	substantively
Theobald	*Works*, ed. Lewis Theobald, 1773
Thirlby	Styan Thirlby, MS. notes in eighteenth-century editions of Shakespeare, 1723–51
Tieck	*Dramatische Werke*, ed. Ludwig Tieck, 1831
Tilley	M.P. Tilley, *A Dictionary of the Proverbs in England in the Sixteenth and Seventeenth Centuries*, 1950 (references are to numbered proverbs)
Warburton	*Works*, ed. William Warburton, 1747
White	*Works*, ed. Richard Grant White, 1857–66
Winny	*Measure for Measure*, ed. James Winny, 1964 (Hutchinson Shakespeare)

Biblical references are to the Geneva Bible (1560), with modernised spelling.

INTRODUCTION

Date

An entry in the Revels Account Book records a performance of the play on 26 December 1604. Other pointers indicate that the play's first performance was probably in the same year. In the case of *Measure for Measure*, a play in which allusion to specific events and persons has been recognised, and which also seems to have links to certain closely contemporary plays of which the date of first performance remains uncertain, the discussion of the date is really inseparable from the discussion of the sources. I have therefore presented the full discussion of factors relevant to dating the play along with all the rest of the discussion of the sources at pp. 7–24 below.

There is a possibility that the text as it stands in the Folio includes changes made at a time later than of the first performance, and this is discussed, along with the question of the scribe and conjectures about authorship, in the Textual Analysis, pp. 193 ff. below.

Puritanism, political allusion and censorship

Shakespeare's title announces an idea – measure for measure – and he twice pointedly refers to it in the dialogue. This is in contrast to his sources Cinthio and Whetstone and to his own usual practice. *Measure for Measure* alludes to a famous passage in the New Testament of the Bible, Matthew 7.1–2 – 'Judge not, that ye be not judged. For with what judgement ye judge, ye shall be judged, and with what measure you mete, it shall be measured to you again' – and it takes up issues from the Sermon on the Mount in Matthew 5 and Luke 6 concerning retribution, justice and mercy. St Matthew's version of the Sermon on the Mount alludes to the proverbial concept of retribution as 'an eye for an eye and a tooth for a tooth' (5.38). In Shakespeare's *3 Henry VI* (2.6.55) the head of the Duke of York, which had been stuck by Clifford on the city gates, is exchanged for the freshly severed head of Clifford himself because 'Measure for measure must be answered'; but Christ taught that instead we should love our enemies (Matthew 5.44). If mercy is invoked to render justice temperate (another sense of 'measure') then retribution in turn will be limited to a not-to-be-exceeded measure. If great cruelty is answered by a free outpouring of love, however, the transformation that results is immeasurably joyful.

The passages from St Matthew and St Luke would have been so well known to most Elizabethans that very probably they would have taken the play's title to refer in the first place to those Gospels. Religious issues were sensitive, so such a title would probably arouse some suspicion, not only from religious extremist groups but also from the authorities. The royal proclamation of May 1559 had prohibited stage plays from dealing with 'either matters of religion or of the governance of the estate of the common weale', and this seems to have been interpreted as meaning 'forbidding direct treatment in plays of current public issues or the representation of important living persons'.[1] Topical allusions in the play[2] seem deliberate and obvious; at the same time, however, the mode of allusion is equivocal. In the play itself Shakespeare does emphasise the name of the location as the city of Vienna, a long way away from London, and the religious robes worn in the play are Catholic, which might have been intended to deflect any accusations that the play breaks the law. Shakespeare nevertheless does not allay suspicion that he is making covert allusion to current events, nor apparently does he wish to do so. Thus in 1604 Vienna, the play's setting, would be associated with the efforts of the Holy Roman Emperor to suppress Protestantism in nearby Hungary, and with the successful rebellion of the Protestants there.[3] In this sense therefore the play's emphasis on Vienna is an emphasis on religious extremism, though the oppressors are (perhaps conveniently for Shakespeare) Catholic. In Elizabethan England, on the other hand, it was now mainly Puritan extremism that expressed religious intolerance. The list of English Protestant martyrs collected by Foxe is long – there had been some three hundred during the Catholic Queen Mary's reign – but there were also some two hundred English Catholic martyrs under the Protestant monarch Elizabeth.

Measure for Measure's various plots focus on a law – capital punishment for fornication – that seems the stuff of fantasy and folk-tale, until one recalls not only the historical excesses of many fanatical religious regimes but the fact that in the sixteenth century some extreme English Puritans did indeed advocate the death penalty for fornication, and later, in 1650, during the Commonwealth, the death penalty for incest and adultery was for a short period actually introduced. It was a concession to a century of pressure from Puritan extremists.

Characteristic of this extremist vein in Puritanism is the pamphleteer Philip Stubbes, who, concerned with the general question of order in the state, sees threats everywhere, though in the over-simple terms of ascribing all problems to individuals and their neglect of religious teaching. He proposes in his *Anatomy of Abuses* (1581) that those who commit whoredom, adultery, incest and prostitution should 'tast of present death', though he remarks that his contemporaries are all too likely to be more merciful 'than the Author of mercie him selfe'. Stubbes is unhealthily excited by what he reviles, sadistically urging that those convicted of these sexual crimes should at least 'be cauterized, and seared with a hote yron on the cheeke, forehead, or some other parte' where all could see that they had been

1 Cited by Glynne Wickham, *Early English Stages*, 3 vols., 1959–81, II, part 1, p. 75.
2 See my discussion of these at pp. 21–4 below.
3 It is curious that Hamlet names Vienna as the location for *The Mousetrap* (the play performed before Claudius). He ironically says to the king that *The Mousetrap* cannot give any offence since it does not touch any local personalities, being merely 'the image of an action done in Vienna'.

branded. Stubbes deplores the laxity of magistrates in this respect: they 'wincke at [fornication] or els as looking thorowe their fingers, they see it, and will not see it' (sig. H6^r). These are terms like those Shakespeare's Duke uses when confessing to his previous lax rule of Vienna, and we are again reminded of the Duke when we read Stubbes's survey of rampant vice in sixteenth-century English society, seen as the product of lax upbringing of children: 'give a wild horse the libertie of the head never so litle, and he will runne headlonge to thyne and his owne destruction also ... So correct Children in their tender yeres' (F7^v). This recalls *Measure for Measure*:

> We have strict statutes and most biting laws,
> The needful bits and curbs to headstrong weeds,
> Which for this fourteen years we have let slip ...
>   Now, as fond fathers
> Having bound up the threatening twigs of birch
> Only to stick it in their children's sight
> For terror, not to use – in time the rod
> More mocked than feared – so our decrees,
> Dead to infliction, to themselves are dead,
> And Liberty plucks Justice by the nose,
> The baby beats the nurse, and quite athwart
> Goes all decorum.   (1.3.20–2, 24–32)

Stubbes voices the notorious extreme Puritan hostility to all customary social festivals and entertainments, which he claims only license 'swilling, gulling and carousing', being the occasion for gluttony and drunkenness, riot and sexual misbehaviour. Extreme Puritans believed acting plays to be an offence against religion. Stubbes says stage plays should be condemned and ought to be prohibited: 'If they be of divine matter, than are they most intollerable, or rather Sacrilegious, for that the blessed word of GOD, is to be handled, reverently ... not scoffingly' (sig. L5^r). Furthermore interludes and plays 'paint' before the spectators' eyes examples of all kinds of sin and mischief. Shakespeare, whose sense of the complexities of social structures and relationships is far ahead of extreme Puritan views, evidently had such Puritan invectives ironically in mind when designing and composing the complex debate of *Measure for Measure*. Stubbes may deliver threats: 'beware, therfore, you masking Players, you painted sepulchres' (sig. L5^v), but Shakespeare reverses this in *Measure for Measure*, where public figures treat the world as a stage for their maskings, and the Puritan, Angelo, explicitly confesses his moral hypocrisy when likening himself to a painted sepulchre (2.4.1–17).

    In his eloquent *Anatomie of Absurditie* (1589),[1] Nashe had mocked extremist Puritan pamphleteers like Stubbes and illustrated the chief features by which extreme Puritanism was recognised at the time. Shakespeare seems always to

---

1 Quotations are from Nashe, *Works*, I, pp. 20–2. J.J.M. Tobin has noticed a number of suggestive verbal parallels from *Pierce Penilesse*, some of which he has published in 'Nashe and *Measure for Measure*', *N&Q* (1986), p. 360.

have taken the closest appreciative interest in Nashe's work, and here Nashe's objections to Puritan extremism could well have been recalled to mind by Shakespeare when he was composing *Measure for Measure*.[1]

Nashe objects to the way such Puritans distort scripture: they make extremist polemic against life itself, declaiming against gluttony as if they themselves did not

---

1 Especially, perhaps, in the language and ideas of Pompey, and the verbal quickness of Lucio, although neither of these characters reflects the essential moral probity and humanity of Nashe.

1   Barnardine: 'I swear I will not die today for any man's persuasion.' Act 4, Scene 3: a reconstruction of the court performance at Whitehall, 26 December 1604, by C. Walter Hodges

eat food, against drunkenness 'as though they had beene brought uppe all the dayes of their life with bread and water', and against whoredom 'as though they had beene Eunuches from theyr cradle, or blind from the howre of their conception' (p. 20). Despite all this they enquire into 'every corner of the Common wealth, correcting that sinne in others, wherwith they are corrupted themselves' (p. 21).

Nashe compares them to actors adopting their stage roles; he turns Stubbes's obsession with attire and clothes, and the theatre, against him: 'the cloake of zeale, should be unto an hypocrite in steed of a coate of Maile; a pretence of puritie'. Extreme Puritans are ham actors: 'It is not the writhing of the face, the heaving uppe of the eyes to heaven, that shall keepe these men, from having their portion in hell. Might they be saved by their booke, they have the Bible alwaies in their bosome, and so had the Pharisies the Lawe embroidered in their garments' (p. 22). All Nashe's writings were banned in 1599 by official decree; another irony for Shakespeare to accommodate.

Moves were also intermittently made throughout the period to suppress plays, arrest actors and playwrights, and close theatres. The city authorities associated theatres with public disorder; the court was suspicious of plays because of their potential for political comment. Shakespeare personally, and his own plays (apart from *Richard II*), seem to have escaped punishment,[1] but Shakespeare and his company of players often needed the protection afforded by aristocratic sympathisers and patrons at court and in the Privy Council. Certainly it is clear from the trouble over *Sejanus*[2] (in which Shakespeare acted), and over the riskily topical *Tragedy of Gowrie*,[3] that in 1603–4 topical political allusion in plays was a serious matter. *Measure for Measure*, as a play no less concerned in its own way with the state and its government, and following in the same playhouse both *Sejanus* and *The Malcontent*, might well arouse the suspicion of the authorities. Perhaps it was for this reason that the threat to Lucio of execution for slander (and his last-minute reprieve) comes so very prominently right at the end of the play, a sign of the commended temperance, but also firmness, of the ruler.

Shakespeare does place obvious compliments to James I in *Measure for Measure*,[4] but it is worth noticing that they are incidental to the play's action, and the play's force does not depend upon them. Queen Elizabeth in 1586 had pointed to the power – and also the danger – which the public role of monarch had in common with that of the actor: 'We princes, I tel you, are set on stages, in the sight and view of all the world' (see 1.1.68 n.). Shakespeare seems nevertheless to have contrived

---

1 Nevertheless, seven years before *Measure for Measure*, in 1597, the London authorities had made major moves against the players. One occasion was the performing at the Swan theatre by Pembroke's Men of the play *The Isle of Dogs*, which was held to contain lewd and seditious matter. Its part-author, Thomas Nashe, was forced to flee London. His co-author, Ben Jonson, and Thomas Kyd were thrown into gaol. In another move the mayor and aldermen of the city induced the Privy Council to prohibit plays within the city and for three miles outside in the County of Middlesex, and two playhouses, the Theatre and the Curtain, were ordered to be pulled down. On 22 June 1600, the Privy Council order allowed that acting plays was 'not an evill in ytselfe' and might indeed 'with a good order and moderation be suffered in a well governed estate'. They conceded to city pressures in ordering some playhouses to be pulled down, but directed that two should be allowed. For the censorship of the deposition scene of *Richard II*, and a performance associated with the Essex rebellion of 1601, see the New Cambridge edition: Andrew Gurr (ed.), *R2*, 1984, pp. 6–7.

2 Jonson had to answer a charge of treason for writing *Sejanus*. See p. 23 n. 4 below.

3 This play was suppressed in 1604, apparently as a direct result of royal displeasure. Chamberlain speculated in a letter, referring to the play, that the reason was because 'it be thought unfit that princes should be plaide on the stage in theyre life time' (see p. 23 n. 4 below).

4 See the discussion below, pp. 21–4.

penetrating questions in this play about the Prince and the State,[1] force and fraud, about the actor and the ruler, even if he did also practise self-censorship.[2]

The sources and their shaping

Measure for Measure is based on folk-tale materials of an ancient and common European stock: these are the stories of the corrupt magistrate and the infamous bargain, of the disguised ruler, and of the substituted bed-mate. These stories each have the characteristic moral and emotional charge of primitive folk-tale. By the time he came to write *Measure for Measure* Shakespeare was already familiar with the sophisticated and psychologically realistic versions of such tales in the Italian novelle of Boccaccio and his followers.[3] He could confidently plan to combine several such stories by modifying their respective tone and force.

CINTHIO

The chief source for *Measure for Measure* is G.B. Giraldi Cinthio's *Hecatommithi* (1565, reprinted four times and then again in 1593, translated into French in 1583–4 and Spanish in 1590). The story of the corrupt magistrate and the infamous bargain is central to Shakespeare's play, and it is helpful to begin with Cinthio's version, even though it is not the earliest known,[4] because Cinthio brings out its complex intellectual and structural tension, and gives it a detailed naturalistic setting.

Cinthio's story[5] is set in Innsbruck (not, as in Shakespeare, Vienna). Juriste, the equivalent of Shakespeare's Angelo, is sent to rule Innsbruck by Maximilian, the Emperor of Rome, whose close friend he is. Juriste is warned by the emperor that he cannot hope for pardon if he offends justice, but (as Cinthio observes) Juriste, though pleased with the appointment, is not a man who rightly knows himself. Still, Juriste rules Innsbruck well for a long time, until he decrees that a young man

---

1 The use of the term 'Prince' in *Measure for Measure* may be intended to be recognised as an allusion to the treatise *Il Principe* (*The Prince*), a study of the science of power and the art of secular government by Niccolò Machiavelli (1469–1527). *Il Principe* was first published in 1513. Machiavelli's comedy *Mandragola*, with its equivocal friar-confessor and ironic story, first appeared in print in 1513 also.

2 On this speculative topic see the recent study by Annabel Patterson, *Censorship and Interpretation*, 1984.

3 Seven novelle by Boccaccio and his successors provide major sources for Shakespearean plots. Bandello is a source for *Romeo and Juliet* (1595) and *Much Ado* (1598); Ser Giovanni for *The Merchant of Venice* (1597); *Othello*, written very close to *Measure for Measure*, probably in 1603, also uses Giraldi Cinthio, and *All's Well*, probably later but possibly as early as 1603, uses Boccaccio. For a discussion of Shakespeare's whole concern with novelle, see the discussion by Leo Salingar, *Shakespeare and the Traditions of Comedy*, 1974, pp. 298–325.

4 Bullough, in the section on *Measure for Measure* (II, 399–524), prints an analogue from St Augustine and another from Thomas Lupton's book *Too Good to be True* of 1581. A number of historical parallels have been suggested, among them an interesting one in a letter from Vienna of 1547 printed by Lever in an appendix. For a discussion of such analogues, see Lever, pp. xxxv–vi and nn., and Eccles, pp. 387–92.

5 This following summary is based on the translation by Eccles, pp. 378–87.

accused of rape be beheaded (by contrast in Shakespeare Angelo is not seen ruling well and the pace is very quick). The young man's sister comes to plead for him. (This part of the story runs parallel in Shakespeare.) The sister is eighteen, beautiful, sweet-voiced, eloquent, and has been educated in philosophy. Her name is Epitia. She pleads that her brother is young – only sixteen; that he loves the woman he wronged and is ready to marry her; and that anyway the law is drawn up to strike terror rather than to be enforced. Juriste, she says, should apply equity and show himself merciful, not harsh. Juriste is impressed only by her beauty. He agrees to a stay of execution but privately determines to satisfy his lust for Epitia. She goes to her brother in prison, who asks her to plead for him once more. When she visits Juriste again he rejects her plea – unless she gives herself to him. She answers that her brother's life is very dear to her, but even dearer is her honour. (This corresponds to Shakespeare.) Juriste then says that if she does give herself to him, he might marry her. He tells her she must decide by the next day. Epitia goes to her brother in prison and begs him to prepare for death, since she cannot sacrifice her honour. He appeals to her on the grounds of natural feeling, their blood kinship, their personal affection for each other, and says it is certain that Juriste will marry her because she is so beautiful and gifted. Epitia then agrees to give herself up to Juriste's bargain and brother and sister embrace in tearful reconciliation. (In this and the following events Shakespeare differs.) Next day she tells Juriste her decision and he promises her brother will be saved. Then, after dining with Epitia and before taking her to bed, he secretly gives orders for the brother to be beheaded. Next morning he lets Epitia go home and promises that he will send her brother home to her.

The gaoler has the brother's body placed on a bier with the severed head at its feet, covered in a black cloth, and sent to Epitia, who, shocked and stricken with grief, but steadied by philosophy, pretends she is resigned to the situation; as soon as she is left alone she expresses her grief, and then meditates vengeance. Recalling the emperor's reputation for justice, she resolves to complain directly to him. She puts on mourning and travels alone and in secret to Maximilian. At the climax of her tale to the emperor she gives so great a cry and her eyes so fill with tears that the emperor and his lords stand 'like men pale as ghosts for pity'. (In the final phase there are close parallels to Shakespeare.) Juriste, without knowing why, is summoned and confronted suddenly with Epitia. The emperor sees Juriste is stricken by conscience and dismay, trembling all over. Epitia repeats her accusation, weeping, and calls on the emperor for justice. At first Juriste tries to flatter her but Maximilian rebukes him; then Juriste declares he had her brother beheaded to uphold the law. Epitia replies that Juriste has committed two sins where her brother committed one. Juriste pleads for mercy, Epitia for justice. Maximilian decrees that Juriste marry Epitia. After the marriage Juriste supposes his troubles are over, but Maximilian now decrees that he must suffer execution since he had her brother's head cut off. Now Epitia, who has been so inflamed against Juriste, suddenly has a change of heart – she decides that having accepted him as her husband she cannot now consent to his execution because of her. The emperor is deeply moved and the goodness he sees in her persuades him to grant her plea. So Juriste's life is saved and, recognising her generosity, Juriste lives with Epitia henceforward in love and happiness.

Cinthio then puts this exemplary tale in perspective: there is an audience, a group of ladies, who then discuss it. They find it hard to decide whether the justice or the mercy pleases them more; at first they would be happy if the rape of Epitia were punished, but it seems no less praiseworthy that her plea for mercy for Juriste should succeed. The more experienced conclude that mercy, in tempering punishment, is a worthy companion to royal justice, and leads to a certain moderation in the minds of princes.

There are two other novelle in Cinthio's *Hecatommithi* which should be noted; novella 52 tells of a governor who fails in his attempt to blackmail the wife of a merchant and dies confessing his corruption, and in novella 56 a tailor's wife, under the same kind of pressure from the judge, appeals successfully to the duke, who condemns the judge. Both these women, it will be noticed, refuse to surrender, unlike Epitia – but like Shakespeare's Isabella.

Cinthio later wrote a drama,[1] *Epitia*, on the subject, in neo-classical form, and made some significant changes to the story: he added a sister of Juriste named Angela who pleads for Juriste's life at the end, and there is a captain of the prison who disobeys Juriste's sealed letter commanding the beheading and saves Epitia's brother's life by substituting the head of a murderer who resembles him. These features are closer to Shakespeare. It is the revelation that her brother's life has been saved that changes Epitia's heart and makes her finally plead for Juriste's life.

Both Cinthio's versions of the Epitia story, though containing horrific events, atrocious cruelty and shocking surprises, show a lively intellectual interest in the arguments for and against mercy, and these arguments are related to the social and psychological factors influencing the protagonists; moral judgement is tempered by equity, or to put it another way, the general principle is shown to be in need of scrupulous modification by the particulars of a given case. Shakespeare's treatment of the story is in these respects like Cinthio's.

WHETSTONE

By contrast when we turn to *Promos and Cassandra*, the early Elizabethan treatment of the Epitia story by George Whetstone (1578), a tone of Puritan authoritarianism is struck right at the beginning in the play's supplementary title: 'Devided into two Comicall / Discourses. / In the fyrst parte is showne, the / unsufferable abuse, of a lewde magistrate: / The vertuous behaviours of a chaste Ladye: / The uncontrowled leawdenes of a favoured / Curtisan. / And the undeserved estim- ation of a pernici / ous Parasyte. / In the second parte is discoursed, / the perfect magnanimitye of a noble Kinge, / in checking Vice and favouring Vertue: /'. Whetstone's dramatisation[2] applies the presentational conventions of Morality drama to give an essentially typical, external account of character and situation, but

---

1 In 1573; it was published in 1583 after his death.
2 *Promos and Cassandra* was apparently not performed. Whetstone got it published as he was leaving on a long voyage; he was aged 28. He later published a novella version of the same story in his *Heptameron of Civill Discourses* (1582, reprinted in 1593 with the title *Aurelia*).

in being designed for practical performance on an Elizabethan stage, Whetstone's play did present Shakespeare with a model providing many ideas for dramatising and staging the narrative; it may well be that a number of scenes in *Measure for Measure*, especially those of public ceremony, were influenced by Whetstone. Whetstone emphasises his demonstration as showing 'the confusion of Vice and the cherising of Vertue', justifying the comic elements he adds to the story since 'with the scowrge of the lewde, the lewde are feared from evil attempts'. The play is dedicated to Fleetwood, the Recorder of London, whose duties involved him in trying to clean up the London underworld – an exasperating business, as the frequent tone of complaint in Fleetwood's letters shows.[1] Whetstone shows little curiosity about the social or psychological aspects of criminality, but his additional characters exhibit a vitality and humour which constitute a stronger challenge to Puritan attitudes than he apparently recognises. Furthermore, in accepting the structural conventions of English stage comedy of the time, Whetstone transmits the effect of counterpoint between the main plot concerning noble characters and sub-plots of trickery and low comedy, so that the comic episodes not infrequently give an ironically critical reflection of events in the main plot. A vivid instance of this is the sexual bribing of the corrupt official Phallax by the Courtesan abetted by her servant Rosko (a prototype for Shakespeare's Pompey), which parallels the bribe Promos offers Cassandra – that he will save her brother and perhaps marry her if she gives herself to him.

Promos the Deputy does not simply enforce the law – he revives a law that a merciful magistrate has allowed to fall into neglect. The condemned young man Andrugio has not committed rape but anticipated marriage, sharing a love relationship with his partner, who is here given a speaking part and a name. Shakespeare follows Whetstone here. At the opening of *Part 2* she has a solo scene before the supposed tomb of her beloved in the temple, expressing her grief and melancholy in an emotional speech and a mournful song. This gives an additional focus of sentiment to the story which Shakespeare may have thought valuable. The young man she mourns is saved by a sympathetic gaoler who substitutes a head, but (unlike that in *Epitia*) it is mutilated beyond recognition. Shakespeare again follows Whetstone. The young man then departs to hide disguised as a hermit in the woods. Only on learning of his sister's distress at her new husband Promos's impending death does he return.

Whetstone makes important additions of conventional Elizabethan kinds, in sub-plots and characters, to extend the themes of justice and government, which possibly influence Shakespeare. Whetstone's visualisation, in terms of Elizabethan staging, of these episodes of city life, prison, and the Royal Entry, could well have influenced Shakespeare and may indicate the kind of detail with which *Measure for*

---

1 See the letters of Fleetwood in Thomas Wright, *Queen Elizabeth and her Times*, 1838, e.g. pp. 164–6. G. Blakemore Evans quotes some vivid letters from Fleetwood in his anthology, *Elizabethan-Jacobean Drama*, 1987, pp. 8–9, 238. Fleetwood thought that the existence of theatres was the cause of much of the civil disorder he had to deal with day after day. He seems not to have been mollified, in the long run at least, by having Whetstone's play dedicated to him.

Measure's setting was realised in performance in 1604. He features the city's mayor, sheriff, aldermen, and upright officers, and directions call for the sword of justice, the keys of the city, the mace, royal letters patent, a proclamation, citizens' petitions, perhaps even the executioner's axe (*Part 2* 5.518). Recalling the Tudor interlude Vice, a favoured officer of Promos called Phallax perverts justice and develops a blackmail and bribery racket. Phallax is in turn sexually bribed by the Courtesan, who has been put out of business by Promos's strict rule. She is eventually arrested by officers of the law in the wake of the king's return and Phallax's downfall.

Whetstone makes the heroine Cassandra's first interview with Promos take place in the presence of the Sheriff, and follows it with a scene in which Phallax dispatches his henchmen as spies to detect likely citizens as targets for blackmail. Soon follows a partly comic macabre prison scene with the hangman, 'a great many ropes about his neck', commenting on his increased work-load under the Deputy. Then a procession of bound prisoners, including a woman and a gipsy, enters on its way to execution, led in a penitential hymn by a 'Preacher'. These dramatic emphases are taken over by Shakespeare, though his treatment differs very distinctly in particulars. Promos himself, in the final act of *Part 2*, is shown led by halberdiers in procession to execution, and passing Cassandra and Polina dressed in mourning.

In these ways Whetstone finds means to embed the Epitia story in a more fully realised city setting, and to develop parallels to the main plot. This too may have influenced Shakespeare's overall design. Significant effects are won through costume, as when the 'brave' gown of the Courtesan contrasts with the sombre mourning of Cassandra and Polina – something stressed when the Courtesan angrily resists when she is at last arrested: 'how now, scab? Hands off my gown!' Cassandra uses disguise as a page when going to Promos's bed, a romance motif like Andrugio's disguise as a hermit of the woods. He appears disguised again, in a 'long black cloak', in the final scene. The king's return is formally spectacular, accompanied by aldermen in red gowns and the sword bearer; Promos presents him with the sword of justice, the mayor presents him with 'a fair purse', and musical entertainment is performed during which the king is seen seriously talking with some of his council before leaving 'leisurably'. A later, equally formal scene presents the king receiving petitions for justice, when Cassandra makes her appeal in public.

Furthermore, in handling the narrative, Whetstone shows concern to create effects of melodramatic thrill and surprise which evidently interested Shakespeare, especially at this point in his career when tragi-comedy was a focus of his attention. A minor instance is the stage direction for the Gaoler's entrance '*with a dead man's head in a charger*' which comes directly after Cassandra's solo scene lamenting her loss of virginity. Only after her scene of shocked reaction does Whetstone reveal (to the audience only) that Andrugio is indeed still alive. A similar pattern is apparent in the conclusion in *Part 2* where the grief of Polina and Cassandra seems complete, Cassandra having given her condemned husband a last kiss as he proceeds to execution, and having sung her song of mourning, when a page enters to announce the astonishing news that her brother lives. Moreover Whetstone makes regular use of soliloquy as a means to depict the inner struggles of his chief characters, another feature paralleled in *Measure for Measure*, especially in Angelo's soliloquies at the end of 2.2 and the beginning of 2.4, and although his grasp of personal psychology is perfunctory (he makes virtually no use of imagery, and the rhetorical structure of the soliloquies is awkward) still there is some emotional force, as when in *Part 1* 3.1 Promos struggles with himself before Cassandra's second interview:

> Do what I can, no reason cooles desire,
> The more I strive, my fond affectes to tame:
> The hotter (oh) I feele, a burning fire
> Within my breast, vaine thoughts to forge and frame.
> O strange effecte, of blind affected Love.

Here, as in other crucial moments in the main plot, Whetstone achieves a forceful succinctness in the opening which is dissipated in what follows; another instance is Cassandra's outburst at the end of this interview:

> What tongue can tell, what thought conceive, what pen thy grief can show?

Shakespeare evidently knew *Promos and Cassandra* for some years before he wrote *Measure for Measure* (there is an allusion to it in *Love's Labour's Lost* of 1594),[1] so we may conjecture that external events and circumstances prompted his decision to base a play on it now, in 1603–4. The most important public events of the time concerned the accession of the new monarch James I in 1603. The city of London devised elaborate festivities of welcome for the king, and certain playwrights were involved in pageants at the triumphal arches erected for the royal entry to the city[2] first planned for the day of his coronation but delayed by an outbreak of plague and eventually accomplished the day James I opened his first Parliament, 15 March 1604. A Royal Entry of this kind features in *Promos and Cassandra* too.

Shakespeare, as a member of the leading company of actors in London, was directly involved in the new monarch's accession; James I honoured the company by becoming their patron, and their name changed from the Chamberlain's Men to the King's Men. With other leading players Shakespeare participated in the Royal Entry procession.[3] The King's Men would be invited to perform plays at court, and it was necessary for Shakespeare to take account of the new monarch's tastes and interests; *Measure for Measure*, a play on the theme of justice and temperance in princes, seems to be Shakespeare's first response.

---

1 See Richard David (ed.), *Love's Labour's Lost*, 1951, nn. to 5.1.113, 141, 500, 753, and Salingar, *Shakespeare and the Traditions of Comedy*, pp. 274–5, 304.

2 See illustration 2. See also John Nichols, *The Progresses, Processions and Magnificent Festivities of King James I*, 4 vols., 1828, 1, 325–99, for a full account.

3 Shakespeare and eight fellow actors wore the livery of grooms of the king's chamber in the

2   Triumphal arch erected in London for the Royal Entry of James I in 1604. From Harrison's *Seven Arches of Triumph* (1603–4)

procession of 15 March 1604. The king proceeded to Temple Bar from the Tower through a series of specially built ceremonial arches (paid for by the Freemen of the City) devised by Jonson, Dekker and others. The king had a canopy borne over him by eight knights and was preceded by two marshals on horseback, each attended by six suitably attired men. The route was railed, the livery companies having spread their streamers, ensigns and bannerets on top of the rails all the way from Marke Lane to Temple Bar. An oration was delivered by the Recorder of London and the king, queen and prince were presented with cups of gold. The conduits of Cornhill, Cheap, and Fleet Street 'that day ran with claret wine very plenteously', as Harrison puts it in his *Seven Arches of Triumph* (1603–4), reprinted in Nichols, *The Progress . . . of King James I*, 1, 328–34. The Fenchurch or 'Londinium' arch had gates 12 feet wide and 18 feet high.

3   Angelo, Escalus: 'Happy return be to your royal grace.' Act 5, Scene 1, as presented on a public playhouse stage: the tiring-house as triumphal arch: a possible reconstruction by C. Walter Hodges

SEVERUS

If events in the city of London in 1603–4 could have recalled Whetstone's play to Shakespeare's mind, the new monarch's declared interest in the ethics of government, in his newly reprinted work *Basilikon Doron*,[1] could have reminded Shakespeare of another work of Whetstone's, *A Mirrour for Magistrates of Cyties* (1584). There Whetstone is concerned with London and the urgent need to reform its vice and corruption, particularly brothels and gambling. Whetstone compares London's corruption to that of imperial Rome. Sir Thomas Elyot in *The Image of Governaunce* (1541) had recalled the commendable reform campaign of the Emperor Severus, who sometimes visited his city incognito, disguised in the 'habite of scholer of philosophie' or sometimes as a merchant, to observe the people and the conduct of the officers of the law. In repeating[2] this, Whetstone urged the need for 'informers' to report offenders, and Lever persuasively suggests that Shakespeare's 'Duke of dark corners' may have been suggested by Whetstone's phrase for such informers, 'visible Lightes in obscure Corners'.[3]

Severus, it is evident, became a model of the high-principled reforming ruler, while at the same time, as Elyot's description of his disguising shows, he conformed to a legendary type in folk-tale, and this aspect is exploited in a number of Elizabethan comedies featuring monarchs in disguise.[4] However, the potential of the disguise plot for subjecting the person in disguise to disconcerting home-truths about his own shortcomings (obvious in Shakespearean comedies such as *Much Ado*) is not seriously exploited in relation to the disguised-ruler story before Shakespeare; in the anonymous *Famous Victories of Henry V* it is interesting to notice a scene in which members of the watch in the city of London are seriously presented discussing the outrageous conduct of the future king; this perspective evidently interested Shakespeare, and is accommodated among other perspectives on monarchy in his two *Henry IV* plays. In fact Shakespeare seems to have been the first Elizabethan dramatist to use the disguised-ruler story as a frame plot, for in the *Henry IV* plays he shows the future Henry V, Prince Hal, consciously choosing to re-enact the role of the disguised ruler, choosing to adopt the disguise of a prodigal and so observe the people and the officers of the law,[5] in the mode of Severus, as a prelude to thorough reform. The psychological pressure and

1 Privately printed in Edinburgh in 1599, reprinted in London in 1603 in a number of editions. Bacon's remark that it fell 'into every man's hand' (*Works*, ed. Spedding, Ellis and Heath, 14 vols., 1857–74, VI, 278–9) is cited by Schanzer, *The Problem Plays of Shakespeare*, 1963, p. 122.
2 See Mary Lascelles, 'Sir Thomas Elyot and the legend of Alexander Severus', *RES* 2 (1951), 305–18, and the same author's *Shakespeare's 'Measure for Measure'*, 1953, pp. 101–2.
3 Lever, p. xlv.
4 On this topic see V.O. Freeburg, *Disguise Plots in Elizabethan Drama*, 1915, reprinted 1966, and Rosalind Miles, *The Problem of 'Measure for Measure'*, 1976, pp. 125–60. Rowley in *When You See Me You Know Me* (1604) presents Henry VIII going one night in disguise to observe his city's 'government'. He meets a constable, a murderer and some prisoners, and gets involved in a fight, but the episode recalls non-satiric popular plays rather than other disguised-ruler plays of 1604; Marston's *The Fawn*, probably written in 1604 after *The Malcontent*, indicates that this type of satiric play was fashionable.
5 See *1H4* 1.2.195–217.

political riskiness involved in the scheme are explored with hitherto unexampled intelligence and imaginative power in the *Henry IV* plays.

It is important to notice, at the same time, that while the analogy with Severus is a high compliment, Shakespeare had demonstrated in *Henry V* that when disguise removed the protection of rank a prince could find himself facing extremely awkward questions posed with unwonted clarity and directness. In this sense, the disguised-ruler tale offered intellectual interest of the same high order as that of the corrupt magistrate, and comparison with two plays by contemporaries of Shakespeare, Middleton's *The Phoenix* and Marston's *The Malcontent*, helps to illuminate the degree to which Shakespeare exploited the sheer intellectual interest of the material.

THE PHOENIX

There is no certainty about the date of Middleton's comedy *The Phoenix*, though it seems to be early Middleton. The title page of the first edition of 1607 declares it to have been played by the Paul's boys 'before his Maiestie', and Chambers thought this could have been on 20 February 1604, but earlier dates have also been plausibly proposed.[1] The chief similarity with Shakespeare's play is in the overall frame plot: the ageing Duke of Ferrara has been a lax ruler for 'seven, nay seventeen years' (1.1.106) and complaints against corruption have been neglected. His son Prince Phoenix apparently goes on a long journey abroad, but in fact adopts disguise to fulfil a plan 'to look into the heart and bowels of this dukedom and, in disguise, mark all abuses ready for reformation or punishment' (1.1.99). With Fidelio (a trusted confidant), Phoenix witnesses or becomes agent in a series of minor intrigue plots. There are references to many popular topics of Elizabethan satire, as when a groom at an inn justifies accepting an unsavoury clientele: 'if we should not lodge knaves, I wonder how we should be able to live honestly: are there honest men enough, think you, in a term-time to fill all the inns in the town?' Other episodes concern a jeweller's adulterous wife, a corrupt lawyer, and a Justice who is the focus for a series of instances of wrongful manipulation of the law. Interspersed soliloquies from Phoenix *in propria persona* deliver sombre moral meditation on what he observes. Phoenix contrives to engineer the exposure of a plot among courtiers to overthrow his father, the Duke; in a final trial scene he appears in disguise, and confesses that he has been an accomplice in several plots; when the guilty courtiers come forward to arrest him they are themselves exposed by a document Phoenix has already handed to the Duke. Dramatic tension is created by suspense in this scene, which concludes in the revelation of Phoenix's true identity and the completion of the disguised-ruler frame plot.

Because what is simple in Middleton is complicated in Shakespeare it has

---

1 See E.K. Chambers, *The Elizabethan Stage*, 4 vols., 1923, III, 439. R.C. Bald proposed 1602 in 'The chronology of Middleton's plays', *MLR* 32 (1937), 36.

recently been argued[1] that it is more likely that *The Phoenix* is the earlier play. Phoenix undertakes to travel in response to a villain's suggestion, and the preceding lax rule is his father's; in *Measure for Measure* the Duke himself devises the deceptive scheme of travelling abroad, and his purpose is to observe both abuses in Vienna and Angelo's conduct as magistrate; the Duke also emphasises that he himself is at fault for the years of lax rule. Shakespeare interiorises within his Duke elements that in the Middleton play are mainly of narrative consequence: the figure of authority is distinct from the disguised observer, who is young, and whose schemes are wittily contrived to preserve his moral integrity, maintaining a distance from the somewhat compromised mature Duke. The ironic tone of the dialogue concedes that corruption is inevitable, though the upright maintenance of law is vindicated; but despite the serious nature of some of the issues, this play is more exuberant than might have been expected if Middleton were responding to *Measure for Measure*. There are certainly close connections between the two plays at the beginning and at the end but the dramatic styles are quite distinct. The question of which came first remains uncertain but indications do suggest Middleton. Comparison makes clear how much more morally and psychologically complex the situation in Shakespeare's play is, where the roles of Phoenix and his father are fused in the Duke, and then this plot is entwined with other plots producing parallels and interconnections which have no equivalent in Middleton, where the frame plot is used to allow the exhibition of folly and vice in a sequence of episodes connected by the common presence of Phoenix.

THE MALCONTENT

In the case of *The Malcontent* there is also a frame plot, but this is not at first apparent, since the duke-in-disguise is already established in the role of Malevole when the play opens, and the audience do not learn of his other identity until 1.3.155 when he is left alone on stage and delivers an expository soliloquy. In the middle of the play Malevole is involved in counter-intrigues to prevent a number of murders; he conceals from certain characters that these murder plots have failed, so that their moral dispositions should fully respond. The political action in the play is violent, and concludes in the toppling of a tyrannous usurper who holds sway at the beginning. As in Shakespeare's version the action places stress on characters' attitudes to sex as a guide to their moral and social condition and psychological motivation; the bawd Maquerelle cynically but forcefully complains of a lady's chastity that it 'had almost brought bed-pressing out of fashion'. *The Malcontent* is emphatically concerned with courtly ambition, flattery, and tyranny; but Malevole reclaims Pietro, Aurelia and Ferneze to virtue, and does not deign to punish his enemies with the worst penalty after recovering his power. In contrast to

---

1 See the argument by Thomas A. Pendleton, 'Shakespeare's disguised duke play: Middleton, Marston, and the sources of *Measure for Measure*', in *Fanned and Winnowed Opinions, Shakespearean Essays Presented to Harold Jenkins*, ed. John W. Mahon and Thomas A. Pendleton, 1987, pp. 79–97.

Shakespeare's play, however, this is achieved *not* through his own successful plots, but rather through a popular uprising against his usurping enemy, a providential and surprising outcome, perhaps intended to be recognised as the counterpart of the individual spiritual reclamation to virtue which he achieves with certain characters.

Some features of language, structure and narrative suggest links between *The Malcontent* and *Measure for Measure*. It needs to be taken into account that both *The Phoenix* and *The Malcontent* were written for the so-called Children's Companies, the troupes of boy actors at Paul's and Blackfriars. It may be that this explains, in Middleton's play, a brightness of style, the witty plotting, and the emphatic youth of Phoenix himself, features which contrast, as we have noted, to *Measure for Measure*. *The Malcontent* is a special case, however, as it was acquired by Shakespeare's company, and certain additions were made before it was performed by the King's Men. Shakespeare, as the chief playwright and a sharer in the company, would probably have been involved in approving the additional material written for the Globe performance of *The Malcontent*, and there are a number of apparent verbal echoes of Marston's play in *Measure for Measure*.[1] Although it is uncertain whether *The Phoenix* preceded *Measure for Measure*, it is much more probable that Shakespeare did know *The Malcontent* when he was writing *Measure for Measure*.

Marston's play was published in 1604 and entered in the Stationers' Register on 5 July; it cannot have been written earlier than the publication of its chief source, *Il Pastor Fido*, in 1602. It seems likely that since the Induction must have been written after the actor John Lowin joined the King's Men, this must have been after 12 March 1603 when he is recorded as still with Worcester's Men: he is listed in the cast of *Sejanus*, which was performed before the end of 1603.[2] This would indicate that *The Malcontent* was probably performed by Shakespeare's company in early 1604. Like *The Phoenix*, its disguised-ruler frame plot tends to separate the character in disguise (here Malevole, a bitterly pessimistic railer) from Altofront, the figure of authority, but although in Marston's play Malevole is a vividly realised presence and Altofront is somewhat static and remote, they are one person according to the narrative. The style of performance in the Children's Companies did not favour the representation of fully realised personalities, but Marston is clearly, in any case, imaginatively drawn to Malevole and gives

---

1 The verb 'touze', which occurs in *The Malcontent* at 3.3.62, 3.5.19 and 4.5.145, is used only once by Shakespeare, in *MM* 5.1.307. The proverb 'there are but a pair of shears between us', only once used by Shakespeare (*MM* 1.2.23), is in *The Malcontent* at 4.5.116. For references to the 'burr' and 'serpigo' in *MM* 4.3.165 and 3.1.31, compare *The Malcontent* 2.3 in successive lines, 31 and 32. Isabella's phrase 'the heavy / Middle of the night' (4.1.31–2) is parallel to Marston's Mendoza in 2.5.88, 'the immodest waist of night'. A parallel between Marston's *Satire IV* 107–8, 'Why thus it is when Mimic Apes will strive / with Iron wedge the trunks of Oakes to rive', and Isabella's reference to an 'angry ape' and splitting an oak in the same speech (2.2.120–4) seems clear, though it does not directly reveal evidence of a knowledge of *The Malcontent*, nor does the reference to the title of a poem by Marston at 3.2.45. I owe some of these points to Lever and to Pendleton, 'Shakespeare's disguised duke play'.
2 See G.K. Hunter (ed.), *The Malcontent*, 1975, p. xliv, n. 2.

Altofront less life. In the middle part of *The Malcontent* Malevole is involved in counter-intrigues against murder plots, and these correspond in their darkness of tone to elements in the Angelo–Isabella narrative in *Measure for Measure*. If Shakespeare was already thinking about dramatising the Promos and Cassandra story when *The Malcontent* came to his attention, he might have seen the usefulness of the disguised-ruler frame plot in allowing him to articulate in effect a double main plot, so outgoing Marston's play.

THE MODE OF TRAGI-COMEDY

The Malcontent reflects its source, *Il Pastor Fido*, in structure and mode, and Guarini's work deliberately sought the creation of heroism and pathos associated with tragedy. Shakespeare's narrative in *Measure for Measure* is composed of distinct though parallel stories, and he needed a means of uniting them in a conclusion where their strikingly diverse tones and modes might be given resolution. It is not only in his sources but in his methods that Shakespeare recalls Italian precedent, for the fashionable interest in Jacobean London in tragi-comedy, associated with the publication of *Il Pastor Fido* in 1602, should not obscure the fact that experimentation with genre and the invention of hybrid forms are the very stuff of sixteenth-century Italian drama as well as characteristic of Shakespeare. Furthermore Shakespeare was evidently greatly interested in the new mode of tragi-comedy, and *The Malcontent* offered an example of how the Italian drama might be adapted; this could have added fuel to Shakespeare's further development of hybrid dramatic forms, his versions of tragi-comedy, in which Italian novella narrative, satiric and comic depiction of the contemporary social scene in England, and mixtures of elements of tragedy and romance, might be flexibly combined in dialectical treatment of major problems of moral and social philosophy. At the time Shakespeare wrote *Measure for Measure* he also produced *Othello*, a play astonishingly different from it; yet both link to *Much Ado*, they utilise common elements and all are based on Italian novelle – but to extremely various effect. If *Othello* can be recognised as a lyric tragedy wrought from the stuff of cinquecento Italian comedy and elements of romance, *Much Ado*, a romantic comedy, can be seen to combine English popular comedy with Italian and Plautine elements and a tragi-comic strain.[1]

Like *Much Ado*, *Measure for Measure* has two major plots. Terence in *Andria* had combined two plots and defended the principle *as* a principle, that of *contaminatio*. The dramatist Caro in 1543 praised himself for interweaving three plots in *Gli straccioni*, and in the later sixteenth century in Italian *commedia erudita* the principle

---

1 In Shakespeare names are often important, and several names in *Measure for Measure* significantly recall previous plays: Claudio is the opposite of his namesake in *Much Ado About Nothing*, who thinks a dowry very important and rejects his bride in church; Juliet is secretly married, as in *Romeo and Juliet*, a play which like *Much Ado* and *Measure for Measure* has a friar who devises an elaborate deception concerning someone supposedly dead; and *Much Ado* develops from *Romeo and Juliet* the form of extremely complicated and exciting final scene, which Shakespeare again utilises in *Measure for Measure* and *All's Well That Ends Well*.

of *contaminatio* led to the practice of deliberate combination of generically incompatible elements – comic, tragic, romantic – not merely multiple intrigues. These hybrids were often strong in romantic elements and episodes of heroism and pathos usually associated, by Renaissance theorists, with tragedy exclusively. The travelling players of the *commedia dell'arte* borrowed from the printed literary texts of *commedia erudita* in revitalising their scenarios for improvisation, as well as performing the written plays.[1] Both kinds were composed from a repertory of conventionalised narrative motifs, plot situations, scenic forms, set characters, set situations and dialogues and attitudes, such as the inamorata as transvestite page to her beloved, the rigged trial of claims to valour or virility, the debate between rustic and elegant figures in pastoral guise. These might be chosen in various combinations and emphases to figure in narratives composed of individual units from the stock of romance and folk-tale; the concern with new and surprising combinations was emphatic.[2]

In order to bring his two main plots in *Measure for Measure* to a conclusion generating the maximum excitement, wonder and astonishment, Shakespeare adds the Mariana plot, a narrative motif from another novella, one by Boccaccio.[3] In his handling of the Angelo–Isabella story he had already chosen a version of the corrupt magistrate story in which the reaction of the condemned man's sister to the bribe is a surprising refusal. The sister's high principles seem to point to a tragic outcome. With the addition of Mariana Shakespeare provides for increased strangeness. The pastoral setting of the Mariana plot suggests its marked generic association with pastoral tragi-comedy. The treatment of the Mariana story is strongly romantic. The description of the place of assignation in 4.1.25 ff. is remarkably unlike the language of the rest of the play, with its Gothic 'circummured' and 'planchèd' and the obvious erotic allegorical significance of the place and action described. The song is consonant with this mode, but sufficiently unexpected to prompt some scholars to suppose it not part of

---

1 See also Salingar, *Shakespeare and the Traditions of Comedy*, pp. 190–1, and Louise George Clubb, 'Shakespeare's comedy and late cinquecento mixed genres', in *Shakespearean Comedy*, ed. Maurice Charney, 1980, pp. 129–40.

2 This experimental interest in hybrid forms and modes is more dynamic than routine sixteenth-century English mingled comedy with its noble romance and popular low comedy and its mixture of barely co-ordinated elements, topical and musical. Such medleys, or romantic fantasies with low comic sub-plots, were a popular staple of the first amphitheatre playhouses in their early years (1567 was the year the Red Lion opened, Burbage's Theatre opened in 1576 and the Curtain the next year). Whetstone in 1578, like Sidney, Gosson, and others, mocked these popular comedies for their artlessness, but the attacks presumably indicate that the plays were liked by audiences. See Andrew Gurr, *Playgoing in Shakespeare's London*, 1987, for an account of the development of different kinds of audience at the time. For sixteenth-century English comedy, see Madeleine Doran, *Endeavours of Art*, 1954, Louise George Clubb, 'Italian comedy and *The Comedy of Errors*', *Comparative Literature* (1967), pp. 240–52, and Salingar, *Shakespeare and the Traditions of Comedy*.

3 *The Decameron*, the ninth novella of the third day, written 1348–58; Shakespeare may have come across the motif in the English version by William Painter in *The Palace of Pleasure* (1566, published again in 1569 and 1575). The successful use of the 'bed-trick' by the heroine in the Boccaccio story, Giletta, not only ensures the consummation of her marriage to her unwilling husband, it also brings her pregnancy and two sons.

Shakespeare's design. Yet the Duke's account of how Mariana's dowry was lost in the wreck with her brother Frederick, who drowned on the 'perished vessel' (3.1.200–12), is an obvious romance motif, recalling the story of Antonio in *The Merchant of Venice*, to go no further. Between this and the social and psychological realism of the Angelo–Isabella story, there is an incompatibility; but it is evident that Shakespeare deliberately chose this. The tale of the substituted bed-mate was susceptible of a wide variety of treatment.[1] It is its strong romance atmosphere here which is Shakespeare's firm hint that unexpected and conflicting elements, in new and surprising combinations, are building to a climax he defies us to anticipate.[2] The bed-trick motif adds to the concern with providence – and perhaps miracle – in *All's Well* (which like *Measure for Measure* touches the serious and noble in its exciting climax of multiple disclosures) but it has a more central place there. In *Measure for Measure* it is used to connect the two major plots, and to give a decisive new ingredient to the last phase of action.

CONTEMPORARY ALLUSIONS

The question of what constitutes a source for a play for Shakespeare is complex, especially when, as a mature dramatist, he has his own previous work before him; it has therefore seemed important to cast the net wide in this survey. Traditionally in such studies pride of place is given to written texts and specific verbal parallels, but in shaping a play a dramatist may well adapt structural patterns and stagecraft from other plays, features not of a verbal, but a physical and visual language of theatre. In addition, a dramatist may imitate in his play episodes and characters from the real life of the time; in the case of *Measure for Measure* it is hard to deny certain events of 1604 the status of minor sources in this sense. I shall now discuss some probable sources and allusions which illustrate the complex interplay of these different categories – written imaginative literature, staged plays, historical events – and point to their close connection with the dating of the play. The matters now to be discussed strongly indicate 1604 for the first performance.

When, after James became king in 1603, the city of London was preparing for the Royal Entry to the city which took place in early 1604, Shakespeare might have remembered that Whetstone's play showed similar preparations. A carpenter in the play is instructed to erect a stage, in preparation for the king's entry, as 'St Anne's Cross', and the Merchant Taylors are assigned 'Duck Alley' for their pageant of Hercules. On his arrival the king is shown being welcomed at a formal reception. Whetstone seems to have London in mind here, though he calls his city 'Julio', and his king is King of Hungary. A number of specific allusions to James I have been suggested. James I's book *Basilikon Doron* was naturally the subject of much attention when it was reprinted in 1603, the year of his accession (Bacon said the book was in every man's hand). It emphasised the importance of

---

1 See E.A.J. Honigmann's excellent essay 'Shakespeare's mingled yarn and *Measure for Measure*', *Proceedings of the British Academy*, 1981, pp. 101–21.
2 That the substituted bed-mate story is also used for *All's Well* does not prove that Shakespeare only knew of such a story from his reading of Boccaccio.

temperance. Acknowledging the element of public display required of a prince, James stressed nevertheless that a prince should show virtue in action and cultivate it as a private inward state, warning against hypocritical outward show and empty words. He also confessed that he had been insufficiently strict at the beginning of his rule, and expressed strong disapproval of 'unreverent speakers';[1] these are elements which Shakespeare gives special emphasis in his Duke at the beginning and end of *Measure for Measure*, and which were no doubt intended to be recognised as allusions to the new king.

It has been argued that certain of the narrative elements at the beginning of *Measure for Measure* need not be supposed to derive from Middleton's play, being available in a prose narrative by Barnaby Riche, *The Adventures of Brusanus Prince of Hungaria* (1592).[2] This romance offers a king whose sudden departure, actually to travel his kingdom disguised as merchant, leaves his subjects prey to conflicting rumours about him. He encounters a braggart courtier who fails to penetrate the disguise and later charges the supposed merchant with treasonable talk; there is a trial scene before the king's son, and finally the king is recognised and the courtier banished.

While Shakespeare may have known Riche's story, I believe those sources already in dramatic form would have been more likely to have a strong influence on him. But furthermore the allusion in the play to Hungary points perhaps more plausibly to current events than to the suggested source, Riche's *Adventures of Brusanus*. This brings under consideration a further type of source, events in real life at the time of the play's composition. 'The Duke of Holst is here still procuring a levie of men to carie into Hungarie', wrote John Chamberlain from court on 10 December 1604. This duke was Queen Anne's brother, Ulrich of Holstein. Hungary was at this time partitioned between the Turks and the Holy Roman Empire, and Turkish support was given to the new King of Hungary, a Protestant, who was installed in 1604. Such events seem to be alluded to in the dialogue between Lucio and the Gentlemen in 1.2 of *Measure for Measure*.[3] It is likely that such allusions would be more appropriate at court than at the Globe, and it is now accepted that the entry in the Revels Accounts – 'By his Ma[tis] plaiers. On St. Stiuens Night [i.e. 26 December 1604] in the Hall A Play called Mesur for Mesur. Shaxberd.' – is genuine,[4] and that this court performance was preceded by public performance at the Globe.

1 See the discussion by Schanzer, *Problem Plays of Shakespeare*, pp. 120–5, building on David L. Stevenson, 'The role of James I in Shakespeare's *Measure for Measure*', *ELH* 26 (1959), 188–208, as well as earlier scholarship by George Chalmers (1799) and Louis Albrecht (1914). Lever cites several passages from *Basilikon Doron* on pp. xlviii, xlix and li. A further excellent discussion is in Josephine Waters Bennett, *'Measure for Measure' as Royal Entertainment*, 1966, pp. 82–104.
2 The relevance of Riche's tale as a possible source is suggested by Bullough, and he prints extracts on pp. 524–30.
3 This was first noted by Bennett, *'Measure for Measure' as Royal Entertainment*, pp. 10–11, in 1966, and seems almost certain. If so, this would be further evidence that whatever revisions were made to the text of the play elsewhere, the dialogue at the beginning of 1.2 was written in 1604. See the Textual Analysis, p. 199 below.
4 See Alfred Stamp, *The Disputed Revels Accounts*, 1930, and E.K. Chambers, *William Shakespeare*, 2 vols., 1930, II, 331.

Lever noticed the possible relevance of attempts to secure peace with Spain, which James I pursued during 1604 and which was ratified on 19 August, following a conference attended by delegates from Spain and the Austrian Netherlands on 20 May 1604.[1] Lever, unaware of the evidence of Chamberlain's letter about the Duke of Holstein, supposed the allusion in 1.2 of the play to be solely to the peace with Spain, but quotes some significant comment in Stow's *Annales* on the anxiety among those 'pretended gallants, banckrouts, and vnruly youths' who stood to benefit from continuing war with Spain. Stow speaks of their being 'setled in pyracie', which would be a closer confirmation of Lever's case had it not been first published eleven years later. Stevenson cites an account from a tract, *The Time Triumphant*, entered in the Stationers' Register on 27 March 1604, describing a would-be secret visit by James I and his queen to observe the Royal Entry decorations in the city.[2] A rumour of the royal visit spread and a crowd pressed, causing the king to take refuge in the Royal Exchange and rebuke them. This account was claimed by Robert Armin, a member of Shakespeare's company, as his own work, based on the observations of Dugdale, under whose name it was published. James hurried through the coronation procession, which was taken as evidence of his dislike of crowds, and Shakespeare's Duke may allude to this in the play's opening scene.[3]

SEJANUS

Some features of the plot in *Measure for Measure* suggest derivation from Jonson's play *Sejanus*, which was performed by Shakespeare's company, and with Shakespeare playing a part, in late 1603. The scheme whereby a number of letters surprises and confuses Angelo seems to recall the letters by Tiberius which have a similar effect on Sejanus, and in both cases the scheme leads directly to the catastrophe. Shakespeare's Duke, like Jonson's Tiberius, professes public honour to the deputy he is about to destroy (Tiberius does so in a letter).[4] At a key moment in the trial scene in 3.1 of *Sejanus* (which has general analogies with the structure of 5.1 of *Measure for Measure*) Silius protests 'is he my accuser? / And must he be my judge?' This seems to be recalled in *Measure for Measure* 5.1.166–7. The parallels to *Sejanus* might point to a date near the beginning of 1604 for *Measure for Measure*. There may be direct allusion to the king's treatment of some

---

1 Lever, pp. xxxi–ii.
2 Noted in Stevenson, 'The role of James I', pp. 191–2.
3 James's hurry is mentioned by Thomas Dekker, 'To the Reader', in *The Magnificent Entertainment* (1604), quoted in Herford and Simpson (eds.), *Ben Jonson*, 11 vols., 1925–52, x, 387. See Bennett, '*Measure for Measure*' as Royal Entertainment, p. 80.
4 This was noted by Hart (1905). The suspicion that *Sejanus* contained satiric allusions to King James and his court led to the arrest of Jonson, though he was released and not proceeded against. Another play about conspiracy was *The Tragedy of Gowrie*. It is referred to in a letter dated 18 December 1604 and evidently dramatised the affair which, according to the official version by James I, involved an attempt on the king's life: James suppressed all other witnesses' accounts. The play was evidently also suppressed; nothing more is heard of it. Perhaps, as Chamberlain speculates in the letter referring to the play, it was suppressed because 'it be thought unfit that princes should be plaide on the stage in theyre life time' (cited by Bennett, '*Measure for Measure*' as Royal Entertainment, p. 107).

of the Raleigh conspirators, as R.A. Shedd supposed. Shedd[1] describes some instances in which James I in 1603–4 dispensed justice in person with the aim of demonstrating the importance of mercy; in the case of the Raleigh conspiracy James sent a letter on the very morning fixed for the execution of one group, secretly reprieving them. The prisoners were brought out to the scaffold, then taken back to their cells without explanation, then brought out again to hear a speech condemning treason and stressing the mercy of the monarch who had saved their lives. Here the king evidently needed no lessons from the playwrights in tragi-comic suspense endings.

The play

UNDERWORLD AND SUB-PLOTS

The play was probably first performed at the Globe Theatre on Bankside, near the brothels or 'stews', so that the original audiences could have had personal experience of seeing 'corruption boil and bubble' on their way to and from the theatre. The alehouse and house of resort owned at the beginning of the play by Mistress Overdone is sited in the suburbs, immediately outside the city proper.[2] In the suburbs a livelihood is made from what the city excludes, suppresses and exudes, but the suburbs witness also to the evils produced by the city. These things are openly apparent in the suburbs of the city just as they are in the sub-plot of this play, where disease, poverty and degradation are obvious and contempt for the law is outspoken, but the conditions in which the inhabitants have to survive are also shown to be harsh: having no money, being thrown out of work, catching disease, being arrested, these are the repeated and feared experiences of their daily lives. Lies and scandal and rumour, theft and deceit and illegitimacy, contaminate relations between them, but they devise nevertheless outside the law a kind of crooked simulacrum of the official system which seems to produce a crude normality, and a means to survival. Many critics have been troubled by the impression of a disorder, and a latent anarchy, more rooted, defiant, and aggressive than might be thought compatible with 'festive' (that is, ultimately reconciliatory) comedy.[3] It is not until the end of Act 4 that an audience is likely to be able to

1 Robert A. Shedd, unpublished dissertation at the University of Michigan, 1953, cited by David L. Stevenson, *The Achievement of Shakespeare's 'Measure for Measure'*, 1966, who quotes Dudley Carlton's description, p. 161. See also Bennett, *'Measure for Measure' as Royal Entertainment*, pp. 98–9 and n. 57.

2 In 1603 the Bankside was reported to the Privy Council as being full of 'theeves, horsestealers, whoremongers, cozeners, coneycatchers'; Dekker said it was a 'contynuall alehouse' (cited by E.J. Burford, *Bawds and Lodgings*, 1976, pp. 152, 154, 157). The theatrical impresario Henslowe owned land and brothels on Bankside, including the triple brothel, the Bell, Barge and Cock, next to the Rose theatre. The major brothel-owner on Bankside was the Bishop of Winchester. The actor Edward Alleyn later acquired the Bell, Barge and Cock, among other brothels. Alleyn founded a chantry chapel and a school at Dulwich where prayers are still said for his soul (the present writer is a former pupil).

3 The term 'festive' occurs in the title of the influential study by C.L. Barber, *Shakespeare's Festive Comedy*, 1958. Northrop Frye defines the essential movement of comedy as towards 'an individual release which is also a social reconciliation' (*English Institute Essays*, 1948).

recognise a dramatic pattern in which the sub-plot episodes serve to reflect aspects of the play's central knot of concerns, and it is indeed to falsify experience of the play as it unfolds if one ignores the impressions of ingrained anarchy in the lower levels of the city's life.

In *Measure for Measure* there is a polarisation of social life into opposed extremes: on the one side serious and strict isolation – the court, the nunnery, the moated grange, the prison cells in which Claudio, alone, and Juliet, alone, are shut up – and on the other side promiscuous – not to say contagious – crowding: the alehouse, the house of resort, the streets.[1] Angelo's clean-up campaign sweeps all the low life off the streets but ironically serves only to transform the common prison (as Pompey remarks) from a house of correction to a house of resort.

At first sight there would appear to be a clear contrast between the play's upper and lower social strata – a distinction in which moral and physical health are to be attributed to the upper stratum, where law is respected, whereas crime, sin and physical disease infect and deform the lower stratum, where instinct rules. Shakespeare makes use of a visual code, a sign system, contrasting the physical appearance of the figures of authority – the Duke, Escalus, Angelo – to that of Pompey and Mistress Overdone.

These city characters are presented in the conventions of Elizabethan comic stereotype, which owe much to Morality tradition as well as satire.[2] The types are fixed, and their function in comedy depends upon their fixity. This fixity helps illustrate the economic and class interests which form or deform them into their types. Thus Pompey, fittingly for the servant of gluttony and lust, is physically gross (Thersites in *Troilus and Cressida* 5.2.55–6 refers to 'the devil Luxury, with his fat rump and potato finger'). Mistress Overdone is worn out, old, lame. In the eyes of the Church these two are servants of sin, in the eyes of the magistrate they promote unlawful drunkenness and prostitution. Yet it rapidly becomes clear to an audience that matters are more complex and paradoxical, for Pompey's trade demonstrates the seeming inseparability of sinfulness from life-sustaining instincts.[3] He serves natural instincts – thirst, hunger, sexual desire – but in cir-

---

1 The city of London had certain specific markets: meat at Smithfield, fish at Billingsgate, money at the Royal Exchange – the building of the Royal Exchange by Sir Thomas Gresham is featured in the Jacobean play by Heywood, *If You Know Not Me You Know Nobody (Part 2)* (1605). Jonson's comedy *Bartholomew Fair* (1614), which has significant allusions to *Measure for Measure*, features the Smithfield market people and their trading practices, observed by a foolish Justice in disguise.

2 The depiction of city life need not exclude the family unit, as Jonson's *Every Man In His Humour* (1598) or Dekker's *The Shoemaker's Holiday* (1599) witnesses, but it is true that city comedies tend to concentrate on the improvident gallants seeking wealth through marriage, around whom lawyers and other kinds of cheats and thieves, prostitutes and keepers of alehouses and houses of resort (brothels), ply their trade. See Brian Gibbons, *Jacobean City Comedy*, second edn, 1980.

3 Pompey and Mistress Overdone have a commercial parody of marriage, in some ways like that of the Peachums in John Gay's *The Beggar's Opera* (1728). Peachum works on both sides of the law and explains to his daughter that he never could have lived comfortably for so long with her mother if they had actually been married (1.8.13–15). Peachum's first song would have made sense to Pompey:

    Through all the employments of life
    Each neighbour abuses his brother;

cumstances where they cannot avoid becoming the sins of drunkenness, gluttony and lust.

The issue of healthy instincts bringing disease and sin in their satisfaction is of general importance in the play as a whole, though seeming at first to be confined to distasteful figures like Pompey. The case of Claudio and Juliet, of better social rank, illustrates the wider significance of this issue, while the cases of Angelo – and, even more strikingly, Isabella – illustrate the difficult terms in which the play confronts an audience with the issue, showing that extreme abstention from appetite, too, brings its own forms of corruption, distortion and abnormality – an almost perverse paradox. The paradoxical structure of the play's design begins to emerge very early, when it is shown how the dominant claims of instinctive nature in the lower ranks make them able to nourish a sympathy for the blighted youthful hopes of Claudio and Juliet, and this sympathy reveals that the lower ranks have a better grasp of common justice and humanity in this case than the educated Angelo does. According to Angelo's severe interpretation of the letter of the law, the spirit of love is mortally sinful.

An audience is shown the unhappy stage image of the young and well-liked Claudio shamed by public arrest, and the sight of his young, pregnant wife also arrested will induce immediate sympathy. Later episodes reveal, however, that both Claudio and Juliet (as they confess) consummated their union knowing they were offending against the law. This shows Shakespeare's method of first eliciting a reaction from an audience, and then forcing it to reconsider its judgement and feelings about characters and issues.

Mistress Overdone is the first woman seen on stage; she is closely followed by the young, pregnant Juliet.[1] The visual contrast between the affirmative and vulnerable image of love and fertility, and the physically and morally corrupt old woman, seems obvious and extreme. Yet it soon becomes clear that from the point of view of the law and the Church Juliet is, though young, also an image of vice and sin. Mistress Overdone's title of married woman may be hollow (worn out, as it were, by repetition), and as we see later it is no protection against being arrested, but Juliet too has no certain title to respectability as a married woman and she too has no protection against being arrested. Though Mistress Overdone and Juliet are contrasted as opposite images of womanhood, there emerge disconcerting similarities between them.

In the society of the play, the upper stratum, the serious characters, are educated in the concepts of religion and the law (although they too may offend),

> Whore and rogue they call husband and wife,
> All professions be-rogue one another.
> The priest calls the lawyer a cheat;
> The lawyer be-knaves the divine;
> And the statesman, because he's so great,
> Thinks his trade as honest as mine.
> Quoted from the edition by Edgar V. Roberts, 1968.

1 For a discussion of the textual problem associated with the entry for Juliet in 1.2, see Commentary to 1.2.96–7 and discussion in the Textual Analysis, p. 198 below.

they respect the principle of authority and they practise reasoned disputation in speech that is highly articulate. The lower stratum's comic characters lack education, they use local vernacular to assert impulsive or instinctual needs or convictions directly from their own personal position. The play, having made these contrasts very clear, then goes on to interrelate the serious and the comic plots and in so doing brings out unexpected complexities in the process. While the marked differences between upper and lower generate much dramatic energy, the surprising similarities stimulate an audience to a vigorous process of mental and emotional debate and reconsideration.

The use of the comic mode makes obvious the contrast between the upper and lower social groups, and there are episodes of irresistibly hilarious, exuberant mirth in the low-life part of the play; but this does not signal an intention on Shakespeare's part to trivialise issues, nor does it imply a simple moral condemnation. It is one property of comedy's caricature and exaggeration to make patterns exceptionally clear and distinct. The comic underworld in *Measure for Measure* is a critical mirror in which we recognise, inverted, the structures and assumptions central to the play's serious action. But comedy in this play is distorted and strained by the use of the grotesque so that comedy's jovial, festive, reconciling spirit cannot gain release, its exuberant energies remain disruptive and dark, locked as they are in a struggle for survival, the central action of the play.

CARNIVAL AND JUSTICE: WORD-PLAY AND SELF-DEFENCE
In the play's second scene the jokes touch on painful matters – 'thy bones are hollow' – 'which of your hips hath the most profound sciatica?' – thus bringing to the surface repressed fears, but at the same time expressing a communal, spirited resistance to them. The reliance in the comic parts of the play on popular proverbs, slang, indecencies and informal types of language gives a dominantly vernacular flavour to these episodes. Jokes need above all to be shared – they deal in common experience, they express a basic communal solidarity both in celebration and in misery. The jokes about the appetites of hunger, thirst and sex in the low life of the play contrast with the crushing effect of guilt and nausea at instinct, as it is expressed in the serious main plot by Angelo and Claudio, for instance in 1.2.110–12:

> Our natures do pursue
> Like rats that ravin down their proper bane
> A thirsty evil, and when we drink, we die.

Even Elbow shares in the companionship common to the comic characters, for all his effort to detach himself from the others as a righteous man. He is incapable of disentangling himself from his local communal society, as his absurd aspirations to educated discourse show, and while at a simple level Elbow's assumption that 'respected' means 'suspected' is a comic confusion of opposites (demonstrating that he is an imbecile compared to Pompey), at another level it also points to the precise inversion of upper-class assumptions by the lower class. The well-off cannot afford not to be respectable, they risk everything if they are suspected of crime: but the poor can rarely afford to be respectable, they are always suspected because it is known they can barely survive without crime.

Pompey contrasts to his companions in being able to manipulate different levels of discourse. This reflects the play's general concern with argument and rhetorical skill, and Pompey's nimbleness in word-play is a mark of his general resourcefulness. In the trial in 2.1 he rapidly develops a full-scale burlesque of legal procedure by building on a parody of Elbow's confusing manner. Elbow strays into irrelevant digressions, made harder to follow by disjointed syntax and over-emotional delivery:

He, sir? A tapster, sir, parcel bawd, one that serves a bad woman, whose house, sir, was, as they say, plucked down in the suburbs; and now she professes a hot-house; which I think is a very ill house too. (2.1.58–61)

Elbow shows that he completely fails to understand either the rules of logic or of court procedure: he cannot set out an argument coherently and, unwittingly, even conveys the impression that his wife (whom he says he 'detests') is the cause of suspicion that the house is a brothel. Pompey disrupts the proceedings too, but does it purposely, first interrupting Elbow with a joke on his name to unbalance his testimony and soon interrupting again to have his say. He is determined to prevent anyone else talking, and so weaves an interminably fluid maze of not-quite-relevant narrative. It is obsessively packed with detail (Pompey here takes his cue from Elbow) and it vividly suggests the atmosphere of Mistress Overdone's house: 'He, sir, sitting, as I say, in a lower chair, sir – 'twas in the Bunch of Grapes, where indeed you have a delight to sit, have you not?' but the precise enumerations of detail are all, like the 'prunes', pure red herrings: 'we had but two in the house, which at that very distant time stood, as it were, in a fruit dish, a dish of some three pence'. In fact this irrelevant account can be translated, according to the many indecent double meanings Pompey implies, to mean that Elbow's wife entered the house in search of sexual pleasure and found Froth, who had just paid for the whore he had enjoyed. The Justice can hardly acknowledge this set of innuendoes without losing his linguistic dignity, so to speak, and allowing the proceedings to go out of his control. If the law accepts Pompey's subversive discourse it may also be trapped into accepting his assumptions.

Pompey's testimony grows ever more elaborate, digressions unfold within digressions – 'and I beseech you, look into Master Froth here, sir; a man of four score pound a year; whose father died at Hallowmas' (108–10) – so that a judge either loses patience and gives up (as Angelo does) or risks succumbing to the story in which everyone is a familiar acquaintance of dear Mistress Overdone in her friendly local and none of them would hurt a fly. Pompey concludes his formidable demonstration of how to run rings round the law by defying the magistrate Escalus openly:

I thank your worship for your good counsel; but I shall follow it as the flesh and fortune shall better determine. (2.1.216–17)

4   The trial of Froth and Pompey
a In Peter Brook's 1950 production, with Sir John Gielgud as Angelo, Geoffrey Bayldon as Froth and
George Rose as Pompey
b In Jonathan Miller's 1974 production

Pompey generally conforms to the spirit of Carnival,[1] uninhibited, spontaneous, mocking, inverting authority's forms and procedures, always choosing the erratic, the discrepant, not the logical or the consistent or coherent. The scene serves more generally as comic burlesque, in anticipation, of the play's main events. Thus Elbow tells Angelo here that Pompey and Froth are 'benefactors' when he means 'malefactors' and calls them 'precise villains'; in the very next scene Angelo will reveal himself as a precise villain; his pose of beneficence and piety will be used as a cloak for profane and criminal intent. Furthermore Elbow's emotional claim that his wife has been indecently propositioned – a charge easily evaded by Pompey – anticipates events in the final act of the play where the passionate accusation by Isabella and the even more improbable-sounding claims of Mariana seem to be shrugged off by Angelo. The comic mode of 2.1, with the laughter it generates in an audience, allows the pattern of ideas and rhetorical techniques to be clearly recognised. At the same time the different cases of Pompey and Angelo need different treatment by justice. The temperate conclusion of Escalus, that Pompey should continue in his courses until he is proved to have committed some offence (2.1.158–60), is a measure against which to judge the new law's severity, as well as the Duke's previous laxity.

Pompey's sense of the city in terms of its physical substance challenges legal and religious concepts of society. His language concentrates on the material stuff of life and on existence in terms of sensory impressions, and he even responds to other people primarily in terms of their physique and physical capacities. He associates the inadequate mind of Elbow with the holes in his clothes – 'he's out at elbow' – and Mistress Overdone's physique with the treatment her ninth husband gave her – 'Overdone by the last' (subsequently he says she has become a pickled carcass of beef (3.2.50–1)). When in prison Pompey names the inmates and evokes the city's turbulent trading activity, in brown paper, old ginger, peach-coloured satin, copper spurs, puddings, shoe-ties, half-cans and pots. Some of these objects metamorphose into people who are vigorously conjured up drinking and eating, capering, gambling, stabbing to death. Angelo's austere decree is at once translated by Pompey into stark terms of the knife, gelding and spaying, whereas brothels, his livelihood, become fields of wheat, fertile seed-beds. To him the body's pleasure is to be warm; it is all the same whether it is by the fire in the Bunch of Grapes or wrapped in a judge's furred gown. Pompey's word-play insists on the underlying physical and instinctual rather than the abstract and rational connotations of words, and such a view of life resists denial or suppression. Hence Pompey's speech is full of irrupting innuendoes, his behaviour breaks the rules of politeness and he is the spokesman for two ancient professions (publican and prostitute) where the line between legal and illegal remains notoriously uncertain.

There is a direct connection in these terms between Pompey and Lucio,

---

1 For a fuller discussion of the idea of Carnival as the communal expression of protest by the poor and oppressed through the forms of seasonal festival, see M.M. Bakhtin, *Rabelais and his World*, 1968. A more recent study directly concerned with Shakespeare is François Laroque, *Shakespeare et la Fête*, Paris, 1986. See also Barber's earlier study, *Shakespeare's Festive Comedy*.

although Lucio's greater social mobility exposes him to more complex moral responsibilities, and subjects his wit to more searching criticism of its cruelty and amorality. In the serious engagement with issues of truth and conscience, anarchic wit can be made to seem superficial, if not brutal, like Pompey. Lucio's mobility displays his facility in a wide variety of verbal and social styles. He enjoys moving among contrasting groups, but he has a taste for the sordid and the perverse. He says of Angelo 'when he makes water, his urine is congealed ice' (3.2.96–7) and of the Duke 'he would mouth with a beggar though she smelt brown bread and garlic' (3.2.155–6). This is fantasy, physically visualised; it lacks Pompey's straightforwardness. Lucio enjoys gossiping with anyone, he is chameleonic in adapting to interlocutors, he will say anything to entertain or surprise them. Hobbes's epigram, 'words are wise men's counters . . . but . . . the money of fools', would be politic and equivocal enough to appeal to him – indeed it is an irony that he finally traps himself in a moment of unguarded, uncharacteristic truth-telling when showing off to 'Friar Lodowick'.[1]

ANGELO AND ISABELLA: WORD-PLAY AND SELF-BETRAYAL

There is point in concentrating for a moment longer on the matter of language, before going on to consider characterisation more generally. The characters in the upper social group in the play share an educated, highly developed, and also highly conscious linguistic capacity, but within this group individuals vary significantly. Normally Lucio's intuition is highly alert and picks up many subtle ambiguities, whether verbal or otherwise. This contrasts illuminatingly with Angelo, who like Isabella and the Duke commits much unconsciously revealing word-play while also exercising a general rhetorical skill. To begin with Angelo. In 2.1, when discussing severe law with Escalus, Angelo says justice concerns itself with what it has access to, it cannot treat what is concealed. This concern with concealed crime, broached by Escalus, is unconsciously clothed in sexual language by Angelo:

> what's open made to justice,
> That justice seizes . . .
>   'Tis very pregnant,
> The jewel that we find, we stoop and take't   (2.1.21–4)

In his first scene with Isabella, 2.2, Angelo uses the same metaphors to describe the preternatural powers of his justice to perceive hidden crimes

> in a glass that shows what future evils –
> Either now, or by remissness new conceived,
> And so in progress to be hatched and born –   (98–100)

Isabella is similarly prone to use, unconsciously, sexually suggestive language: she cries

---

1 See 4.3.158 ff.

> I would to heaven I had your potency,
> And you were Isabel: (2.2.68–9)

her choice of word influenced by her contradictory feelings about her brother's potency (in connection with his sin) but also perhaps registering the subliminal awareness of Angelo's sudden sexual attraction to her, even perhaps of hers to him. Isabella's subsequent challenge to Angelo:

> Go to your bosom,
> Knock there, and ask your heart what it doth know
> That's like my brother's fault. (2.2.140–2)

has two ironic effects: first it strikes, unwittingly, at Angelo's guilt for his past treatment of Mariana, and secondly, to an Angelo now caught in desire for her, it tantalisingly puts into words directly what he does desire, so that now he himself can confess his guilty desire to himself. Though still secret (in an aside), what is significant about his response is that it consciously plays on the ambiguous meaning of the word 'sense':

> She speaks, and 'tis such sense
> That my sense breeds with it. (2.2.146–7)

For Angelo sexual desire, even when he is seized by it, remains 'foul', Isabella, though an object of lust, is named 'virtuous', 'the sanctuary', 'good', 'a saint', and again 'virtuous' (2.2.166–89). For her part, Isabella can speak of her female body in arousing sexual terms when next she comes to plead:

> Th'impression of keen whips I'd wear as rubies,
> And strip myself to death as to a bed
> That longing have been sick for ... (2.4.101–3)

To her the physically sensuous is transfigured in the exaltation of martyrdom, the violation only exalts the purity of faith's ecstasy: but to Angelo the erotic suggestion is overpowering, determined as he is to talk not of her soul but of her giving up her 'body to such sweet uncleanness' (2.4.53) as (he thinks) did Juliet with Claudio. The extended hypothetical discussion with Isabella about submitting to sexual intercourse with him, and her intense and close physical presence to him, charge his language with erotic word-play from her first remark, unconsciously tantalising,

> I am come to know your pleasure

and his reply, in which he confesses his inhibitions about putting desire into words:

> That you might know it would much better please me
> Than to demand what 'tis. (2.4.32–3)

Angelo plays again on the word 'sense' ('Your sense pursues not mine' (74)) then (82) says he will 'speak more gross' to be 'receivèd plain'. This sexual double meaning is unconscious, but at 41–5 his comparison of the begetting of an

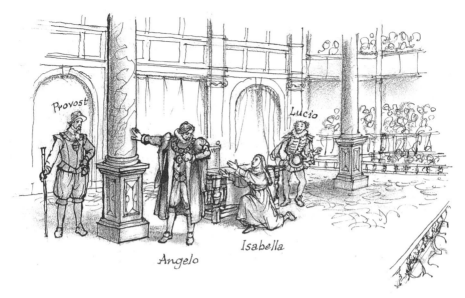

5   Isabella: 'Gentle my lord, turn back.' Angelo: 'I will bethink me. Come again tomorrow.' Act 2,
Scene 2: a reconstruction of a performance on a public playhouse stage, by C. Walter Hodges

illegitimate child to the forging of money, to 'coin heaven's image / In stamps that
are forbid', is a graphic and deliberate sexual metaphor which Isabella also adopts
later when she says women

> are soft as our complexions are,
> And credulous to false prints.   (2.4.130–1)

From this point on in the scene Angelo becomes increasingly violent in his passion,
and increasingly explicit both in uncovering his criminal desires and in putting
them into shockingly direct, deliberately clear physical terms which also consciously convey cruel sexual sensations:

> I have begun,
> And now I give my sensual race the rein.
> Fit thy consent to my sharp appetite,
> Lay by all nicety and prolixious blushes
> That banish what they sue for, redeem thy brother
> By yielding up thy body to my will,
> Or else he must not only die the death
> But thy unkindness shall his death draw out
> To lingering sufferance.   (2.4.160–8)

An intense mixture of conscious and unconscious word-play is apparent in the
tightly strained soliloquy Angelo speaks in 4.4, when he confesses his guilt for the
death of Claudio (as he supposes) and the rape of Isabella:

This deed unshapes me quite, makes me unpregnant
And dull to all proceedings. A deflowered maid,
And by an eminent body that enforced
The law against it? But that her tender shame
Will not proclaim against her maiden loss,
How might she tongue me? Yet reason dares her no;
For my authority bears of a credent bulk,
That no particular scandal once can touch
But it confounds the breather. He should have lived,
Save that his riotous youth with dangerous sense
Might in the times to come have tane revenge
By so receiving a dishonoured life
With ransom of such shame. Would yet he had lived.
Alack, when once our grace we have forgot,
Nothing goes right: we would, and we would not. (4.4.18–32)

This is the only occasion on which he speaks of his personal reaction to the 'bed-trick' in which, it should be recalled, he loses his own virginity while committing (in his own mind) rape. The speech expresses his sense of the inseparability of his political potency, as Deputy, and his sexual potency, both no sooner discovered than lost through the crime of the ransom and the betrayal. The 'deed' which he says 'unshapes' him is both the killing of Claudio and the rape (as public betrayals of his duty as Deputy they are inseparable in his mind). At the same time the 'deed' is the personal sexual act (so Pompey uses the verb 'done' in 1.2.72–3).

Guilt leaves him bereft of ideas in confronting the crisis of the Duke's return, but a strong awareness of his body and physiology is apparent here, and further in the unconscious ambiguity of the syntax in 'A deflowered maid, / And by an eminent body that enforced', where the line end seems to make 'enforced' relate back to 'maid', though the sentence when completed makes 'The law' the verb's object. The speech is a fierce effort to confront his guilt and confess it; the proliferating unconscious sexual play in the language is a witness to the depth of Angelo's disturbance, too profound and turbulent for his conscious thought to bring out and shape: Angelo knows this, partly, as his very use of the verb 'unshape' reveals.

EXCHANGES

The association of honest money-making with human fertility is celebrated as straightforwardly positive in other city plays of the period, such as Dekker's *The Shoemaker's Holiday*, which features a tremendous communal feast, with the king present, to mark the opening of the Leadenhall Market as inaugurating civic growth and increase. *Measure for Measure* is concerned with the interrelations in love and in commerce which constitute society; it is also concerned with religious and state law as they seek to regulate those interrelations. The names of Mistress Overdone's customers recall the great variety of commerce which the city's markets exchange; in Mistress Overdone's alehouse these customers themselves exchange money, for goods, and for the services of the whores who ply their trade there. In the underworld of the city poverty forces people to trade whatever they can in order to survive, whether it be goods, or services, or even their own bodies. Poverty may force them to offend against the rules which forbid certain kinds of exchange on moral grounds. Poverty or sinfulness may induce them to trade dishonestly, make unfair bargains or break the rules of fair exchange.

Shakespeare's design of *Measure for Measure* gives central focus to Angelo's offer of an unfair exchange – saving Claudio's head from the axe if Isabella surrenders her maidenhead to him. Angelo doubles his crime by determining to cheat Isabella by taking Claudio's head once Isabella has kept her side of the bargain. This central focus is given visual emphasis by the episode in which the executioner is seen preparing, and by the bringing on stage of an actual severed head. The play's dénouement involves the disclosing, by unhooding, of the head of the Duke, by unveiling, of the head of Mariana, and by unmuffling, of the head of Claudio. These actions are the reverse of 'heading' in the sense of 'to behead' or execute, just as they serve to expose the precise frustration of Angelo's schemes against Claudio, against the Duke-in-disguise, and against his former betrothed Mariana.

The story of Mariana is significant in developing the implications of love in relation to other kinds of exchange, since Angelo broke off with Mariana when her dowry was lost in a wreck at sea. Marriage, as the play reminds us, involves money changing hands as well as the mutual exchange of vows and bodies in love. The point is repeated for emphasis, too, for Claudio and Juliet delayed their official marriage 'only for propagation of a dower': Juliet's lack of a dowry made them delay the church wedding ceremony[1] and left them exposed to Angelo's severe imposition of the law. Angelo claims to ensure that all moral corruption will be rooted out of the state, and as we have seen he describes the illegitimate begetting of children in terms of forging counterfeit money, coining 'heaven's image / In stamps that are forbid'. Shakespeare devises a pattern in which lack of money induces Claudio and Juliet clandestinely to coin *heaven's* image, beget a child. The

---

1 The statement of Claudio about his marriage at 1.2.126–30 could have sounded familiar to lawyers of the time, since it raises an issue of ecclesiastical law special to England. A free choice of marriage partner was permitted in English law, though the influence of parents, relatives and 'friends' could be great. A private contract was legal, even with no witnesses, though the Church strongly recommended that a marriage should be solemnised in public and in church. A couple were deemed married if they exchanged vows in the present tense (*per verba de praesenti*), while a promise to marry in the future (*per verba de futuro*) was deemed binding unless specific conditions which were agreed at the time were not fulfilled. The case of Claudio and Juliet, according to Claudio, is that vows *de praesenti* were exchanged and the marriage was physically consummated; all that was missing was that it remained secret and unsolemnised in church. This clandestine marriage exposed them both to the charge that they were not married, thus raising an issue often provoking court cases – see Martin Ingram, 'Spousals litigation in the English ecclesiastical courts *c.* 1350–1640', in R.B. Outhwaite (ed.), *Marriage and Society*, 1981. He quotes a case from 1641 which almost exactly echoes Claudio's words in 1.2.126–30. The case of Angelo rests upon his claim that his vow *de futuro* was conditional, and that the conditions were not fulfilled, so that his unilateral withdrawal from the contract was justified. Evidently Mariana did lose a dowry; but Angelo's claim that her reputation became scandalous is not supported in the play – indeed it is contradicted by Isabella (3.1.202–3). See also 5.1.207 n.

force of this metaphor is understood when we recall that the Book of Common Prayer (1549) declares that in Christian marriage the getting of children is considered lawful profit from the giving of one's body, as is profiting from natural increase in agricultural crops. It is baldly stated. The husband in the service of matrimony is told 'Thy wife shalbee as the fruitful vine, upon the walles of thy house' and 'Thy children like the olife braunches rounde about thy table' (quoting the Psalms). The getting of children outside marriage is forbidden because they may be bereft of religious education and bodily support. The priest has to declare that holy matrimony was instituted 'of God in paradise in the time of mannes innocencie, signifying unto us the misticall union that is betwixte Christe and his Churche'; its causes however are practical: 'One cause was the procreacion of children, to be brought up in the feare and nurture of the Lord, and prayse of God. Secondly . . . to avoide fornicacion . . . Thirdly for the mutuall societie, helpe, and comfort, that the one oughte to have of thother.' The groom is to swear 'withal my worldly Goodes I thee endowe'.

What is striking is that both religious and secular law accept the analogy between commercial valuation and ethical valuation, something evident in the scope of the very word 'valuation', and in the emblem of Justice's scales, symbolic of the weighing of men's deeds and motives to assay their worth, just as real scales are used to weigh coins and assay their true metal and real worth. The Christian doctrine of marriage as set forth in the Prayerbook concedes the importance of worldly wealth as frankly as social custom does, in the institution of marriage and the family. Elsewhere in Christian doctrine the Gospels teach a different lesson, and this is of supreme importance in Shakespeare's *Measure for Measure*: that men should not invest in the material wealth of this world, 'where the moth and canker corrupt, and where thieves dig through, and steal'.[1] Rather it is spiritual riches that should be sought and propagated by men. It is these opposed ideas of wealth[2] which are focused in the language of Isabella and Angelo in 2.2, as when Angelo offers to exchange Claudio's head for Isabella's maidenhead and she in turn offers to bribe him, though in a contrary sense, 'Not with fond sickles of the tested gold' (2.2.154). Later Isabella is clear that she will pay with her body, submitting to torture and death, for virtue:

> Th'impression of keen whips I'd wear as rubies,
> And strip myself to death as to a bed
> That longing have been sick for . . .   (2.4.101–3)

In religious terms this would be a 'cheaper way' than for a sister to exchange a brother's life in this world for eternal torment of her soul. Angelo speaks of the

---

1 Matt. 6.19. Verse 20 recommends: 'lay up treasures for yourselves in heaven'; and 25: 'be not careful for your life, what ye shall eat, or what ye shall drink: nor yet for your body, what ye shall put on. Is not the life more worth than meat, and the body than raiment?' The next chapter concerns judgement, mercy, the 'straict gate' of virtue, and measure for measure.

2 See the chapter on 'Love's wealth' in John Russell Brown, *Shakespeare and his Comedies*, 1957, pp. 45–81, for a study of the metaphor of wealth in relation to spiritual love in Shakespeare's plays.

'treasures' of her body in sensuous, material terms, but Isabella transforms her tortured body's blood into symbols of spiritual treasure, echoing biblical imagery of rubies as she does so.

The play's climax focuses on the issue of exchange and the meting out of due reward and punishment in exchange for the actions that have been committed during the play. When Isabella made her plea to Angelo in 2.2 to save her brother's life, she invited Angelo to see the situation from Claudio's point of view. Had they changed places, Claudio would have shown mercy where Angelo would not:

> If he had been as you, and you as he,
> You would have slipped like him, but he like you
> Would not have been so stern.   (2.2.65–7)

Once the Duke is restored as head of state in Act 5 and Angelo's crimes are exposed, the Duke decrees that to behead Angelo is fair exchange for his beheading of Claudio:

> An Angelo for Claudio, death for death;
> Haste still pays haste, and leisure answers leisure;
> Like doth quit like, and measure still for measure.   (5.1.402–4)

In fact the play begins with the Duke, as head of state, exchanging Angelo for himself – 'be thou at full ourself', he says, conferring the office on him. This is a *measure*, in the sense of 'a course of action, a plan',[1] designed to discover how well Angelo can rule with temperance, *measured* firmness, passing laws, legal *measures*, which will ensure that his subjects' behaviour confines itself to *measured*, not-to-be-exceeded limits. As head of state Angelo must administer justice, involving retribution for offences, measure for measure, and reward for the deserving. Christian doctrine teaches, however, that the highest good is forgiveness for evil, not retribution, and the climax of the play faces Isabella with the choice between asking retribution or forgiveness for Angelo's crimes. Mariana has already chosen spiritual wealth in rejecting the Duke's offer of Angelo's property after his execution to 'buy' her 'a better husband' (5.1.418). She says

> I crave no other, nor no better man.

A further sense of 'measure', one used in *Romeo and Juliet* 1.4.9–10, is 'a dance', and one might see in this movement of reconciliation and uniting the dance-like movement of comedy – the *measure* of tragedy and revenge transformed by the *measure* of love. At the same time these transformations could not have been achieved without the severe risks involved in exchanging places, comparing one judgement with another. A year or so after *Measure for Measure*, in 1605, Shakespeare in *King Lear* brings a king to recognise how powerfully social privilege and position affects such matters:

1 This definition is from *OED* Measure *sb* 21.

see how yond justice rails upon yond simple thief. Hark in thine ear: change places, and handy-dandy, which is the justice, which is the thief?   (4.6.151–4)

In *Measure for Measure* this is an issue affecting everyone, though it is indeed focused on the Duke himself.

THE QUESTION OF THE DUKE

In the sources Cinthio and Whetstone, the ruler is a lofty and remote figure. Shakespeare's Duke, while pretending to leave his city, in fact remains in it in disguise, and becomes intricately and familiarly involved in it. Furthermore Shakespeare invents a character, Lucio, to encourage a critical attitude to the Duke, and though Lucio is obviously an inventive and malicious liar for much of the time, he instinctively senses weaknesses and vulnerability in others; and when the Duke gives up his ducal robes Shakespeare uses Lucio to stress the danger of exposure to injustice when one is powerless. Shakespeare invents a second character, Barnardine, precisely to frustrate the Duke's fanciful scheme to save Claudio. Barnardine's blunt refusal to provide his head throws the Duke into an acute crisis. After all, Claudio is facing death indirectly as a result of the Duke's delegation of power, and only now does the Duke seem to have second thoughts about the desirability of having Angelo 'strike home' in 'the ambush' of the Duke's name.[1]

The Duke is himself thrown on the mercy of Providence, which intervenes in a manner arguably more suggestive of implausible theatricality than religious mystery. Barnardine too is placed in the play to invite criticism of the Duke. In neither Cinthio nor Whetstone does the ruler devise a scheme to save the condemned young man; this is done by the gaoler. Moreover Shakespeare greatly complicates the character of the Deputy and the young man, for Claudio is terrified of death and Angelo is shocked violently by the eruption of lust in himself. The sister accepts the ransom's terms in Cinthio and Whetstone, but not in Shakespeare, who makes her someone not only serious and chaste but very immature in her absolute views. Consequently her meetings with the Deputy are extreme in their repression and then in their release of immature passion (qualifying her virtue and vice), and when she is subject to Claudio's terrified pleas she catches his panic. Isabella and Claudio are young, and inexperienced enough to be severely disturbed by challenges too severe for them. Shakespeare involves the Duke directly in witnessing this, and greatly increases the sense of urgency by telescoping the time-scale of events which, in Cinthio and Whetstone, devolve much more slowly.

All of these changes seem to be devised by Shakespeare to expose the practically risky and morally dubious aspects of the Duke's behaviour to the audience and, perhaps, even to the Duke himself. He keeps Isabella unaware of his true identity

---

1 See 1.3.42.

while disguised as 'Friar Lodowick' and denies her, right up to the last moments of the play, the knowledge that her brother is still alive. In his disguise as Friar he exploits the intimacy of the Confessional in his dealings with Isabella, Juliet and Claudio (a genuine friar would be bound to secrecy). This may be acceptable within the conventions of dramatic comedy, but looks more dubious when seen as an allusion to the Divine Right theory of monarchy, whereby a ruler claims religious authority by his consecration. Shakespeare does not, in any case, stop there in making the Duke questionable; he adds the sub-plot involving Mariana, and presents the Duke inventing the scheme of Mariana and the bed-trick, a further Shakespearean addition which is morally paradoxical as well as humanly risky and generically highly exotic, and it directly implicates Isabella the would-be nun as well as the Duke-as-Friar. It is disconcerting to be reminded of the Friar in Machiavelli's ironic comedy *Mandragola* in one of the most tense episodes of *Measure for Measure*.[1] All in all Shakespeare goes out of his way to make the Duke's role as Friar outrageous in certain ways, as if to highlight difficulties for which there is no precedent in Cinthio or Whetstone. The Duke's is an extravagant piece of bravado, a high-risk venture, and one that emphasises a highly improbable plot. Might all this be thought of as touching on the chief objections to the theory of absolute monarchy advocated by the new king, James I? To treat grave and lofty matters such as these in so profoundly comic a spirit is perhaps a way of concealing from the authorities the real force of dissent the play animates. At any rate nothing could be more clear than that Shakespeare deliberately devises a whole series of episodes, inventing new characters as necessary, to entangle the Duke in practical and personal difficulties, requiring moral choices and personal commitments which a ducal role allows one to evade. He is confronted with the stubborn human realities of life in the city, and the contortions that law imposes on people. In the play's climax he is threatened with torture, he is arrested and manhandled. He is made to feel what wretches feel, if only briefly.[2] It is true that his unhooding restores his authority, but the point is that even compared to the similar plot in Middleton's *The Phoenix* this is a violent episode, whereas it would be quite unthinkable in Whetstone and even in earlier Shakespeare, where in *Henry IV* (1598) or *Henry V* (1599) Shakespeare changes the sources to avoid subjecting Hal to such indignities.

---

1 In Machiavelli's comedy a young man schemes to seduce a virtuous young wife by manipulating, among others, her own mother and her holy confessor, who urges her to accept seduction. The virtuous wife works out a formula which could be seen as sublimely pious or profoundly cynical or plainly honest in saying to the young man 'Since your guile, my husband's folly, the simple-mindedness of my mother, and the wickedness of my father confessor have led me to do what I should never have done of my own free will, I must judge it to be Heaven that willed it so, and I cannot find it in myself to refuse what Heaven wishes me to accept' (trans. Eric Bentley and Frederick May in *The Classic Theatre*, I, 1958).

2 In a year or so, in 1605, Shakespeare would be subjecting a king to every kind of humiliation, including exposure to wind and rain. After King Lear loses his reason and strips off his clothes he perceives the suffering of the beggars, excluded even from the lowest estate of the realm, who are 'houseless', 'unfed', 'ragged', examples of flagrant injustice.

ACTING

A self-consciousness about acting, and theatre, is apparent in Shakespeare's work around the turn of the century, perhaps stimulated by the general popular success of the leading companies at this time; no less significant is the awareness of the idea of the world as a stage, especially for public roles. In the theatre – to judge by *Hamlet*, and the Induction to *The Malcontent*, and *Every Man Out of His Humour* – actors were themselves confident in their art, calling attention to their skill in moving into big roles, and switching suddenly to very different styles in the course of a performance. Shakespeare's Henry V adopts the guise of a gentleman and goes undetected among his men the night before the battle. Tiberius does a polished machiavellian impression of a just and temperate ruler in Act 3, Scene 1 of *Sejanus*, and Jonson has an observer give an ironic running commentary on this skilful deception. Hamlet responds to the impersonation of rightful monarchy by Claudius by adopting the intermittent role of melancholic madman, a performance Shakespeare shows as dazzling in its skills and virtuosity. Close to the time of *Measure for Measure* Marston's Malevole/Altofront offers a demanding double major role, presumably taken by Burbage in the King's Men production. In *Othello*, Iago, another skilful deceiver, confides his plans in advance to the audience, who then watch him act the part of trusted confidant so that he can induce Othello to interpret harmless scenes according to Iago's salaciously ugly version, in which the role of Othello is virtually that of cuckold in a Marston-style city comedy. In both *King Lear* and *The Revenger's Tragedy* a major character – Edgar, Vindice – adopts a new name and character to survive in a world of ruthless court intrigue and corrupt rulers. As the instances show, common themes were treated in a variety of dramatic modes and styles at this time: indeed courtesans, fawns, malcontents and phoenixes all have their place in *Measure for Measure* as well as being the titles of city comedies by other dramatists.

Measure for Measure, much more emphatically than *The Merchant of Venice*, is concerned with law, and must have appealed to a significant section of playgoers at the time, members of the Inns of Court. A number of plays at Blackfriars and Paul's are designed to appeal to law students and lawyers, though none is more attentive to the complexities of the monarch's relation to secular and religious law than *Measure for Measure*, while not even *Volpone*, among plays of the time featuring a trial scene as climax, is so exciting as theatre.

Measure for Measure has several scenes featuring intense legal argument, and there it becomes clear that powerful acting is inseparable from good advocacy. The role of magistrate, as the play's opening insists, requires strength in performance from whoever dons the robes and insignia. The first scene shows the Duke laying aside the role of magistrate and requiring Angelo to dress in borrowed robes. The first view of Isabella is of her discussing the rules of the Poor Clares with a nun of the Order, another public role with its insignia. Isabella is not yet a full member of the Order, Angelo is but a deputy magistrate. He protests at his appointment, asking for a longer period of preparation; Isabella is anxious to be subjected to a stricter restraint: both at first seem uncertain and hesitant, and when confronted by their first challenge in the play, neither begins confidently. Though both well schooled, they lack experience.

Angelo, taking the case of Elbow versus Pompey and Froth, loses patience and control, lapses into silence and hands over in the middle of the proceedings to Escalus. Isabella is slow to react when informed of her brother's plight – condemned as he is to death – and when she actually makes a plea for his life it is a mere token effort, and she seems relieved when Angelo says 'no', and turns to leave.

It is then that the importance of acting, of performance of a role in legal argument, is stressed by Shakespeare, for Lucio takes over to direct Isabella as if she were an actress in rehearsal, instructing her in movement, gesture, pace and emphasis, out of Angelo's earshot but in the audience's hearing, so making the audience read the scene as a skilful acting of a role. Isabella's unconfident beginning of the scene is in the role of sister[1] of one condemned, whereas Angelo is withdrawn behind the official image of authority, invested in the ducal robes. When Isabella uses the argument that beneath his official insignia Angelo is only a man like Claudio, we at once sense a shift to her advantage in the debate: as if suddenly conscious of the authority of the nun's robes she feels destined to wear, she invokes the authority of the Gospels, reducing the magistrate to 'man, proud man', merely 'dressed in a little, brief authority'. The state, its book of law, the magistrate's robes, are secular and temporal: the Church, its book, its gowned sisters – potential martyrs every one – represent a higher authority. Isabella suddenly becomes confident in her performance, she takes the stage as she assumes a public role and seeks to reduce the magistrate to mere nakedness as a man before God's judgement. In the excitement of the moment her plea persuades, though on reflection it may appear less secure. Here, as often in *Measure for Measure*, the power of performance changes the shape of problems.

At the same time, two types of acting confront one another here: Angelo, the logician, cold as a chisel, presenting in few words a seemingly unanswerable case, Isabella, exploiting varying rhythm, a variety of different appeals in a circling movement, stressing the naked humanity of the victim, rapidly exploiting an advantage with thrilling emotion. There is self-consciousness in Shakespeare's presentation of the episode with its on-stage spectators, the Provost and Lucio.

---

1 One should note different senses of the word 'sister': (1) a daughter of the same parents as another person; (2) a member of a religious community of women; (3) *OED* Sister *sb* 3c records 'sisters of the bank' (1550) = prostitutes; compare *The Revenger's Tragedy* 2.2.144–5:

And careful sisters spin that thread i'the night
That does maintain them and their bawds i'the day.

A nun severs her bonds with the specific family into which she is born and becomes a sister of the universal family of mankind, when she takes her vows. The text is ambiguous about Isabella's dress, though Angelo's reaction to her will be more dramatically forceful if she wears religious robes. As a postulant or novice in actuality a woman would probably have worn secular dress outside the convent, but Shakespeare could take dramatic licence with such rules, and the general concern of this play with the official robes pertaining to government, the law and religion (and also the socially typifying dress, recalling the Morality plays, of gallants and prostitutes) might suggest that Isabella was imagined by Shakespeare as wearing a nun's habit.

The focus on legal and ethical points yields a debate played at first according to strict rules. Each advocate deploys trained skill and knowledge; it is law-court theatre.[1] The audience is thus licensed to enjoy the performance as such, and a certain air of unreality may prevail, as if a man's life were not actually, directly, at stake. Soon the strong latent personal bias of both players unbalances their advocacy. Isabella is stung to assert the superior authority of the Church to which she is dedicated: she speaks as if only women were capable of martyrdom, their softness like that of the myrtle is cherished by God who shatters great oaktrees for all their hardness. As she softly pleads to Angelo, 'Go to your bosom, / Knock there', she penetrates the role, and arouses the man. Lucio, the licentious cynic who stage-manages her performance, supposes Angelo a hypocrite and sees Isabella's erotic potential. To Lucio everybody is sexually susceptible; to him Isabella's intensity is a form taken by the repressed libidinousness of her youth, which her beauty nonetheless reveals. In the convent he speaks of 'the wanton stings and motions of the sense' as giving men their 'natural edge', which the austere or celibate seek to 'blunt' by self-denial.

Lucio's judgement reveals his own bias, but Shakespeare devises a situation in which Lucio's different angle of vision increases the complexity of the issue, reveals further facets. His baseness ironically does good, exposing and manipulating Angelo's instability, though putting Isabella dangerously at risk too. It is a scrupulous exercise of moral discrimination to judge the degree of accuracy in Lucio's acute, but always distorted, judgement of others. His innuendoes about the Duke's past, in discounting his public reputation for chastity, plausibly raise questions about the healthiness of the Duke's attitude to love.[2] At the same time Lucio is cruel-tongued, and enjoys the suffering of others – witness his mockery of Pompey, arrested and appealing to Lucio for bail (another ransom) in 3.1. Perhaps the Duke at the beginning *is* suffering from an unhealthy disgust at the body, to judge by his assertion 'Believe not that the dribbling dart of love / Can pierce a complete bosom', as well as abhorrence of crowds, the 'body politic'. If there is some substance in Lucio's insight, when its skew is corrected, it may help us to recognise the Duke as having faults, an imperfect nature – that is, as a man among the ranks of humanity. This does not correspond to James I's view of the absolute monarch's status as above the law.

Considering more widely the issue of role-playing, one notes that the Duke is

---

1 See p. 35 above, n. 1. At the same time it is an instance of the play's large concern with casuistry, the procedure by which the particular circumstances of a case – personal, social and psychological – are taken into account, so that general principles of justice are scrupulously qualified, tempered by equity. The casuistical treatment of such issues was of great interest to religious and moral thinkers as well as lawyers of the time. See Camille Slights, *The Casuistical Tradition*, 1981.

2 A number of questions are raised about the bearing of the past on the present in the play. The information tends to be fragmentary and hence tantalising, though whether this is due to Shakespeare's negligence or calculation cannot be determined. The consequence is that these obscure references require an audience, like a jury, to assess the evidence, evaluating the reliability of the witnesses and the likelihood of their statements as best they can.

impatient to divest himself of his robes and insignia, and no sooner is he free of them in the first scene than he is seeking out the Friar to don his Friar-disguise, and, with it, the opportunity to revel in the devious plotting that goes with the Friar's role in Shakespeare, as in *Romeo and Juliet* or *Much Ado*. Release from the constrictions of being head of state lets the Duke play games of improvisation – wryly recalling the actors of the *commedia dell'arte* – and at the crises of the play he is confronted by dilemmas requiring ingenuity of an order approaching that of the three tricksters in Jonson's *The Alchemist*. There is an ironical parallel between the Duke's response to his role as 'Friar Lodowick' and Isabella's donning a religious gown and by its constraint escaping from her youthful, natural self as Claudio's sister. Though sacrificing ordinary kinship bonds and accepting isolation as a nun – a bride of Christ – she can hope for a respected role in her own right, something otherwise available to a woman only through marriage. Angelo, too, finds donning robes a release for unknown desires. So intense is his private state of repression and isolation that it amounts to self-torture; in his role as Deputy he ambitiously expands the domain to be repressed, decreeing instantly that the whole state be subjected to the same compulsion (as Lucio shrewdly notes). He does at first really resist Isabella, too. Once touched by the idea of sensual gratification which she unintentionally gives him, however, his desire irresistibly swells, but in a distorted form. His intelligence at once sees how public position and power may be used to gratify private, forbidden, violent desire. He exploits the system of law for tyranny. In presenting Angelo's machiavellian plots Shakespeare exhibits the workings of the internal power-system of the state as graphically as Jonson in *Sejanus*. Angelo's desire is infected and it is cruel, its object 'sweet uncleanness', blackmail and rape, not wooing and love. Even the infamous bargain over Claudio's life is broken – a gratuitous kind of theft and therefore especially sweet to his perverse taste.

Angelo goes to recklessly extreme lengths in public as well as private because turning licence into licentiousness produces uncontrollable consequences. Absolute power operates unchecked, beyond the law, and secretly. This is what its consequences are if the ruler becomes corrupt, and this may be why Shakespeare shows the Duke – himself an absolute ruler – once stripped of his power, driven to the most frantic ingenuity in attempting to frustrate the absolute ruler's tyranny. Shakespeare's use of Barnardine to wreck the Duke's scheme brings the Duke face to face with despair. This is not a tragic play, but it offers an analysis of absolutism not in essentials very different from *Sejanus* in this respect. Angelo's corruption seems self-sustaining: he is gratified by watching himself play the devil in the guise of a saint: consciousness of guilt is a desired 'wanton sting', it makes hungry where most it satisfies.

These issues and the questioning mode in which they are presented can be more clearly illustrated by turning to the long final scene of the play. This concerns a formal state occasion, a Royal Entry to the city in which official robes and insignia must be worn for the performance of the public rituals. During the scene a number of disguises are removed before everyone's eyes, one after another, amid mounting excitement: first Mariana's veil, then the Friar's hood, then the muffles from the head of Claudio.

Shakespeare exploits the presence of various kinds of spectator on stage in Act 5 who witness the events from different points of view and offer the audience, through their witness, a sense of the moral complexities, on the one hand, and of the partiality with which each judges, on the other. The reactions of the on-stage spectators can also, in the manner of a classical chorus (though less obtrusively), transmit to the theatre audience an emotional involvement and responsiveness to the increasingly exciting sequence of discoveries in Act 5.

As these visual discoveries are presented to the audience, a series of further disguises and deceptions are also uncovered, revealing how intricate is the interplay between verbal and visual codes, images in language and stage action concerning role and identity, in the play.

PLAYING WITH AUDIENCES

At the beginning of 5.1 the Duke recalls in his formal greeting to Angelo the emphasis he placed, when first appointing his deputy in 1.1, on unfolding Angelo's 'character', his secret 'history'. The theatre audience now in Act 5 know the Duke is fully informed of Angelo's wickedness, so may sense a sharp edge – as sharp as Jonson's in Act 5 of *Sejanus* – in his fulsome commendation of Angelo's performance as Deputy: it is in effect a signal for accusation to be levelled at the Deputy:

> Oh, your desert speaks loud, and I should wrong it
> To lock it in the wards of covert bosom
> When it deserves with characters of brass
> A forted residence   (5.1.9–12)

The anticipation of a full parallel to *Sejanus*, with the disgrace of the Deputy, is signalled, but it does not happen: on the contrary the Duke deliberately frustrates it. This must disquiet a theatre audience and their doubts may also be reflected in the audience of citizens welcoming the Duke. Is the Duke actually evil himself? The wordless but visual reaction of his people may underscore the question, in a stage production of the scene. 'Friar Lodowick''s plan was to destroy Angelo through Isabella's denunciation. This, for all its genuine passion, involves a deliberate lie, and in telling the lie she appears to stumble in her part:

> Justice, oh royal Duke! Vail your regard
> Upon a wronged – I would fain have said a maid.   (5.1.20–1)

Isabella may thus provoke a reaction from the Duke – a flicker of amusement or a start of anxiety. The hesitation, whether interpreted as rhetorically calculated (which is possible) or accidental, calls the audience's attention to Isabella's performing of a role involving deception (and Friar Peter's tactful stage-management shows it too). The Duke's peremptory dismissal of Isabella's accusation against

Angelo horrifies Isabella, and must surprise any spectators who know Cinthio or have taken the hint of the allusion to *Sejanus*. Is the implication that the Duke is himself a tyrant, or suddenly betrayed by a whim into siding with Angelo? An audience may uneasily recall how Lucio said the Duke was perversely devious. With Isabella thus discredited, Angelo must think himself nearly in the clear, and must look more confident, even though still closely observed by the Duke. Shakespeare's aim at this point is deliberately to confuse the audience and keep them anxious: he gives clues which seem to contradict one another, or which are misleading. The more alert the spectator, the more he is likely to be misled. Thus news is suddenly brought that 'Friar Lodowick' is sick 'of a strange fever'. An alert spectator may think this sounds ironically like the fever Ragozine 'conveniently' died of, but then may realise that in any case 'Lodowick' could never appear before the Duke, since they are one and the same person. When Friar Peter announces that the absent 'Lodowick' would have supported Angelo's claim to innocence, Peter himself must be suspected of working covertly against Isabella. This is as bewildering as a Hitchcock plot: and if Peter is an agent of a malign Duke, an audience must feel real anxiety. Shakespeare has deliberately misled them several times in quick succession, and he sows further anxiety with scattered allusions to ominous situations in *Hamlet* and *The Spanish Tragedy* as well as *Sejanus*.

The Duke now turns to Angelo:

> Do you not smile at this, Lord Angelo?   (5.1.163)

This may remind spectators of Hamlet's note on the brazenness of the secretly guilty Claudius.[1] The Duke invites Angelo to conduct a trial and calls for seats to watch it as if it were a play. If the allusion is to the play within the play in *The Spanish Tragedy* (already alluded to at 5.1.20) or *Hamlet*, it will be recalled that justice is not simply affirmed in either, and both end in bloody violence.

Now the Duke invites Angelo to begin his performance as magistrate even though it may prove something of a comedy with such 'wretched fools' in the case. There is ominous emphasis, in the Duke's deliberate words 'be you judge / Of your own cause', which might signal to an alert spectator an allusion to the trial scene in 3.1 of *Sejanus*, where Tiberius, intent on liquidating those no longer useful to him, has a deputy conduct a trial to license judicial murder with a show of rectitude. There, the brave victim Silius defies the blatant and black farce but is obviously doomed:

> Is he my accuser?
> And must he be my judge?

The implied parallel between the Duke and Jonson's Tiberius is a real cause for anxiety. Now Angelo as judge is confronted with a veiled female figure. Her plea is in the riddling form familiar in folk-tale and dramatic romance, far remote from

---

1 The word 'smile' is memorable in *Hamlet* where the prince notes that a man 'may smile and smile and be a villain' (1.5.108).

the court-room demands for no-nonsense evidence of the scene so far. The contrast between the impatient brusqueness of the Duke and Angelo, and the strangely grave veiled figure uttering apparently incomprehensible riddles,[1] is a contrast in styles of theatre as well as ways of feeling and understanding – Shakespeare wishes to keep an audience aware of the element of artifice, playing-as-deception, as the action reaches its climax.

In devising this climax Shakespeare recapitulates important earlier scenes in which key issues of the play are debated. Isabella in Act 2 has two interviews with Angelo; these are recalled in her two appeals to the Duke in Act 5: one appeal is to denounce Angelo, the other to pardon him. On both occasions she is shocked to be rejected, repeating the rejections suffered in Act 2. Shakespeare also recalls the trial scene with Elbow, Pompey and Froth in 2.1. There Angelo affected to find the cause too mean for one of his ambition and high seriousness – although an audience in the theatre may rather judge that he very rapidly loses control to the more experienced Pompey. In mitigation, it may be said that Escalus too, though successful in preventing anarchy from wrecking the proceedings, is outmanoeuvred by Pompey. Both Angelo and Escalus are deceived by Pompey's vulgar appearance and manner into underestimating his skill, his wit, and the force of his point of view.

Now, in Act 5, Angelo seems to be finding it easier to keep order, at any rate under the observing eye of the Duke. When Mariana delivers her riddling appeal, dark-veiled as she is, Angelo has no difficulty in getting the Duke to agree that, like Isabella earlier, this witness is out of her wits (another parallel with Pompey and Elbow in 2.1). Emboldened now, Angelo takes a step too far, offering to uncover the real plot which he suggests was devised by some 'more mightier member' working behind the two women. The Duke excuses himself and abruptly leaves (as did Angelo in 2.1), asking that the case be taken over by Escalus (again as happened in 2.1). Escalus promptly calls on Lucio to testify. Lucio is no grubby tapster, he is a gallant, and Escalus is evidently deceived by his gentlemanly appearance, crediting his slanders against 'Friar Lodowick' and condemning the 'Friar' as dishonest even before he appears to be questioned. This is a piece of flagrant injustice.

When 'Friar Lodowick' is brought in he is at once defiant and aggressive (recalling the doomed Silius in Act 3 of *Sejanus*). He declares loudly that the judge is infamous:

> Respect to your great place: and let the devil
> Be sometime honoured for his burning throne. (5.1.288–9)

This is a bitter insult, and Escalus is provoked to a degree of intemperance by this 'Friar' which nothing earlier in the play leads one to expect. (Pompey, it is true,

---

1 In *All's Well That Ends Well* 5.3 Diana produces some riddles which at first seem completely absurd. For an early Elizabethan example see the drama *Sir Clyomon and Sir Clamydes* where at the end a mysterious and beautiful lady speaks riddles to Sir Clyomon which, when solved, reveal her to be his long-lost beloved.

tried to compromise Escalus back in 2.1, but Escalus seemed easily able to keep
self-control there.) Now Escalus orders torture for 'Friar Lodowick':

> Take him hence; to th'rack with him! We'll touze you
> Joint by joint . . .   (5.1.307–8)

Escalus calls on Lucio to help when 'Lodowick' seems to resist, and Lucio takes
the opportunity with both hands for a physical assault. To break the taboo
associated with holy robes, and to ingratiate himself with a newly arbitrary
magistrate, are added bonuses from Lucio's point of view, but he rips the 'Friar''s
hood off only to uncover the Duke. It is instead, we see, an unmasking of Lucio,
and of Angelo's tyranny. Angelo descends from the seat of justice, an isolated
figure of guilt and shame who asks for death.

The 'Friar''s unhooding is a means also to focus on the situation of Isabella.
She was brought back on stage to be told by the 'Friar' that all was lost, and his
performance, which she then observed helplessly, could only confirm the
desperate view of things. The Duke, once restored to power, gives her some
reassurance, but he still maintains the fiction that her brother Claudio is dead. He
next condemns Angelo, which in turn strikes Mariana with dread. The scene
presents three graphic, isolated figures – Angelo, Mariana, Isabella – in whom the
crisis is concentrated. Then Mariana breaks out of her isolation and appeals to
Isabella. Isabella, in an intense moment, kneels to plead for the man who killed
her brother. This moment when interpreted as Isabella's spiritual transformation
can be wonderful, sometimes overwhelming, for an audience in the theatre. It is
striking, therefore, that it cuts no ice at all with the Duke. He rejects it:

> Your suit's unprofitable. Stand up, I say.   (5.1.448)

The harsh material ring of the word 'unprofitable' seems in itself gratuitously
cruel. What is necessary for the Duke's plot gives pain to Isabella, repeatedly. She
must experience, as deadly earnest, trials an audience is privileged to know are
contrived. Is this to show she is slow to respond from the heart? Or does it show
the Duke as callous? Or just driven by necessity?

Structurally the plot points to affirmative spiritual change at the very end of the
play, in a mood of great excitement, for Isabella, Angelo, and Claudio, each of
whom has been shown earlier in the grip of painful and turbulent moral and
emotional stress. The dramatic action can be recognised as subjecting each of
them to a severe trial confronting them with their own particular faults,
compounded by weakness, and all three reach a crisis in which they are powerless
to control their situation. The main part of the play unfolds these histories at some
length and with a degree of psychological detail that contrasts markedly with the
sudden and compressed ending. This contrast, however, provokes contradictory
interpretations. The question of the relation between guilt and suffering on the
one side, and retribution, reconstitution and reward on the other, may implicitly be
accounted for by the measurelessness of mercy and Christian compassion which,

according to one interpretation,[1] is released in the climax. Nevertheless, neither Claudio nor Isabella speaks the words which could have made such a nobly affirmative conclusion certain. Claudio on being unhooded is shown not the expected axe and execution block but Juliet, and freedom, and life to come. He may also see his sister, who left him to die in prison. They do not speak to each other. There is the brief dialogue in 3.1 suggesting that the Duke-as-Friar wished to mitigate the bitter pain each gave the other, so that all may be assumed to be well between them, but this part of the story is left almost blank. In the case of Isabella it is debatable whether her act of kneeling to plead for Angelo's life shows she has finally learned what true Christian compassion is, and is at last mature enough to fulfil the demands the duties of a nun involve. What then is to be made of the Duke's proposal of marriage, and what is to be made of her silence in response to it?

THE QUESTION OF TRAGI-COMEDY

Romance traditionally invites expectation of development in its characters as they undergo testing experience, as is evident in the young lovers in Sidney's *Arcadia* (1590) or Shakespeare's earlier comedies. Conventionally also in romance, this positive change in certain characters is contrasted to the fixed – and limited – nature of minor characters.

In tragi-comedy Shakespeare and his close contemporaries often present characters spiritually transformed by some intense crisis brought about by melodramatic abrupt turns of plot: sudden disclosures of concealed identity, or of survival of persons supposed dead, or evil schemes averted in the nick of time. Tragi-comedy stresses the peaks and troughs of the emotional trajectory proper to romance; it experiments by accelerating the development of experience proper to tragedy and reversing its thrust, to exert a maximum of stress on the persons in the play and on its significance. By bringing opposed artistic modes into collision in this way, tragi-comedy as a mode in its own right is an unstable, experimental kind of drama, and Shakespeare explores its extremes in this play. Shakespeare's repeated arousing and frustrating of expectation, and the bizarre surprises he springs on an audience, will sweep them away on an emotional switchback while allowing them to glimpse from time to time the artful technique of the dramatist, as reflected in the scheming of the Duke, since the Duke is making, in effect, a play within a play by means of deceit and inspired improvisation.

The Duke seems to have a taste for springing surprises which increases in step with the increasingly risky opportunities presented to him (there is a clear parallel with Angelo here). At the very end of the play it might be plausible to see the Duke, carried away by euphoria at his overwhelming success, overreaching himself

---

1 The essay on the play by G. Wilson Knight, first published in 1930 in *The Wheel of Fire*, was an acknowledged influence on Tyrone Guthrie in producing the play in London in that year, with Charles Laughton as Angelo. Peter Brook's 1950 production took a similar line in its interpretation of the role of the Duke, though emphasising the counter-force of the 'rough' elements. See the discussion, pp. 61–5 below.

by springing one surprise too many in proposing to Isabella – such an interpretation acknowledging the Duke's evasion of a full confrontation, on his own part, with the faults of his nature and actions. Offering marriage to a young woman who has not renounced her commitment to the life of a holy sister, a bride of Christ, might be shown, then, to deserve scornful rejection. A play with a number of parallels to *Measure for Measure*, *The Revenger's Tragedy*, has a surprise ending with a twist in its tail – where in the very last moments the wittily triumphant plotters suffer a fall. On the other hand the design of the analogous Shakespeare play *All's Well That Ends Well*, which had perhaps already been written, shows that Shakespeare was very interested in the motif of the sick ruler mysteriously cured at the hands of a young, idealistic heroine. This motif is pivotal to the plot in *All's Well*. In *Measure for Measure* the Duke's sickness seems to involve an isolation in which are glimpsed misanthropic despair and sexual unease. Shakespeare strengthens the folk-tale suggestiveness of the Duke's disguise role by associating Mariana with it, and thereby invites a further, discrepant interpretation. With the invocation of folk-tale Shakespeare has been supposed by some interpreters to summon the full extent of the pagan tradition behind the sources, and the concern with magic there. If the Duke is a shadow for the role of trickster and priest, both associated with the casting of spells, it may be assumed that transformation and healing compose the play's conclusion. But Shakespeare is not inclined to repeat himself, on the whole, and even in *All's Well* some characters resist healing.

If the Duke proposes, is this because he sees Isabella has discovered that her true destiny is to be a woman rather than a bride of Christ? Or is the Duke hopelessly mistaken? Even if some of the characters are subject to inner change, it may be this offer of marriage is deliberately intended by Shakespeare to show that the pattern is precisely not consistent. Isabella acts in response to pressure from outside in her previous appeals; is it therefore certain that in appealing for Angelo's life she is not once more acting under pressure rather than spontaneously from her heart? Circumstantial evidence could support either view.

When considered on reflection *Measure for Measure* can seem to raise questions too profound and difficult to be accounted for in the chosen mode and form, whereas in the theatre the compelling sway of a dramatic rhythm seems to change an audience's sense of things as it proceeds. In the theatre an audience contributes to, as it is involved in, a performance; even apparently unforgivable actions, such as Isabella's rejection of her brother's agonised appeal (3.1), can be made to seem, by the end of the play, no barrier to reconciliation in the immeasurably joyful mood a performance may create there. On the other hand the emotional violence, and shockingly immoral impulses, released in the first half of the action can be the basis for an interpretation of the whole play as a posing of difficult questions in an ironic form, so that it is received as a 'problem play' or as dialectically presenting intellectual and moral issues in the casuistical tradition. Such an interpretation will find the last-minute climactic resolution in Act 5 too contrived adequately to accommodate the deep personal and spiritual reorientation required of Angelo,

Isabella or Claudio, and will consider the Duke as especially worthy of critical irony.

The art of being a prince, and the art of being a tragi-comic dramatist, are both subjected to serious ironic criticism by viewing them from the perspectives of two dramatically minor and socially marginalised characters, Juliet and Barnardine. There is no doubt something of the baroque in presenting unexpectedly revealing views from such odd angles, but this is the kind of cunning-wrought design which recurs in the late Shakespeare of *Cymbeline*, *The Winter's Tale* and *The Tempest*.

Barnardine and Juliet are remarkable for the clarity with which they assert themselves as individuals, a clarity which renders them immune to browbeating or mystification. In confrontation with the Duke, where in each case a life is at stake, the youthful Juliet and the hardened Barnardine each assert a conviction which makes the Duke appear callous as well as inept in his role and his plotting. With Juliet (2.3) the Duke apparently anticipates that his interrogation will expose, first, her immature confusion at finding herself unmarried and pregnant and, second, her lack of formal religious education and understanding. Instead it is the Duke who rapidly gets out of his depth. Juliet cuts off his moralistic platitudes. Her quiet but succinct statement

> I do repent me as it is an evil
> And take the shame with joy
> (2.3.35–6)

is a perfectly contrite formula, but at the same time it expresses simple joy in love and in pregnancy. The Duke-as-Friar has to tell her then, with the crudest abruptness, that Claudio is to die 'tomorrow'. The official tone exposes the gap between Juliet, who lives by the holiness of the heart's affections, and the public authority's blank heartlessness.

Juliet, as a young pregnant woman, might seem to be powerless, but after this interview it is the Duke who must appear a weaker figure. Barnardine is not a youth but has long experience in resisting the law as well as a natural hostility to being pushed around. He declares he will not die for any man's persuasion (4.3.51), and indeed everyone can see that to execute him to serve the Duke's emergency, which has nothing to do with him, looks suspiciously like a form of judicial murder.

Barnardine is coarse and apparently brutal, but he is so stark in his will to live, an 'unaccommodated man', that his refutation of the Duke (and his fancy plot) is vindicated. His refusal to die exposes the gap between the Duke's bizarre plotting (and the mystical adumbrations of writers of tragi-comedy) and the actual world where men rot away in prison or perish on a scaffold, depending on a word from a prince.

Central to the play is the question of faith versus credulity, love versus deceit. Like the lover, the lawyer or the poet, the playwright uses rhetorical arts to persuade. The mode of tragi-comedy at this time offered extraordinary techniques for manipulating audience response: thus manipulated, audiences might be persuaded – against their normal judgement, perhaps – to believe the strangest transformations, or to accept the strangest extenuating circumstances to justify actions which otherwise were wrong. In certain other tragi-comedies Shakespeare calls attention to the dramatic art and rhetorical techniques of the mode (as he certainly does in *Measure for Measure*) to show an audience that to accept certain kinds of truth must be an act of faith, in life as in theatre. In *Measure for Measure* it remains possible, however, that although an audience is meant to feel tempted to see things as the Duke would have them seen, they should nevertheless think again. Perhaps that is why the figures of Barnardine, brutally instinctive, and Juliet, human and loving, stand out, desiring only to be free from the inhibition or stupefaction of bad law and bad governors.

The play on the stage

Although *Measure for Measure*'s full text presents actors and readers with questions of interpretation which yield various possible answers, nevertheless to perform the full text must at the very least give expression to all the elements – religious, legal, social, personal – which the various plots bring into dynamic interrelation. The judicious cutting of lines of dialogue by 'thinning' can shorten the playing-time without substantial loss or distortion. As a general principle a dramatist expects changes to be made when a new company prepares his play afresh for performance, particularly in a place different from that in which it was previously acted, or in a length of time shorter than his full text requires. The structural robustness of a Shakespeare play, whether considered as a whole or scene by scene, appears to have been designed to ensure that judicious cutting will be possible without substantial distortion of the overall pattern of dynamically interrelated elements. But Shakespeare's constructional unit was the scene, so that the cutting of whole scenes almost always involves some substantial loss or distortion, as does any alteration in the order of scenes. Yet the history of *Measure for Measure* in the theatre up to the present shows a continuing readiness to make substantial cuts and transpositions of whole scenes, and there is also a readiness to cut substantial passages so that characters and episodes can be made to have a significance Shakespeare's full text will not allow.

   Measure for Measure is concerned with public and private issues which were highly sensitive in 1604 and which have so continued to the present, and performances often witness more to the cultural and political climate of the time when they take place than they do to any genuine attempt to confront the full text and full design of the play. At various times from the Restoration (1660) to the 1980s the sexual, or the political, or the religious issues of the play (or all three) have been as far as possible suppressed in order to make the play tame and accept-able, or the play has been made the occasion for strong ideological advocacy, whether it be for sexual liberation[1] or against sex,[2] whether it be in affirming an

1 See the discussion of John Barton's 1970 production at the R.S.C., pp. 67–8 below.
2 The notorious Thomas Bowdler was rather a latecomer, so far as *Measure for Measure* is concerned, in attempting to suppress the play's outspoken concern with sexuality, since the process of

all-powerful incomprehensible Christian deity or advocating a materialist, anti-authority polemic.[1] The play has been adapted to yield melodrama and romantic fairy tale, or to present a hostile view of totalitarian regimes – Capitalist in Brecht's version of 1951, Communist in the Polish production at Cracow in 1956.

Indeed from the beginning of its stage history *Measure for Measure* has been susceptible because of its double plot to radical distortion by adaptation. It is notable how often adapters have reintroduced elements from the sources that Shakespeare deliberately kept out, or have suppressed elements of Shakespeare's design that he took obvious care to emphasise.

After its first recorded performance in 1604 at court there is no specific further record until 1662, when Davenant presented his adaptation with the title *The Law Against Lovers* at Lincoln's Inn Fields Theatre, where the leading actor was Thomas Betterton. This theatre, like others of the time, had scenic resources in the form of backdrops, painted wings and movable shutters. However, scenic locations were general rather than specific, while the actors performed on a projecting forestage in close contact with their audience. Rapid transition from scene to scene was also a characteristic of performance, so that significant links were retained with theatrical custom in Shakespeare's time. Taste had changed significantly in other ways, however. Davenant disdained the socially inferior characters and their language in *Measure for Measure*, but he approved the more courtly conversation of gentlemen and ladies in Shakespearean comedy, especially Beatrice and Benedick in *Much Ado About Nothing*, which accords with Restoration taste. Davenant exploited the fact that *Measure for Measure* has a double plot like *Much Ado About Nothing* by entirely removing the underworld characters and plots from *Measure for Measure* (except for Lucio) and replacing them with Benedick and Beatrice. He invented a younger sister for Beatrice, Viola, who danced and sang. The effect may be suggested by noting one song's opening line, 'Wake all the dead! What hoa! What hoa!', the fact that she sang a chorus with Benedick, Escalus and Lucio, 'Our Ruler has got the vertigo of State', and that she danced a saraband with 'castanietos'. Pepys saw the production and liked her dancing and singing 'especially'.[2]

In splicing together the two plots Davenant is indifferent to Shakespeare's concern with the play's overall tone and mood, with a general harmonic scheme within which changes of key are carefully calculated. Davenant instead makes blunt substitutions, simplifying character, toning down conflict, diffusing intensity. He begins by presenting Angelo as Lord Protector, which is a manifest allusion to the Puritan rule of Cromwell, who had only ceased to be Lord Protector four years earlier; but this political allusion is not followed through in the rest of the play. Benedick is spliced into the *Measure for Measure* plot by making him Angelo's

suppression began with Davenant's cutting of the low-life episodes and their emphasis on prostitution and disease. The full text was not restored to the stage until the present century.

1 As in the adaptation by Brecht, 1951, or that by Howard Brenton at the Northcott Theatre, Exeter, in 1972, or that by Charles Marowitz, discussed at p. 69 below.

2 Pepys recorded his visit to see the play in his diary on 18 February 1662.

brother and substituting him for Escalus in pleading for Claudio's pardon; later, after this fails, the episode from *Much Ado*, in which Beatrice challenges Benedick to act when her cousin is abused, is adapted: Beatrice now urges Benedick to steal a signet and contrive a forged pardon for Claudio.

Davenant also alters the plot of *Measure for Measure* itself, making Angelo a simpler, weaker figure: in a final interview he tells Isabella he was only testing her, never intended to have Claudio executed, and has already sent off his pardon. Isabella does not believe him, but it turns out to be true. Davenant contrives incidents and dialogue to fill out the gaps created by his cuts (including Mariana) and to give Beatrice and Benedick something to do, since the Duke is no longer a key figure masterminding the action.

This adaptation is an early instance of the way Shakespeare's characters generally are thought of as separable from the dramatic text in which he presents them, and are given fresh narratives and situations. It also prefigures many musical and operatic adaptations of Shakespeare's plays generally from Purcell up to Bernstein. Richard Wagner in fact wrote an opera based on *Measure for Measure*, *Das Liebesverbot* (1836). In this version Isabella rouses the people of Palermo to revolt against the German viceroy and free Claudio. Wagner records[1] that the Magdeburg police objected to the opera's title but when told that it was modelled on a very serious play of Shakespeare's they permitted its performance, though under a new title.

That Shakespeare's play as it stood in the First Folio was not acceptable to Restoration taste was not disputed by Gildon, author of the next adaptation, *Measure for Measure, or Beauty the Best Advocate* (1700). Gildon has the novel idea that instead of splicing Shakespeare's *Measure for Measure* with his *Much Ado*, he will splice it with the dramatic opera *Dido and Aeneas*, music by Purcell, libretto by Tate.[2] Gildon follows Davenant in cutting the underworld characters (even Lucio after Act 1) and episodes to make way for the added material; he inserts parts of Purcell's opera at intervals in the first four acts of *Measure for Measure*. The play's emotional and intellectual complexity is generally simplified and weakened.[3]

Even after cutting and adapting, the discrepancy between Shakespeare's drama-

---

1 Cited in Eccles, pp. 480–1.
2 *Dido* was first performed in 1689. Purcell's wonderful music could have imbued the name of Tate with a degree of fame, but it is his fate to be remembered rather as the adapter of Shakespeare's *King Lear*, to which he supplied a different ending.
3 Angelo here begins in full authority, and the Duke makes his first appearance much later; his dramatic significance is considerably diminished, and he definitely does not marry Isabella at the end. Emphasis is placed on the melodramatic villainy of Angelo, who is from the first moment attracted to Isabella, without any inner struggle; he is prompt to stress the lurid torments he will impose on Claudio if she does not give herself to him. Both Angelo and Claudio are already properly married, to Mariana and Juliet respectively, before the dramatic action begins, which tones down the significance of the bed-trick and prepares for Claudio's scene with Isabella: he begins by expressing terror of death, and induces a violent response from Isabella, but then confesses this was merely a preliminary to asking her to take care of Juliet after his death. Isabella's hysteria turns to sweet contrition. This episode is followed by operatic episodes from Purcell ending with Dido's superb lament 'When I am laid in earth'.

turgy and Purcell's remains obvious, but at least Gildon seeks to match some qualities in Shakespeare with Purcell's dramatic music,[1] whereas Davenant's use of Beatrice and Benedick could only produce discords. Restoration audiences might have been expected to appreciate Gildon's adaptation, but in fact the version of *Measure for Measure* which held the stage for the main part of the eighteenth century was Shakespeare's own text, though heavily cut. The idea that the play could be performed as Shakespeare wrote it (though shortened) was tried for the first time since the Restoration in December 1720. The famous actor Quin gave a performance as the Duke in a production at the Lincoln's Inn Fields Theatre which used a text exclusively Shakespeare's except for eight lines added at the end. The text was heavily cut, however, as the acting edition of Tonson (1722) reveals.[2] The part of Lucio is much weakened (possibly in deference to Quin's wishes, as he was playing the Duke) and much of the low comedy is removed, including the first part of 1.2, the Froth–Pompey trial in 2.1, and Pompey's speech in prison in 4.3. This pattern of cuts recurs in later acting editions such as that of 1778, suggesting that they were the rule. Quin played the Duke in performances of *Measure for Measure* every year up to 1734 at Lincoln's Inn Fields, and again for his benefit at Drury Lane in 1737, which indicates that it was now established as an important part in Shakespeare, while Mrs Cibber, who played Isabella for the first time opposite Quin in his benefit performance, went on to play Isabella many times and make it an important female role.[3] Thus the Duke and Isabella became the leading roles in the play in the eighteenth century; Mrs Yates had success in the 1770s with Isabella, and Henderson played the Duke opposite her from 1780. Then in 1783 Mrs Sidddons won acclaim for her Isabella at Drury Lane, and her brother J.P. Kemble played opposite her for the first time in 1794. The next year Kemble's acting edition of *Measure for Measure* was published, containing some new alterations to the text.[4]

Kemble's rearrangement substitutes simple narrative for the method of alternating different strands of plot and groups of characters whereby Shakespeare raises contrasts between social and moral attitudes right from the beginning.

1 In his study *Shakespeare and the Artist*, 1959, pp. 24–5, W. Moelwyn Merchant recalls having heard an experiment in which Gildon's text was spoken in combination with the playing of the appropriate parts of a recording of the opera *Dido and Aeneas*. The experiment was considered surprisingly successful.

2 Noted by Miles, *The Problem of 'Measure for Measure'*, p. 106.

3 *Measure for Measure* was acted in London 69 times between 1700 and 1750, and a further 64 times up to the end of the century, while there had been further performances in British cities including Bath, Liverpool, York and Salisbury. In Dublin, after Quin first performed it in 1738 with Mrs Cibber, it was performed 31 times up to 1837. Comparable figures for the most popular Shakespeare play on the London stage in the eighteenth century are 601 for *Hamlet*. *Measure for Measure* ranks nineteenth in popularity. (See C.B. Hogan, *Shakespeare in the Theatre, 1701–1800*, 2 vols., 1952–7.)

4 This version reverses the order of 1.2 and 1.3; it moves the Froth–Elbow–Pompey trial to follow 2.2. It cuts 2.3 (the Duke's scene with Juliet) as well as the Duke's speech in 1.1, 'I love the people'; it also cuts Angelo's soliloquies in 2.2 and 2.4. It cuts the moated grange episode, all 4.5 and 4.6, and removes bawdy from the dialogue in general. At the same time it adds a reconciliation between Claudio and Isabella in the final scene, and rewrites the concluding speech.

6 *Mrs Siddons as the Tragic Muse* (1784), by Sir Joshua Reynolds. Sarah Siddons played Isabella at Drury Lane in 1783 at the age of 28

Kemble's changes to Act 2 also have the effect of providing a prolonged scene of serious emotion (the Elbow–Froth–Pompey material does not intervene as in Shakespeare), which no doubt gave scope to Mrs Siddons for a display of grand and classical acting, the large sweep of which is prepared for by the brief Angelo–Escalus dialogue beginning 2.1. By transferring the Pompey–Elbow–Froth trial to follow 2.2 Kemble smooths out the ironic dialectic provided by the contrasting low comic mode, and devastating counter-arguments, of Pompey; thus in making an acting opportunity for Mrs Siddons as Isabella, Kemble simplifies the emotional experience offered to the audience, and reduces the intellectual content. Kemble's cutting of the Duke's interview with Juliet and the soliloquies of Angelo avoids some intense and painful emotion – perhaps because this might distract attention from the female lead, Isabella – and generally gives the play a smoother, more conventional narrative and emotional shape, largely bereft of specific religious or political questions (although it does retain the Elbow–Froth trial scene). The text was combed for explicit allusions to sexuality, and in removing Angelo's soliloquies the intensity of concern with corruption and disease is played down.

Mrs Siddons is commemorated in a great portrait by Reynolds (who turned to Michelangelo for inspiration) as a superb and maturely dominant figure. She was famed for her neo-classical, 'ideal' acting style, and she last played Isabella in 1811–12 at Covent Garden, so weakened by age that when she knelt in the last scene before the Duke she could only get up again with his help. Shakespeare's text indicates the youthfulness of Isabella – 'for in her youth / There is a prone and speechless dialect' – and she is usually played as young in modern productions.

Measure for Measure was played with decreasing frequency as the nineteenth century wore on. Its emphasis on sexuality, disease and poverty in low life, and intense, painful emotion, might well cause discomfort to increasingly urban middle-class audiences, sanctimonious about the family and marriage, anxious about class, sexually prudish or prurient, unused to thinking when at the theatre. As early as 1809–10 a regular member of the company at Bath 'had in the previous season advertised Measure for Measure in her benefit bills, but was firmly told that it was an indecent play and she had to change it for – of all things – The Provoked Husband'.[1]

Macready had some success as the Duke in a performance he mounted in 1824, and though the play was not again performed in London (except once, in 1829) until a significant production by Phelps in 1846 at Sadler's Wells, Macready's general influence was seen then. Macready became famous for a direct emotional acting style in Shakespeare, seeking closer fidelity to the text.[2] Phelps himself had

---

1 See Arnold Hare, 'A Victorian provincial stock company', in R. Foulkes (ed.), *Shakespeare and the Victorian Stage*, 1986, p. 262, and John Genest, *Some Account of the English Stage*, 1832.

2 He restored some cuts and removed non-Shakespearean accretions, and he introduced more realistic scenery. The Sadler's Wells Theatre benefited from the 1843 Theatres Act which removed the monopoly of spoken drama from the two patent theatres, Drury Lane and Covent Garden, both of them cavernously large and hard to act in. Sadler's Wells apparently addressed itself to the middle

wanted to play Angelo in his 1846 production, but when it became clear that this would mean another actor named Bennett taking the Duke, Phelps changed his plan: he thought Bennett, too much in the stiff Kemble style, would make a pompous Duke; accordingly Phelps took the Duke himself and left Angelo to Bennett.[1] This shows Phelps's concern for the more varied and particular style, but it also shows that the Duke was still the key role, while Angelo was so insignificant that Bennett could do no harm with it. *The Athenaeum* commended Phelps's bowdlerisation of the text (7 November 1846): 'not an offensive phrase left'. The new 'realism' did not extend to restoring the play's low comedy or the conventional extensive cuts.

Attention to historical period accuracy in scenery and costume is a feature of Phelps's work, but it was taken to extreme lengths by Phelps's rival Charles Kean at the Princess's Theatre. At this period designers and scene-painters shared many of the precepts and methods of the Pre-Raphaelite painters, and there is a painting by the Pre-Raphaelite Holman Hunt of Claudio and Isabella, begun in 1850, soon after Phelps's production. Hunt took the interior from the Lollards' prison in Lambeth Palace, following the Pre-Raphaelite concern with authenticity; the painting has been seen in relation to contemporary stage design,[2] with 'all the appearance of a theatrical box-set, with a backcloth of sky and trees visible through the window, itself carefully exploited as a source of "natural" light'. To some degree in tune with changing styles in acting, the Pre-Raphaelites shared ideals of more 'real' and particular representation, and their portraits were seen as substituting intensity for vehemency, self-repression for expansive and gesticulatory display. A *Manchester Guardian* critic wrote about Hunt's *Claudio and Isabella* as a moment in performance: 'The artist has chosen the moment when the first doubt of Claudio's courage grows up in his sister's brain. You can see the slow flush of scorn still striving with doubt in her eyes, and in every lineament of her noble face.'[3] Here the Shakespearean scene is valued for its particular detail and intensity; thus the critic at least imagines an ideal of acting remote from that of the eighteenth century. Probably the contrast in acting as it was actually presented in the theatre in the 1840s with the 'old' school was only relative, since the claim of greater naturalism is recurrent in every generation of actors since; and certainly an incipient Victorian sentimentalisation of Shakespeare's heroines is already to be glimpsed. The particular historical realism of the scenery would soon require vast and cumbrous masses of painted canvas, elaborate costumes and properties, necessitating reduced acting-time and prolonged intervals for scene-changes interrupting the rhythm of performances. Audiences would even applaud

and lower classes of theatregoers, with a repertoire of classics. Particularly in acting style, but also in costume and scenery, there was a move from the generalised and conventionalised to an emphasis on the 'real', on more varied emotion and particularisation. See Russell Jackson, 'Shakespeare on the stage from 1660 to 1900', in the *Cambridge Companion to Shakespeare Studies*, 1986, p. 201.

1 Shirley S. Allen, *Samuel Phelps and the Sadler's Wells Theatre*, 1971.
2 Richard Foulkes, 'Charles Kean's King Richard II', in *Shakespeare and the Victorian Stage*, p. 47.
3 Cited by Foulkes in *ibid.*, p. 46. See illustration 7 overleaf.

7   *Claudio and Isabella* (1850–3), by W. Holman Hunt

impressive scenery when the curtain rose – indeed a stage-manager might appear, bowler-hat in hand, to receive the audience's applause for the scenery, before the actors could begin. *Measure for Measure* offered the scene-painters little scope, which perhaps further contributed to its infrequent stage production in the period.

Shakespeare's concern with conscious theatricality, and the opportunities his texts afford for direct playing with an audience, were ignored and suppressed in the 'pictorial' style, and it is significant that when revolution came in the form of William Poel he chose the now rarely performed *Measure for Measure* to begin it. In 1893 he presented the play on a reconstruction of an Elizabethan stage (that of the Fortune) in the Royalty Theatre. The adaptation did not extend to lighting or to the auditorium or its seating. *The Times* reported that the performance 'proved at least that scenic accessories are by no means as indispensable to the enjoyment of a play as the manager supposes'. The flowing continuity between scenes that Poel achieved, according to other witnesses, was a revelation.[1] Poel produced other Shakespeare plays in reconstructions of Elizabethan playing conditions and returned to *Measure for Measure* in 1908 at the Gaiety Theatre, Manchester. The reconstruction of the Elizabethan stage was within the proscenium arch. The reviewer C.E. Montague wrote[2] that Poel's swift transition from short to long scenes exposed the destructive results for Shakespeare's dramatic rhythm of 'pictorial' staging, where short scenes are 'scurried through' by actors at the front of the stage, a canvas landscape scene 'swelling out at them behind', while the next heavily elaborate set is prepared behind it. Montague also writes acutely on the limitations of the production: 'the essence of the Elizabethan theatre was the fusion or interpenetration of stage and auditorium, and the essence of modern theatre is their separation by the proscenium arch'. Poel's production at the Gaiety was only 'a picture of an Elizabethan stage seen through the frame of a modern proscenium', it was not 'the Elizabethan sensation of having an actor come forward to the edge of a platform in the midst of ourselves'.

Interaction between spectators and performers was the essence of the Edwardian music hall, but because of its proletarian associations it was not easily acceptable for Shakespeare; nevertheless, when Poel's production was seen at Stratford one reviewer[3] wrote of 'the actors being constantly to the front', and since he says the stage projected 'beyond its usual limits' (presumably forward of the proscenium arch) there may have been a tendency to play out to the audience. The performance basically was still within a picture-frame stage with scenery – even though the scenery did represent the Elizabethan Fortune theatre stage.

Poel became famous and influential for his ideas about the speaking of Shakespeare: Basil Dean, the Claudio in this production, recalled Poel's insistence on his method of 'incantation', on speaking the verse 'both musically and

1 Cited by Robert Speaight, *William Poel and the Elizabethan Revival*, 1954, p. 93.
2 *Ibid.*, p. 97.
3 *Leamington Courier*, 24 April 1908.

8   William Poel's production of *Measure for Measure* at the Royalty Theatre, 1893

intelligently . . . he achieved a total effect of surge and sweep quite unlike anything I had heard before'.[1] Nevertheless, the text was extensively cut.

The vicar of Stratford-upon-Avon protested when Poel's *Measure for Measure* was announced there, but reviews of the production in the Leamington and Stratford papers defensively harped on it as 'a moral play': the *Stratford Herald* (24 April 1908) said Miss Allgood's Isabella used so much art 'that passages most naked in their descriptive realism [i.e. on sexual matters] were covered by the veil of her delicacy'. The *Leamington Courier* defended the play's 'great purifying influence'.

After Poel's experimental productions of several Shakespeare plays it was Harley Granville-Barker who between 1912 and 1914 at the Savoy Theatre presented virtually uncut texts of a number of the plays – though not, unfortunately, *Measure for Measure*. The plays were performed with continuous action and rapid speaking on a stage built out over the orchestra pit, against an abstract backdrop of curtains and hard white light. W. Bridges-Adams showed his response to Granville-Barker in the production of *Measure for Measure* at Stratford in 1923, with a virtually complete text, only one interval and swift transition from scene to scene, facilitated by a relatively simple set: a grey Norman arch, one side draped in scarlet for court scenes, with two cell doors and a grated window for prison scenes, and a large canvas backdrop depicting rolling fields for the last scene. Reviewers in *The Times*, the *Telegraph* and the *Morning Post* agreed that it was not a good play

1 Cited by Speaight, *William Poel*, p. 96.

and noted that it was rarely acted; they connected this with its being an 'unpleasant' play rather than a 'pleasant' one – terms borrowed from Bernard Shaw, significantly enough. Shaw wrote devastating reviews of the heavily cut 'pictorial' productions of Shakespeare in the 1890s and he appreciated the experimental work of Poel. In 1898 he implicitly compared his own work, the *Plays Unpleasant*, to 'such unpopular plays as *All's Well*, *Measure for Measure* and *Troilus and Cressida*' where 'we find [Shakespeare] ready and willing to start at the twentieth century if the seventeenth would only let him'.[1]

The *Daily Telegraph* noted[2] of the Bridges-Adams production that 'the Stratford audience, to its infinite credit, never turns a hair at this practically uncut version' and the reviewer, keen to show himself an advanced thinker, describes Angelo as 'a pathological study in the effects of sex-repression, rather of a piece with the missionary in that horribly clever story "Rain" by Mr Somerset Maugham'. The *Birmingham Post* thought the current stage censor would be most likely to prohibit this of all Shakespeare's plays for its 'audacity and outspokenness' and considered Lucio's slanders would be 'impossible in a new play'. (Censorship was not abolished until 1968 in Britain.)

Two years later in 1925 Nugent Monck produced *Measure for Measure* as part of his cycle of Shakespeare in simulated Elizabethan conditions at the Maddermarket Theatre, Norwich; then the productions by Tyrone Guthrie in 1930 and 1933 showed the play's potential for dealing with issues of strong interest to modern audiences and paved the way for the breakthrough achieved by Peter Brook at Stratford in 1950. Brook achieved a firmly coherent production of the play, with an extremely young Isabella, Barbara Jefford, full of burning conviction as an ardent, innocent novice; rather than righteous anger she showed a softer humanity, condemning 'proud man' with 'an air of bitter discovery rather than cynical denunciation';[3] nor was she cold or withdrawn in her interviews with Angelo. Gielgud, after his renowned Hamlet, gave Angelo 'suppressed and twisted nobility': at one point Isabella grasped his hand in fervour and Gielgud showed, 'subtly, the response of the awakened Angelo. His voice was somewhat less sure, his motions not flagrantly but just perceptibly less steady. The audience was aware of the change. Isabella was not.'[4] With Gielgud playing Angelo rather than the Duke, Brook's production might seem to follow Guthrie's of 1933, which had a memorably frightening Angelo in Charles Laughton; but Brook had a powerful Duke too, played by Harry Andrews, an actor commanding effortless authority, who here gave the Duke human warmth, and 'whose charm of manner could convince us of his integrity and wisdom'. He spoke the couplets at the end of Act 3 ('He who the sword of heaven will bear') naturally, 'as a rumination, moving, as well as in character'.[5]

1 George Bernard Shaw, *Plays: Pleasant and Unpleasant*, 1898, I, xxi.
2 26 April 1923.
3 Richard David, 'Shakespeare's comedies and the modern stage', *S.Sur.* 4 (1951), 129–39.
4 *Ibid.*
5 *Ibid.*

In fact Brook made a large number of cuts[1] which affected the interpretation of the main characters and substantially changed the action of the final scene; these cuts reinforce the emphasis implicit in the casting. The Duke lost a good deal of his dark-corner manipulative aspect: he did not confess 'I have strewed it in the common ear' nor did he explain that Angelo is to 'strike home' while he himself is to evade being directly involved; Lucio's comment that the Duke has deliberately deceived many gentlemen (1.4) was also cut. Later the Duke-as-Friar's interview with Juliet lost the exchange in which Juliet has the fine reply 'I do repent me as it is an evil / And take the shame with joy.' Isabella lost lines which show her in a less than admirable light, such as 3.1.184 ff., 'I had rather my brother die by the law than my son should be unlawfully born.' Brook cut the Duke's conspiratorial speeches in this part of the play to enhance his dignity and probity. Further important cuts included the Duke's speech 'Oh place and greatness' (4.1) as well as 'music oft hath such a charm / To make bad good'; the Duke's continuing deception of Isabella in Act 5 about her brother was cut, as was the Duke's direct offer of marriage – 'and say you will be mine'. Barnardine's Act 5 entrance and pardon were also cut; while this left emphasis more directly focused on the major characters, it reduced the universality of forgiveness and of the Duke's magnanimity. These cuts tended to present the Duke and Isabella rather in their own view of themselves, while protecting them against evidence jeopardising this view.[2]

Brook reinforced the admirable characteristics of Isabella and the Duke, and gave Angelo a context in which agonising struggle demonstrated his 'twisted nobility'; and he gave this area of the play a less devious plot. What Brook did to the scenes of low life was to make them a genuine counterweight; this demonstration of their power is of major importance, marking the modern rediscovery of the play's full design.

The set was a single permanent double range of high arches, receding from the centre of the stage to the wings on both sides upstage. 'These arches might remain open to the sky in those scenes where some air and freshness is required – the convent at night . . . Mariana's moated grange . . . and the [final] street scene.' Yet in a moment 'their spaces could be blanked out, with grey flats for the shabby decorum of the courtroom, with grilles for the prison cells'.[3] This is reminiscent of Bridges-Adams, not least in its concern with swift scenic transitions. Downstage, Brook had a permanent heavy postern gate for minor scenes or for those (such as the visit to Claudio) which require a cramped setting. Richard David's account suggests that this permanent set had a continuous 'shadowy' presence giving coherence to the whole play, emphasising the cramped space in which

---

1 For a convenient list of all the prompt-book cuts by Brook, see A.J. Harris, '*Measure for Measure*, A Stage History and an Interpretation'. Unpublished M.A. thesis, University of Birmingham, 1959, Appendix II.
2 Ralph Berry, *Changing Styles in Shakespeare*, 1981, p. 39; and Herbert Weil, Jr, 'The options of the audience: theory and practice in Peter Brook's *Measure for Measure*', *S.Sur.* 25 (1972), 27–37.
3 David, 'Shakespeare's comedies and the modern stage'.

9 Peter Brook's 1950 production at the Shakespeare Memorial Theatre, showing the versatile set
a The prison
b Claudio (Alan Badel) and Juliet (Hazel Penwarden) in Act 1

major scenes of confrontation – Lucio–Isabella, Isabella–Angelo, Claudio–Duke, and so on – were played. Moreover, 'at any moment the whole span of the stage might spring to life and remind us of our bearings in the play'. The progress of Claudio and Juliet to prison 'with all corrupt Vienna surging and clamouring about them' was one such scene; another was an amplification of Pompey's account of the denizens of the prison in Act 4: this presented the prisoners 'processing through the central hall of the prison, [and] brought its holes and corners for a moment into relation with each other'. Barnardine emerged from a pit, and this pit was used to 'tumultuous' effect for a general exit at the end of his scene in Act 4. Several reviewers noted the suggestion of Breughel in the low-life costumes and sets – how the prison scenes recalled not the 'usual Dickensian or eighteenth century stage-prisons' but the 'wheels, fires, the whips and racks of a still crude epoch'.[1] The *New Statesman* reviewer remarked that the staging had the effect of bringing action forward to the front of the stage. Pompey, Elbow and Abhorson, instead of being reduced to 'circus clowns and fantastics', made their 'proper effect'[2] as natural 'characters'; the outrageous mob was 'extremely loud and energetic'. Brook wrote[3] that this 'Rough' world is opposed to the 'Holy' world with which it co-exists: 'Isabella's plea for grace has far more meaning in this Dostoevskian setting than it would in lyrical comedy's never-never land.' In seeing the play in these terms it was logical for Brook to make the cuts he did, exaggerating the opposition between high and low, holy and rough, rather than acknowledging the more complex interweaving of qualities in both, and the manipulatory initiative and moral embarrassments Shakespeare imposes on his Duke. Brook's achievement in giving full and outrageously energetic scope to the play's low life is a milestone, and although his cutting altered the final scene, it ensured a powerful impact: after Mariana made her plea to Isabella to join her in supplication for Angelo's life, a very long and intense pause ensued before she finally knelt to plead for the man she believed had had her brother killed. 'Her words came quiet and level, and as their full import of mercy reached Angelo, a sob broke from him.'[4] In this production Brook used no music save for a tolling bell and herald's trumpet, and the couples merely walked off at the end, hand in hand, in silence from the stage. Brook wrote: 'when this play is prettily staged, it is meaningless – it demands an absolutely convincing roughness and dirt'.[5]

The Brook production achieved fame and influenced productions of the play for years. It became usual to have a single unchanging set, throwing emphasis on the actors, with swift transitions from scene to scene and little or no music. The emphasis on an authoritative Duke as the central figure persisted even in the 1960s, although there were hints from time to time, throughout the period, of interest in a more ironic view of the play as a whole. Still, it was not until 1970 that

1 T.C. Worsley, *New Statesman*, 1 April 1950.
2 David, 'Shakespeare's comedies and the modern stage', p. 137.
3 Peter Brook, *The Empty Space*, Pelican edn, 1972, p. 99.
4 David, 'Shakespeare's comedies and the modern stage', p. 137.
5 Brook, *The Empty Space*, p. 99.

a major production emphatically presented a generally ironic view of the play.

It is all the more striking, therefore, that directly in 1950 Harold Hobson[1] recorded his dissent from Brook's interpretation. Hobson granted the impressiveness of Harry Andrews in the role of the Duke and the sheer charm and dignity with which he won the audience over, but to Hobson this showed the Duke to be much more an actor, a master of deception, than a profound man of integrity. Hobson wrote that Andrews's Duke, 'so fine and frank in appearance', spoke 'in so manly a fashion that one forgets he is a masquerader and an eavesdropper, a practical joker, and a liar'. Brook's cutting of the text, it might be added, helped an audience to forget this, and a later production by Anthony Quayle in 1956 also cut the text to protect the Duke from seeming too devious and to enhance his nobility. The Duke-as-Friar in Quayle's production bore a staff surmounted by a large cross giving marked medieval visual emphasis to stress the allegorical element; his compassion was evident when he knelt to comfort a distraught Isabella after her scene with Claudio, and when Isabella knelt to plead for Angelo's life in the final scene it was the Duke, his face 'illuminated with joy',[2] who was the centre of interest. This Isabella was an austere figure, spiritually dedicated. Her struggle was with her faith, and when Claudio was unmuffled at the end she crossed herself before rushing to his arms. A further consequence of the approach in terms of divine allegory in productions of this period was to see Isabella and Claudio rather emphatically young and having less autonomy, while Angelo became recognisably a victim of sexual psychosis (in a 1962 production he was seen scourging himself, and Tynan in the *Observer* described him as 'a classic sado-masochist').

Brook had made a famous effect by prolonging Isabella's intense silence as she struggled with her conscience before kneeling at last to plead for Angelo's life. Margaret Webster, who directed a production in 1957, spoke of the important interpretative possibilities of silence in the play,[3] and her approach points forward to the detailed, psychological naturalism and ironic mode of the 1970s, in which a concern for close fidelity to the text uncovered many subtleties of characterisation and a number of intense moments of fear, pain, surprise and joy. The trend towards psychological naturalism shifts away from matters of absolute principle, of the allegorical aspect of the Duke on one side and the low life on the other.

Margaret Webster presented an authoritative Duke showing a 'flicker of

1 Harold Hobson, *Sunday Times*, 19 March 1950.
2 *The Times*, 15 August 1956. An attempt to interpret the play in the opposite way was made by John Houseman at Stratford, Conn., and New York in 1956, but although this farcical version in terms of a Strauss operetta gave a wholly comic Duke with some consistency – the Duke-as-Friar was a 'bespectacled bearded dodderer rather like a Mack Sennett comedian' who reacted extremely when overhearing abuse of the Duke (*Montreal Star*, 10 July 1956) – nevertheless, it proved impossible to give life to Angelo, Isabella and Claudio while employing this exclusively light comic mode. In this sense the production witnesses to the marked variety of dramatic and theatrical styles Shakespeare exploits in *Measure for Measure* and to the very damaging effect, for the play as a whole, of ignoring the relationship between its distinct modes.
3 Margaret Webster, *Shakespeare Without Tears*, 1955, cited by Jane Williamson, 'The Duke and Isabella on the modern stage', in Joseph G. Price (ed.), *The Triple Bond*, 1975, pp. 149–69.

a

10   Peter Brook's 1950 production.

a Mistress Overdone (Rosalind Atkinson) and Lucio (Leon Quartermaine), with the First and Second Gentlemen (Robert Hardy and Robert Shaw)

b The Duke (Harry Andrews) overhearing Claudio and Isabella (Alan Badel and Barbara Jefford)

b

humour'[1] in 1957, and reviewers noticed the lightness of touch and the moments of absurdity delicately conveying Shakespeare's ironic view of 'what is equivocal in the Duke's behaviour'. The director thought the Duke, who 'does quite a lot of listening and quite a lot of learning as he listens', is a part 'for an actor of imagination who has the ability to project unspoken thought'.[2]

To identify the Duke's silences, as well as the ironic discrepancy between his actions and his words, as a space deliberately created by Shakespeare for the actor to fill, is an important insight.

John Russell Brown, writing in 1962,[3] distinguishes between an actor's use of a pause to convey thought or feeling and the use of a pause merely to direct attention to a single line of text or to the placing of the actors at an important moment on stage. In John Barton's production in 1970 Angelo (Ian Richardson) is 'busy at his desk in II, ii, when Isabella is first admitted. "You're welcome" he announces tonelessly, then looks up, *sees* her, and continues, "what's your will?" The pause is not a long one, but a lot of work is done in it.'[4] Later, in 2.4, Isabella is again

1 *Punch*, 20 Nov 1957, cited by Williamson in 'The Duke and Isabella'.
2 Webster, *Shakespeare Without Tears*, p. 249.
3 John Russell Brown, 'Acting Shakespeare today', *S.Sur.* 16 (1963), 143–52.
4 Peter Thomson, 'The Royal Shakespeare season 1970 reviewed', *S.Sur.* 24 (1971), 63–73.

announced: 'seated on his desk, he pulls a chair towards him with his foot, and indicates with a flick of the right hand that she should sit'. This very handsome, tight-lipped, icy Angelo eventually turned physically violent, seizing her hair and pulling her down on to the judgement table and stroking her body from breast to groin. The Duke in this production was meant as a study in inconsistency from the very beginning, when he appeared in Holbein cap, bespectacled and pipe-smoking, with a desk piled high with dusty books. Taking over as Deputy, Angelo showed fastidious distaste for the dust as well as the books and when next seen, in 2.2, the desk was clinically bare: it separated him from Isabella psychologically as much as it expressed his bureaucratic power, and when Isabella in 2.4 moved round to take his place she acquired psychological superiority over him with the exchange of places. Silence was used to memorable effect at the very end of this production too, but at a different point from Brook. Barton had aimed at an 'open-ended'[1] interpretation of Isabella's wordless response to the Duke's proposal of marriage: Isabella was to remain alone on stage, 'wondering, puzzling about what she should do'. Reviewers interpreted this in various tones but concurred that it was a rejection of marriage: Isabella reacted with silent dismay in one view,[2] but in another by 'glaring at the audience, silent rage written all over her high forehead and stubborn chin'.[3] This reviewer saw the production as 'feminist', perhaps reading into the performance the sexual politics of the day, perhaps recording the mood of a particular performance and audience response. Ralph Berry points out that even the most acute critics of earlier decades, including Empson, take it for granted that Isabella accepts the Duke because that would have been the invariable way they saw it acted in the theatre.[4] Barton noted that the text gives no indication that she assents. His Duke, after a long pause of silence after the proposal, uttered a resigned 'So', put on his glasses,[5] and departed with all the others, leaving Isabella alone on stage, staring out at the audience in silence before making a solitary exit.

Since Brook showed how the elements of passionate idealism, self-dramatisation and uncertainty in Isabella could be made consistent and convincing if the character is very young, a number of subsequent productions have also presented very young Isabellas. In 1962 a young Judi Dench played the part but never wore religious robes – indeed one reviewer[6] was struck by her wearing 'so low-cut a gown'. He accepted the idea of secular dress as plausible since 'the lady has not yet

1 John Barton, interviewed by Gareth Lloyd-Evans, *S.Sur.* 25 (1972), 66.
2 This was suggested in the programme note as a possible way for the character to react and some reviewers understood Estelle Kohler's Isabella in these terms; other intelligent reviewers felt there was more confusion: Benedict Nightingale in the *New Statesman* (12 April 1970) commented, 'Does Barton mean to imply that Isabella finds the Duke as Machiavellian as everyone else, or what? It isn't clear, hasn't been prepared for and (I suspect) isn't justified.'
3 D.A.N. Jones, *Listener*, 9 April 1970.
4 Berry, *Changing Styles in Shakespeare*, p. 41.
5 This detail is recorded by Jane Williamson in 'The Duke and Isabella', p. 169. Benedict Nightingale thought Barton's interpretation strained the text; Nightingale felt 'So' means 'Now that's done' rather than (as Barton would have it) 'too bad'.
6 Philip Hope-Wallace, *Manchester Guardian*, 11 April 1962.

taken her vows' but felt that in Shakespeare's conception Angelo is tempted partly by the very fact of her wearing the nun's habit. Some recent Isabellas have worn secular dress, some religious.

Though the issue of sexual politics has been inevitably implicit if not explicit since the Barton production, Barton failed to present the low life with conviction, although it was one of Brook's major achievements to do so. The text of these scenes has not been severely cut in productions since Brook, but interpretation has tended to be weak. In the mid 1970s an effort to make the social and political issues central is seen in certain major productions, such as those by Keith Hack, Jonathan Miller and Charles Marowitz; a production of 1987–8 by Nicholas Hytner reveals the recent influence of designers, on the one hand, and an interesting attempt to respond to the play's socio-political concerns, on the other.

Although the productions in the present discussion took place in Britain, the general features correspond to productions in West Germany, where the play has been frequently performed since 1950, as well as to those in North America, which are regularly reviewed in the journal *Shakespeare Quarterly*.

At the Open Space in 1975 Charles Marowitz presented a version of the play more heavily adapted than any since Davenant. Marowitz restored features from Cinthio and dispensed with most additions since Cinthio (except Lucio). His Isabella accepts the ransom and gives herself to the Deputy, but her brother is beheaded nevertheless. There is no Duke-as-Friar, no Mariana, and no low life. At the same time there are some new features: Isabella is denied justice at the end, and a corrupt Duke condones the Deputy's guilt; a new character, a Bishop (incorporating aspects of Friar Thomas and the Duke-as-Friar), is equally ready to support this 'Establishment cover-up', as the jargon of the period would phrase it. Although superficially this production might seem to be a social and political satire, its central emphasis was rather on sexual psychology. Marowitz freely redistributed lines and speeches from their position in Shakespeare's text, dismantling scenic structure, narrative sequence and characterisation. With a collage of lines he made a kind of dream-sequence suggesting Isabella's sexually turbulent condition, and his dramatic structure concentrated on abrupt shock, both in events and character-revelation.[1]

The cartoon-like exaggeration and crudity exemplified by Marowitz is an extreme instance of a more general impatience with full-scale Shakespeare in the 1970s, a time of much interest in 'poor theatre', of small-scale touring theatre groups acting much-abbreviated texts with very small casts on shoestring budgets in improvised playing-spaces. It was also a time of spreading interest in 'theatre-workshop' style, improvisatory exploration of the text in the teaching of Shakespeare. Keith Hack, who had worked at the Glasgow Citizens' Theatre and admired Brecht, produced *Measure for Measure* at Stratford in 1974 to a chorus of violent critical disapproval; though the performance may have failed, its aim

---

1 This account of Marowitz's production is based on *The Marowitz Shakespeare*, 1981, Catherine Itzin's review in *Plays and Players*, July 1975, and Marowitz's article in the *Guardian*, 28 May 1975.

was intelligent:[1] to insist on the poverty of the material circumstances of the play's Vienna, and on the intellectual poverty underlying well-worn 'bourgeois' interpretations of the play in terms of individual conscience and the view of society as the rulers see it. Hack conceived the play as a fable of social oppression. The costumes were felt to recall Georg Grosz, who had designed for Brecht, and the theory of the alienation effect is discernible in the overall conception, which, Peter Thomson concluded, was to present 'a *performance* of the events of *Measure for Measure*': The R.S.C. actors impersonated a discontented stock theatrical company, 'jaded professionals going through the necessary motions of a performance they would willingly have avoided'. They had to make do with available scenery (none could be afforded for Mariana, who was placed at the top of a high step-ladder for want of anything better). The air of shabby poverty was increased by a wire grid at the back of the acting area and bare scaffolding downstage of the proscenium arch. The poor set and costumes showed, on the one hand, that everyone in Vienna is poor, on the other that the company of jaded actors was underpaid by its actor-manager, who played the role of Duke as a heavy villain of melodrama. Specific alienation effects began with 'lethargic' opening music which went on too long, and fidgeting actors; a very large male actor played Mistress Overdone, and did a parodic strip-tease in order to change into a nun's habit for the scene with Isabella: here the exposure of the theatrical doubling of roles also pointed to Viennese perverted sexuality as being in league with an established Church. For the final scene the Duke with golden hair descended on a ramp labelled 'deus ex machina'; his over-acting was intended to undermine the audience's belief in the happy ending. The chief point of the alienation was to represent the story as ideologically committed to oppression of the under-privileged; the actors disliked acting this conformist rigmarole (as they saw it) which only confirmed the political – and hence artistic – nullity of professional theatre, especially in its tired passivity in recycling the classics. It was ironic that this production failed to give the low-life characters substance: rather than their emotional reality being demonstrated, they remained (except for Lucio) mere caricatures without conviction.

Jonathan Miller's 1974 production emphasised the play's setting in Vienna, not as the city of Freud but of the political pre-Nazi time, with Schönberg-style music and a drab institutional setting, the higher officials dressed in black suits with stiff wing-collars (recalling the dress of Neville Chamberlain coming back from Munich with his piece of paper). In fact the drab set was due to a small budget (its doors came from a building site) but a reviewer wrote[2] that 'Given the bureaucratic abuses of power that were to follow this particular period of Viennese history' this production took the audience into 'deeper moral waters' than most. In 1975 in Canada Robin Philips[3] quite independently set the play in the Vienna of

---

1 I am persuaded by Peter Thomson's account in *S.Sur.* 28 (1975), 137–49, and what follows is based on Thomson.
2 Peter Ansorge, *Plays and Players*, March 1974.
3 See Ralph Berry, *On Directing Shakespeare*, 1977, pp. 92–9.

1912 to make an explicit point of the relevance of Freud, whose city Vienna was. Philips, like Miller, identified sexual repression as the core of the play, together with an awareness of corruption in high places and the feminist issue. Philips had considered setting the play in the Berlin of the 1930s since the 'seamy side of life' there could work for the low-life episodes, but discarded the idea because of an 'authoritarian element' associated with that Berlin which he felt to be too strong for what the play's text suggests; Vienna, on the other hand, implied decadence, a sophisticated, knowledgeable upper class, and a state which was not a major power, so that there was more time for intrigue. Philips remarked: 'I would not be surprised to find that Freud or Ibsen were devoted to *Measure for Measure.*' These Freudian interpretations of the characters in the light of determinism diminish attention to the religious doctrines alluded to in the text and the action, as well as to the spiritual ideals of which the characters speak with feeling. Together with an interest in Freudian theory these productions also witness to the sociological and political concerns of many modern directors.

Such was the case in Nicholas Hytner's 1988 production of *Measure for Measure*, which opened with a stage dominated by two classical columns, down the side of which ran post-modern industrial metal service ducts. This set later revolved to reveal on its reverse side (in an architectural strip-tease, said one reviewer[1]) a modern city street, with steam escaping from manholes as in Brooklyn and an underground public lavatory in more British style, the focus of much murky trade in varieties of sex and drugs. In the final scene there was a concrete fascist-modern arch. The guards had a distinctly military look and the crowd was prominent. Augmenting this emphasis on public events in political terms, the pressure of public life was also significant in the psychological interpretation of the Duke himself. This interpretation included elements of many recent versions of the role: the Duke was uneasy and very much a human being, not divine; he found humour in improvising when in difficult situations; he was using his disguise role as an escape from the intolerable pressure of being in the public eye, as a means to therapy, and one reviewer[2] saw in his delivery of the speech 'Be absolute for death' 'a therapeutic self-analysis'. He finally engineered a successful outcome of his schemes but he was still personally uncertain enough to bungle the proposal to Isabella. The impression of documentary realism in the gleaming steel prison and the street scenes rendered the bleak alienation and implicit violence of modern cities: but there was little warmth or humanity and no sign of real rebellion. Characteristically for its period, the production tended not to illuminate the religious aspects.

The play's rhythms, the scale of emotion and the texture of the language, the development of thought and argument, can be damaged or obscured by unsuitably dominant settings and visual emphases which call inappropriate attention to themselves. Shakespeare stresses social and political issues in his design and

1 Irving Wardle, *The Times*, 13 November 1987.
2 Michael Billington, *Guardian*, 13 November 1987.

makes them integral elements in his characterisation, but they are inseparable from intellectual and spiritual concerns, and it is through acting, not sets or properties, that the interconnected issues find full expression. Shakespeare creates characters who all insist on their substantial presence: this is what makes the play political, in a thorough and radical sense.

NOTE ON THE TEXT

This edition is based on the first published text of *Measure for Measure*, in the First Folio of 1623, where it appears fourth in the Comedies section after *The Merry Wives of Windsor*. All these four first plays in the Comedies section were set from transcriptions (which are not extant) prepared by the professional scribe Ralph Crane. Crane is known to have interfered with his text, both consciously and unconsciously, when its meaning was obscure to him, and he also imposed his own habits of spelling and punctuation. Thus Shakespeare's text of this play is mediated to us by a transcription that may partly obscure the nature of its copy, as well as by a process of printing in which changes, errors and omissions may have been made in following Crane's transcription. The fuller account of this, together with a discussion of the main hypotheses about the copy Crane was given to transcribe, is set out in the Textual Analysis, pp. 193–211 below. Here it may be appropriate to note, briefly, that although the evidence surveyed presents some riddles, presumably due to Crane's having effaced telling features of his copy, nevertheless the Folio text of the play seems on the evidence to represent Shakespeare's completed version, though perhaps with some changes after its original completion.

The Textual Analysis also offers some discussion of verse and prose in the play and the associated question of displaying short verse lines as linked or unlinked, so that most of the specific cases can be briefly recorded in the collation without burdening the Commentary. The Commentary offers some account of the complex word-play which is an important dramatic feature of the play, and attends to complexities of grammar which are as remarkable for their dramatic as their linguistic interest, if not more so.

Routine interventions to be made by a modern editor in a critical edition such as this one concern regularisation – of spelling, speech headings, stage directions. In supplying missing stage directions, or amplifying inadequate directions, however, an editor in effect presents a performable version of the text. In the case of *Measure for Measure*, this involves making decisions about staging left open in the Folio. The notes and collation make clear the nature of these editorial interventions.

Measure for Measure

LIST OF CHARACTERS

VINCENTIO	*the Duke*
ANGELO	*the Deputy*
ESCALUS	*an ancient lord*
CLAUDIO	*a young gentleman*
LUCIO	*a fantastic*
Two other like gentlemen	
PROVOST	
[JUSTICE]	
FRIAR THOMAS	
ELBOW	*a simple constable*
FROTH	*a foolish gentleman*
[POMPEY	*tapster and pimp, working for Mistress Overdone*]
ABHORSON	*an executioner*
BARNARDINE	*a dissolute prisoner*
[VARRIUS	*a gentleman, a friend of the Duke*]
ISABELLA	*sister to Claudio*
MARIANA	*betrothed to Angelo*
JULIET	*beloved of Claudio*
FRANCISCA	*a nun*
MISTRESS OVERDONE	*a Bawd*
[*Attendant Lords, Officers, Servants, Citizens, a Boy*]	

The Scene Vienna

Notes

The list of characters is printed immediately after the end of the play under the heading 'The names of all the actors' in F. Pompey is listed as *'Clowne'* and 'Justice' and 'Varrius' are omitted.

VINCENTIO The name only occurs here; possibly Crane omitted it from the SD at 1.1.0. No such name appears in the known sources and analogues. The historical figure Vincenzio Gonzaga, Duke of Mantua 1587–1612, was often in Vienna or fighting in Hungary. He had a wife who became a nun after their divorce, but he was in character quite unlike Shakespeare's Duke, English travellers reporting him 'given to more delights than all the Dukes of Italye' (1592) and 'much delighted with Commedies and Mistresses' (1610). He was a patron of a company of players and of Monteverdi, Tasso and Rubens (K.M. Lea, *Italian Popular Comedy*, 1934, I, 83–8, 276–8, II, 342–3; Maria Bellonci, *A Prince of Mantua* (trans. S. Hood), 1956, cited by Eccles, p. 3). K. Muir (*N&Q* (1956), pp. 424–5) supposes there may be significance in the fact that Erasmus, *Colloquia*, 1571 edn, p. 504, has a Friar called Vincentius and another called Barnardinus. But Shakespeare had already used the name Vincentio in *The Taming of the Shrew*, and it was by no means an uncommon name in the drama of the period, while Marlowe in *The Jew of Malta* had named a friar Barnardine. Perhaps more remarkable is that none of the names in *Measure for Measure* suggest Vienna, they are all either Italian, English, or Latin.

ANGELO The characterisation 'outward-sainted' (3.1.88) by Isabella, and 'angel on the outward side' (3.2.234) by the Duke, indicates the inward devilishness hidden under his name; as Schanzer notes, he is also a false coin, not a genuine 'angel', a ten-shilling gold coin of the time (*The Problem Plays of Shakespeare*, 1963, p. 94).

ESCALUS The name occurs in *Rom.* and *AWW*. As Eccles notes, a pun on 'scales of justice' would be more evident if the accent were on the second syllable and the medial vowel long. Nevertheless such a pun may be suspected, as the idea is strongly present: see for instance 3.1.239.

CLAUDIO This is the name also given to a character in *Much Ado* who thinks a dowry very important and falls easy prey to jealousy, shamefully disgracing his bride-to-be. See above, p. 19 n. 1.

LUCIO The Italian word means 'light', perhaps alluding to his morals and his wit. He puns on the word's senses of 'bright' and 'wanton' in 5.1.276. The epithet 'fantastic' may be the scribe's. The word 'fantasime' occurs in *LLL* meaning 'one full of fancies'. Overbury, *Characters* (1614), has 'A Phantasticke. An Improvident Young Gallant'.

PROVOST 'An officer charged with the apprehension, custody and punishment of offenders' (*OED* sv *sb* 6).

FRIAR THOMAS The name occurs only in a SD, as does that of Francisca, a nun; Shakespeare may have written their names there with the intention, later abandoned, of using them in the dialogue. It is possible to argue that Thomas enjoys the Duke's confidence whereas Peter does not, and that Shakespeare intended them to be differentiated. No doubt the parts were doubled, and the costumes identical, which lends weight to Johnson's suggestion that '*Friar Thomas*, in the first act, might be changed, without any harm, to *Friar Peter*.'

ELBOW Possibly intended to be a very old man (the Duke calls him 'father' at 3.2.11), hence stooped and bent like an elbow. Other allusions in the text play on his poverty, 'out at elbow', and his inept attempt to rely on the law, 'lean upon justice' (2.1.56, 46).

FROTH Said to be of 'four score pound a year' (2.1.109–10) which, if true (Pompey is the informant), is a substantial sum, making Froth a typical Jacobean prodigal-gallant, empty-brained (mere froth) and addicted to ale. Escalus seems not to credit this identity, to judge by his questions at 2.1.164 and 166.

POMPEY Named 'Pompey' in the dialogue but listed as 'Clowne' in the SDs SHs and 'Names of all the actors'. His full name is Pompey Bum (2.1.185), beginning pompously, ending basely. Allusion to his trade (he is a pimp as well as a tapster) may also be heard in his name. Costard in *LLL* presents the hero 'Pompey the Big' (5.2.550).

ABHORSON That he is abhorrent, and a son of a whore (*ab* = from, *hor* = whore, popular etymology like that in 'abominable', 'from man') seems not fully realised in his characterisation; but his trade is gruesome.

VARRIUS He has no speaking part, and is only referred to in the SD at 5.1.0. He is not in the list 'Names of all the actors' in F. Lever notes that there is a messenger called Varrius in *Ant.* 2.1, and suggests Shakespeare recalled the name Varius, father of Severus. There is a Varrius in Plutarch. The name, like others mentioned in 4.5 – Flavius, Valencius, and Crassus – is in a Latin not Italian form. See Textual Analysis, p. 202 below.

ISABELLA Possibly, as G.K. Hunter notes (*SQ* 15 (1964), 167–72), named in allusion to Isabella, sister of St Louis of France, founder of the convent of Poor Clares; the order in England observed the 'Isabella rule'. The Poor Clares are referred to at 1.4.5. The form of the name in F is most often 'Isabell'. In *AWW* Lavatch names his possible future wife as 'Isbel'.

MARIANA This is also the name Shakespeare gives the lady who warns against masculine enticements and seduction of maids in *AWW* 3.5.

JULIET The name of the heroine of Arthur Brooke's *Romeus and Iuliet* (1562), in which the Prince of Verona is named Escalus. Brooke's poem is the chief source of *Romeo and Juliet*.

FRANCISCA The name appears only in a SD, like Friar Thomas.

OVERDONE The verb 'do' can mean 'copulate with' – the worn-out whore becomes a bawd: Pompey says at 1.2.92 that she has served to exhaustion. 'Overdone' is also the name of her ninth and last husband (2.1.173 and n.).

THE SCENE VIENNA This location was presumably added by the scribe Ralph Crane. Vienna is identified in the dialogue in the first scene at 22; but scenes take place outside the city walls and at the moated grange as well as in the city.

MEASURE FOR MEASURE

1.1 *Enter* DUKE, ESCALUS, LORDS

DUKE Escalus.

ESCALUS My lord.

DUKE Of government the properties to unfold
    Would seem in me t'affect speech and discourse,
    Since I am put to know that your own science   5
    Exceeds, in that, the lists of all advice
    My strength can give you. Then no more remains
    But that, to your sufficiency, as your worth is able,
    And let them work. The nature of our people,
    Our city's institutions, and the terms   10
    For common justice, y'are as pregnant in

Title] MEASURE, For Measure. F   **Act 1, Scene 1** 1.1] *Actus primus, Scena prima.* F **8–9** But . . . work] F; Put . . . work *Rome*; But that to your sufficiency you joyn / A will to serve us as . . . work *Hanmer*; But that. To . . . work *Sisson* **10** city's institutions] *Italic in* F

Act 1, Scene 1

3 properties essential qualities (*OED* Property *sb* 5). Taken together with 'unfold', a play may be suspected on 'property' in the theatrical sense: any portable article of costume or accessory used in acting a play.

4 affect love (*OED* sv $v^1$2); Lever suspects 'practise artificially', which would develop the theatrical hint in the preceding line.

4 discourse pompous dissertation or sermon (*OED* sv *sb* 5).

5 put to know obliged to recognise.

5 science knowledge (and skill) in a particular field.

6 that i.e. the essential qualities of government.

6 lists limits (*OED* List sb^3 8); and perhaps playing on the sense 'catalogues' (*OED* List sb^6).

7 strength intellectual powers. There is the additional sense of ducal authority.

8–9 But . . . work i.e. but that you use your natural ability supported by authority, keeping a balance between the two.

8 sufficiency authority.

8 worth virtue, moral integrity.

8 able empowered (*OED* sv *v* 3), given legal authority (*OED* sv *v* 4b).

8–9 Line 8 is hypermetrical and rhythmically faulty. F may represent faithfully what Shakespeare wrote, presenting the Duke as ambiguous and deliberately vague; moreover obscure and elliptical expressions are frequent throughout the play. Emendation seems unwise. Editors have usually sought to eliminate ambiguity and to contrive metrical regularity. Warburton interprets the general sense 'put your skill in governing to the power which I give you to exercise it, and let them work together'. Dr Johnson suggests a minimal emendation, omitting 'as' and reading 'abled' ('invested with power'). It is questionable whether 'that' is a pronoun or a conjunction and to what 'them' refers. Does 'to' imply a missing verb?

10 city's institutions established laws and customs (*OED* Institution *sb* 6), with the added sense, written legislation: 'institute' could mean a digest or treatise of jurisprudence, as that by Justinian (*OED* sb^3). Italicised in F.

10–11 terms . . . justice i.e. conditions of the administration of justice (*OED* Term *sb* 10) and technical expressions used in courts of law (*OED* Term *sb* 13).

11 pregnant well-informed, resourceful, quick in comprehension (*OED* sv adj^2 3).

79

As art and practice hath enrichèd any
That we remember. There is our commission,
From which we would not have you warp. Call hither,
I say, bid come before us Angelo.   15

[*Exit a Lord*]

What figure of us think you he will bear?
For you must know, we have with special soul
Elected him our absence to supply,
Lent him our terror, dressed him with our love,
And given his deputation all the organs   20
Of our own power. What think you of it?
ESCALUS If any in Vienna be of worth
To undergo such ample grace and honour
It is Lord Angelo.

Enter ANGELO

DUKE   Look where he comes.
ANGELO Always obedient to your grace's will   25
I come to know your pleasure.
DUKE   Angelo:
There is a kind of character in thy life
That to th'observer doth thy history

15 SD] *Capell subst.; not in* F   24 SD] F; *following* comes. *in Dyce*

---

13 commission warrant conferring delegated authority (*OED* sv *sb¹* 3). The Duke presumably hands Escalus a written document.

14 warp deviate, stray from (*OED* sv *v* 19: the first use in this figurative sense).

16 figure represented character, enacted part (*OED* sv *sb* 11); compare *Temp.* 3.3.83: 'Bravely the figure of this harpy hast thou / Perform'd.' Lever sees an allusion to the ducal stamp on the seal of the commission, introducing the 'stamp' and 'coin' images. See note on 'metal' at 48 below.

17 soul intellectual and spiritual power (*OED* sv *sb* 5).

18 Elected Chosen (for a specific function) (*OED* Elect *v* 1).

18 supply make up for; also, fill as substitute; see *OED* sv *v¹* 9, citing Elyot (1548), 'to be in an other mannes steede, to supply an other mannes roume'.

19 The Duke literally transfers the dread power and the robes of the office of Duke, temporarily; with them go the love of the people

for their ruler and his love for them; perhaps the Duke also implies that making Angelo his deputy is a mark of his provisional love. The stress falls on 'Lent' and 'dressed'.

20 deputation office of deputy.

20 organs means of operation.

23 undergo bear the weight of (C.T. Onions).

27 character In the senses (1) obvious sign for all to see, (2) cipher of hidden neurosis. Literally 'character' is a graphic sign or symbol, hence writing, a hand's distinctive style or traits; but Hart points to 'Cipher for hidden or secret writing or correspondence' as in Jonson, *Epigrams*, xcii: 'the sundry ways / To write in cipher, and the several keys, / To ope' the character'. This meaning seems to be confirmed by 29's verb 'unfold', which implies a concealed 'history'. See 1.2.136.

28 observer Perhaps with two senses: 'a mere bystander', and, as Johnson says, 'One who looks vigilantly...a close remarker' (*Dictionary* (1755)).

28 history i.e. personal record, in public office

Fully unfold. Thyself and thy belongings
Are not thine own so proper as to waste   30
Thyself upon thy virtues, they on thee.
Heaven doth with us as we with torches do,
Not light them for themselves: for if our virtues
Did not go forth of us, 'twere all alike
As if we had them not. Spirits are not finely touched   35
But to fine issues: nor. nature never lends
The smallest scruple of her excellence
But, like a thrifty goddess, she determines
Herself the glory of a creditor,
Both thanks and use. But I do bend my speech   40

or private life. It may be that Johnson is right to
suppose the word used loosely in the sense of
future behaviour, predictable on the basis of
observed character (*2H4* 3.1.80–5 expresses this
idea unambiguously); yet the Duke's earlier
questions to Escalus and warnings to Angelo in
this speech suggest that he is concerned with
faults in his character already detected, with his
'psychological history'. It is this which is hinted at
in the equivocal 'fully unfold'.

29 belongings endowments, qualities.

30 thine own so proper so much thy own
property (Steevens).

30–1 waste . . . thee i.e. bestow all your
powers on privately perfecting your own virtues,
and use up your virtues on your own perfection.
There is a firm negative connotation to 'waste'.

32–3 Heaven . . . themselves Recalling Matt.
5.15–16 'Neither do men light a candle, and put
it under a bushel, but on a candlestick, and it
giveth light unto all that are in the house. Let
your light so shine before men, that they may see
your good works, and glorify your Father which is
in heaven.' See also Mark 4.21–4. There is the
proverb 'A candle (torch) lights others and
consumes itself' (Tilley C39) and Bond compares
Lyly, *Campaspe* (1584), Prologue at Court, which
repeats the proverb: 'these torches, which giving
light to others, consume themselves'.

33–6 virtues . . . issues Whiter, *A Specimen
of a Commentary on Shakspere* (1794), notes a
possible allusion to Mark 5.25–30, the account of
the woman cured of an 'issue of blood' when she
touched the garment of Jesus, and immediately
'Jesus did know in himselfe the vertue that went
out of him.' The words 'issue', 'touched', 'vertue'
are repeated, and the phrase 'went out of him' is
echoed in Shakespeare's 'go forth of us'.

35–6 Only the greatest *general* moral causes
can inspire the finest spiritual emotions in us.

(The pointed contrast is between the general
public concern and the merely private and
personal.)

35 finely touched 'affected with fine emotions' (*OED v* 24). There is an allusion to the
'touch' placed on gold coins after they have been
assayed with the touchstone, officially marking
them as fine, and hence approved for issue.

36 fine issues 'morally fine causes or deeds',
and alluding via 'touched' to assayed gold coin
issued for general use.

36–40 nature . . . use The lending of talents
by nature recalls Seneca, *De beneficiis* 5; the
analogous parable of the talents (Matt. 25) concerns the talents given by heaven. Compare
Shakespeare's interest in the same idea in the
Sonnets, for instance Sonnet 4 ('Nature's be-
quest gives nothing, but doth lend . . . For having
traffic with thyself alone, / Thou of thyself thy
sweet self dost deceive') and Sonnet 6. The
Duke's own scheme may be seen in the same
light – he lends Angelo his power but uses him
and recoups 'thanks and use' for himself, at the
end of the play making his own position as ruler
more secure and enhancing his own reputation
for justice and mercy. There is a possibility that
we should recognise a suppressed erotic meaning
in 'use'.

37 scruple A very small unit of weight.

39 glory of a creditor i.e. 'the glory due to a
creditor, the thanks of her debtor and her loan's
interest or use' (Capell).

40–1 bend . . . advertise 'address one who
knows more about governing in my place than I
can tell him'. 'Advertise' (stressed here on the
second syllable) means 'inform' (*OED sv v* 4); 'my
part in him' is 'my role as Duke lent to him'.
'Bend' means 'direct, apply' (*OED sv v* 18) but
also 'direct downwards' or 'twist, turn away from
the straight line' (*OED v* 13) and also 'pervert

To one that can my part in him advertise.
Hold therefore, Angelo:
In our remove be thou at full ourself.
Mortality and mercy in Vienna
Live in thy tongue and heart. Old Escalus,   45
Though first in question, is thy secondary.
Take thy commission.

ANGELO   Now good my lord,
Let there be some more test made of my metal
Before so noble and so great a figure
Be stamped upon it.

DUKE   No more evasion.   50

---

48 metal] F (mettle)

---

from the right purpose' (*OEC v* 15). Compare
'wrinkled' at 1.3.5 and n. Angelo is said to be
'strait' at 2.1.9.

42 Hold The grammar presents a difficulty.
The object of 'Hold' may be simply Angelo, the
Duke commanding him to be consistent to his
principles. So, but with explicit irony, Timon
enjoins 'bankrupts, hold fast' (*Tim.* 4.1.8). Angelo
may be assumed, however, to be attempting to
interrupt, as he does a few lines later, and the
Duke could be understood to mean 'stop', 'wait'
(see *Rom.* 3.1.90 or 165, *2H6* 5.2.14), or, simply,
'hold your peace', 'silence'. It is less likely that the
Duke is referring to the actual commission and
handing it to Angelo. Many instances elsewhere
in Shakespeare have 'hold' followed by such a
word as 'there's' or 'here's' or 'take' to mark
the actual giving (*MV* 2.4.19, *AWW* 4.5.44, *H5*
4.8.63, *John* 2.2.92, etc.). The example from *Shr.*
(4.4.17), 'hold thee that to drink', has the direct
object 'that', which is not clearly present here.

43 remove absence (*OED* sv *sb* 5c: the only
example in this sense).

43 at full ourself i.e. in every respect our
deputy. The Duke's use of the royal first-person
plural is frequent in this scene (in 13, 15, 16, 17,
18, 19, 21, 51) although he sometimes uses the
ordinary first-person singular (as in 4, 5, 7, 15,
40, 59). It is not always clear why the latter,
informal style is used, though often it seems to
indicate some purely personal rather than ducal
concern. Perhaps the inconsistency is revealing of
his personality.

44–5 Mortality . . . heart i.e. authority to pro-
nounce sentence of death and freedom to temper
justice with mercy (Evans). 'Live' may be either
imperative or indicative; if the former, the Duke
enjoins Angelo to temperance; if the latter, he

might be understood to be ironically bland,
something an actor could bring out in tone of
voice and manner. For 'mortality' see 4.2.127
and n.

45 For the distinction between 'tongue' and
'heart' see Lucio's remark at 1.4.33 and Angelo's
words at 2.4.4–7. See also 2.2.38.

46 in question Explained in *OED* (Question *sb*
1d) as 'under consideration', and the phrase 'to
come into question' is explained as 'to be thought
of as possible'. Yet in *2H4* 1.2.60 the phrase
occurs with the sense 'on trial, under judicial
examination', and here the emphasis on the word
'question' is likely to attract the audience's
attention: it may be that the Duke's choice of
phrase should be seen as betraying his covert plan
to put the deputies (but chiefly Angelo) on trial.
The fact that Escalus has up to now been
Angelo's senior is stressed here; he remains
confused (79–80) about the extent of his
authority, and the contents of the two commissions the Duke gives are never made clear to
the audience.

46 secondary subordinate (rhetorically balanced against 'first').

48 test Term used of precious metal: to
subject to a process of separation and refining in a
test or cupel; to assay (*OED* sv *v²* 1). Compare
2.2.154, 'tested gold'.

48 metal Also the alternative spelling in
Shakespeare's time for 'mettle' = natural vigour,
spirit, courage (*OED* sv *sb* 3). Angelo employs the
metaphor of assaying gold for testing character.

49–50 figure . . . stamped The metaphor of
coining is here concluded: the assayed gold is
stamped with the royal image and perhaps there
is allusion in 'noble' to the fact that the English
gold coin was originally called the Angel-noble,

We have with a leavened and preparèd choice
Proceeded to you; therefore take your honours.
Our haste from hence is of so quick condition
That it prefers itself and leaves unquestioned
Matters of needful value. We shall write to you,   55
As time and our concernings shall importune,
How it goes with us, and do look to know
What doth befall you here. So fare you well.
To th'hopeful execution do I leave you
Of your commissions.

ANGELO   Yet give leave, my lord,   60
That we may bring you something on the way.

DUKE My haste may not admit it,
Nor need you, on mine honour, have to do
With any scruple. Your scope is as mine own
So to enforce or qualify the laws   65
As to your soul seems good. Give me your hand,
I'll privily away. I love the people,
But do not like to stage me to their eyes:
Though it do well I do not relish well

'having as its device the archangel Michael standing upon, and piercing, the dragon' (*OED* Noble *sb*): 'This was the coin always presented to a patient "touched" for the King's Evil.' The mystical power of the ruler, as God's deputy, is a critical concern of the play.

51 leavened prepared and matured. The action of yeast in dough 'leavens' or produces fermentation, on completion of which baking takes place. Evans suggests that the underlying idea is 'pervaded by the gradual working of judgement'.

53 quick condition urgent nature, 'probably with a play on "quick" as pregnant' (Lever). This accords with the metaphor of 'leavening' at 51.

54 prefers gives priority to.

54 unquestioned undiscussed. A repeated stress on 'question' (see 46 and n.).

55 of needful value important enough to require attention.

56 concernings affairs. Compare the forms 'belongings', 'advisings', 'thankings' all used by the Duke, forming part of a distinct ducal idiolect, perhaps.

59 The unusual word order seems to stress the phrase 'hopeful execution', perhaps with anticipatory ironic effect.

59 hopeful i.e. prompting good hopes.

61 bring . . . way accompany you for some of the way.

63–4 have . . . scruple entertain any feelings of doubt or hesitation, and, perhaps, 'be so punctilious'.

64 scope freedom to act (hence, breadth of authority).

65 enforce . . . qualify compel observance of, or moderate; apply with strict or tempered force (see 4.4.22).

66 soul See 17 n. above.

67 privily secretly, privately.

68 stage exhibit publicly (first recorded figurative use in *OED*; both instances in *Ant.* (at 3.13.30 and 5.2.216) are also in a context of distaste, as Lever notes). The metaphor from the theatre recalls 'properties', 'unfold', 'figure' and 'dress' noted earlier in the scene. Steevens quotes from the 1586 Queen's speech to Parliament: 'We princes, I tel you, are set on stages, in the sight and viewe of all the world.' On the possible allusion to King James I, see p. 23 above. The Duke's claim to shun public events contrasts with his self-presentation in Act 5. See also 3.2.16 and n. for another instance of the Duke's inconsistency.

69 do well If the subject is 'stage me' then this means 'be politically expedient' or 'please them',

Their loud applause and aves vehement, 70
Nor do I think the man of safe discretion
That does affect it. Once more, fare you well.

ANGELO The heavens give safety to your purposes.

ESCALUS Lead forth and bring you back in happiness.

DUKE I thank you, fare you well. *Exit* 75

ESCALUS I shall desire you, sir, to give me leave
To have free speech with you; and it concerns me
To look into the bottom of my place.
A power I have, but of what strength and nature
I am not yet instructed. 80

ANGELO 'Tis so with me. Let us withdraw together
And we may soon our satisfaction have
Touching that point.

ESCALUS   I'll wait upon your honour.

Exeunt

1.2 *Enter* LUCIO, *and two other* GENTLEMEN

LUCIO If the Duke, with the other dukes, come not to composition
with the King of Hungary, why then all the dukes fall upon the
King.

1 GENTLEMAN Heaven grant us its peace, but not the King of
Hungary's. 5

2 GENTLEMAN Amen.

LUCIO Thou conclud'st like the sanctimonious pirate that went to sea
with the ten commandments, but scraped one out of the table.

2 GENTLEMAN Thou shalt not steal?

75 SD] F2; *following 74 in* F **Act 1, Scene 2** 1.2] *Scena Secunda.* F

but if the subject is 'their loud applause', as Evans
believes, then it means 'show their good will'. I
incline to the first possibility.

70 aves shouts of welcome (Latin, *ave* =
'hail').

71 safe discretion sound judgement.

72 affect Implying 'show an affectation' as well
as 'loves'.

74 Lead forth i.e. may they conduct you
(Eccles).

78 look . . . place understand fully the extent
of my duties and office.

83 wait upon attend.

Act 1, Scene 2
1 composition agreement.

7 sanctimonious having the outward appearance of sanctity (first quotation in this sense in
OED).

8 table Tablets of wood or stone inscribed
with the Ten Commandments were set up in
English churches (see *OED* Commandment *sb*
2b, quotation from 1560).

LUCIO Ay, that he razed.   10
1 GENTLEMAN Why, 'twas a commandment to command the captain
    and all the rest from their functions: they put forth to steal.
    There's not a soldier of us all that, in the thanksgiving before
    meat, do relish the petition well that prays for peace.
2 GENTLEMAN I never heard any soldier dislike it.   15
LUCIO I believe thee, for I think thou never wast where grace was said.
2 GENTLEMAN No? A dozen times at least.
1 GENTLEMAN What? In metre?
LUCIO In any proportion, or in any language.
1 GENTLEMAN I think, or in any religion.   20
LUCIO Ay? Why not? Grace is grace, despite of all controversy: as,
    for example, thou thyself art a wicked villain, despite of all grace.
1 GENTLEMAN Well, there went but a pair of shears between us.
LUCIO I grant: as there may between the lists and the velvet. Thou
    art the list.   25
1 GENTLEMAN And thou the velvet. Thou art good velvet: thou'rt a
    three-piled piece, I warrant thee. I had as lief be a list of an
    English kersey as be piled, as thou art piled, for a French velvet.
    Do I speak feelingly now?
LUCIO I think thou dost, and indeed with most painful feeling of thy   30
    speech. I will, out of thine own confession, learn to begin thy

11 Why,] *Pope*; Why? F   14 relish] rallish F

10 **razed** erased.
12 **functions** calling, livelihood.
14 **meat** a meal (*OED* sv *sb* 4b).
15 **dislike** express dislike of.
19 **proportion** metrical or musical rhythm (*OED* sv *sb* 10).
21 **Grace ... controversy** Compare Rom. 11.6: 'And if it be of grace, it is no more of works: or else were grace no more grace.' Lucio shifts the sense of grace from a short prayer before a meal to God's merciful love.
23 **Well ... us** We are both of the same piece (Johnson). A common proverb (Tilley P36).
24 **lists** The edge or selvage of a piece of cloth. Lucio claims the gentleman to be worthless.
27 **three-piled** finest and most costly. Linthicum explains that 'velvet was made also in two piles upon a ground of satin. Since this makes three heights, if the satin ground be counted as one, it is probably the "three-pile velvet" ... in *Measure*.' The comment by 1 Gentleman is ironic, as the ensuing jest shows.

28 **kersey** 'A light-weight, narrow, wool cloth ... Broad-list kersies had a very wide selvedge or "list"' (Linthicum). These wasteful cloths are presumably what the Gentleman refers to.
28 **piled** Plays on the senses 'pilled', deprived of hair, side-effect of treatment for syphilis (the 'French disease') and 'piled', referring to a napped cloth.
28 **French velvet** A play upon 'French' as referring to the French disease and costly imported French velvet cloth. Colman sees an allusion to the patch of velvet used in treating syphilis 'to cover lanced chancres'. Compare *AWW* 4.5.95–8.
29 **feelingly** to the point (with a playful allusion to the pain of syphilis). Evans sees a reference specifically to mouth sores; Lucio exploits the idea, turning it against 1 Gentleman at 32.
30 **feeling** personal understanding.
31 **begin** drink to (see Sonnet 114).

health; but, whilst I live, forget to drink after thee.

1 GENTLEMAN I think I have done myself wrong, have I not?

2 GENTLEMAN Yes, that thou hast, whether thou art tainted or free.

Enter [MISTRESS OVERDONE, *a*] *Bawd*

LUCIO Behold, behold, where Madam Mitigation comes. I have   35
purchased as many diseases under her roof as come to –

2 GENTLEMAN To what, I pray?

LUCIO Judge.

2 GENTLEMAN To three thousand dolours a year.

1 GENTLEMAN Ay, and more.   40

LUCIO A French crown more.

1 GENTLEMAN Thou art always figuring diseases in me, but thou art
full of error: I am sound.

LUCIO Nay, not, as one would say, healthy, but so sound as things
that are hollow. Thy bones are hollow. Impiety has made a feast   45
of thee.

1 GENTLEMAN How now, which of your hips has the most profound
sciatica?

MISTRESS OVERDONE Well, well: there's one yonder arrested and
carried to prison was worth five thousand of you all.   50

2 GENTLEMAN Who's that, I pray thee?

MISTRESS OVERDONE Marry, sir, that's Claudio, Signior Claudio.

---

34 SD MISTRESS OVERDONE] *Dyce; Bawde.* F (*throughout*) 35–6] *As prose, Capell; perhaps as verse,* F:
Behold . . . comes. / I . . . Roofe, / As come to 49 SH] *Dyce; Bawd.* F (*throughout, with variation of spelling*)

32 drink after thee Hart cites Montaigne,
Book 1, ch. 40: 'hee would not drinke after him,
for feare hee should take the pox of him'.

34 whether . . . free i.e. whether diseased or
not, since he has made himself vulnerable to
Lucio's wit if not to disease's inroads on his body.

35 Mitigation So called because she provides
means to appease or mitigate lust.

36 In F there is a space after 'Roofe' and 'As'
is upper-case, but the lines are not metrical.

39 dolours diseases. There is a pun on
'dollars' (apparently pronounced the same), the
name of a silver coin (German 'Thaler') and also
the word used for the Spanish coin, the 'peso'
(which, being worth eight 'reales', was also called
a 'piece of eight').

41 French crown Punning on the coin, on the
crown of a Frenchman's head, and on the
baldness caused by syphilis, the 'French disease'.

42 figuring Evans suggests 'reckoning' (with
reference to the preceding puns on money) and
'imagining'.

43 sound i.e. giving off the resounding noise
of hollow things, as in the proverb 'sound as a
bell'. The bones are affected in the secondary and
tertiary stages of syphilis. In *Tro.* 2.3.18–19
syphilis is 'the Neapolitan bone-ache', and *Tim.*
4.3.151–2 associates money and syphilis: 'Con-
sumptions sow / In hollow bones of men.'

45 Impiety Wickedness.

47–8 Addressed to Overdone, as her response
indicates.

47 profound deep-seated.

48 sciatica hip-gout. Considered as a symp-
tom of syphilis in *Tro.* 5.1.21, where Thersites is
listing the 'rotten diseases of the south'.

49 yonder *OED* says it usually refers to objects
at a distance but in view. Overdone is evidently
referring to Claudio, who is yet to make his
entrance. In this instance 'yonder' evidently does
not imply that 'that man back there' is in view.

50 carried taken forcibly.

52 Marry Indeed. A mild oath, originally using
the name of the Virgin Mary.

1 GENTLEMAN Claudio to prison? 'Tis not so.

MISTRESS OVERDONE Nay, but I know 'tis so. I saw him arrested,
saw him carried away, and, which is more, within these three   55
days his head to be chopped off!

LUCIO But, after all this fooling, I would not have it so. Art thou sure
of this?

MISTRESS OVERDONE I am too sure of it: and it is for getting
Madam Julietta with child.   60

LUCIO Believe me, this may be. He promised to meet me two hours
since, and he was ever precise in promise-keeping.

2 GENTLEMAN Besides, you know, it draws something near to the
speech we had to such a purpose.

1 GENTLEMAN But most of all agreeing with the proclamation.   65

LUCIO Away. Let's go learn the truth of it.

Exeunt Lucio [and Gentlemen]

MISTRESS OVERDONE Thus, what with the war, what with the sweat,
what with the gallows, and what with poverty, I am custom-
shrunk.

Enter [POMPEY]

How now? What's the news with you?   70

POMPEY Yonder man is carried to prison.

MISTRESS OVERDONE Well, what has he done?

---

66 SD *and Gentlemen*] *Capell; not in* F   69 SD POMPEY] *Dyce; Clowne* F *(throughout)*   71 SH] *Dyce; Clo.* F *(throughout)*

---

62 precise … keeping The word 'precise' is
later associated with Angelo, promise-breaker.

63–4 it … purpose it corresponds somewhat
to that conversation we had on the subject (either
of Claudio and Juliet, or of the newly severe law
enforcement).

67 the sweat Johnson probably rightly suggests an allusion to the sweating sickness, a
disease inducing fever, often fatally, of which
there were epidemics in the sixteenth century
(*OED* Sweat *sb* 3b), but thinks more probable an
allusion to the treatment of venereal disease, in
which patients were induced to sweat in sweating
tubs (see 3.2.50 and n.). Capell suggests that 'the
sweat' is plague, but offers no other instances of
the word's use in this sense. Nashe, *The Unfor-
tunate Traveller* (1594), distinguishes sweating
sickness, a fatal plague he describes unforget-
tably, from venereal disease: 'This sweating
sickness was a disease that a man then might
catch and never go to a hothouse.'

68 the gallows Although Lever suggests an

allusion to treason trials and executions at Winchester in connection with the plots of Raleigh
and others, Mistress Overdone may simply be
bemoaning the routine depletion of her customers
drawn from the criminal classes, or the new
proclamation's threat to her trade. On the treason
trials, see p. 24 above.

68–9 I am custom-shrunk i.e. the number
of my customers has shrunk.

71–7 POMPEY Yonder … maid by him
Lever (p. xx) suggests this passage was marked
in the MS. for omission: the compositor found he
was crowded for space in this column (b on F1V,
set by Compositor D or C) because the casting-
off did not allow for the printing of these lines.
See the Textual Analysis, p. 199 below.

71 Yonder man Referring to Claudio, though
he has not yet appeared. Mistress Overdone's
ignorance of Claudio's situation contradicts what
she says in 49 ff. above.

72–3 Pompey takes the slang sense of 'done'
= 'copulate', as in the name Overdone.

POMPEY A woman.

MISTRESS OVERDONE But what's his offence?

POMPEY Groping for trouts in a peculiar river.   75

MISTRESS OVERDONE What? Is there a maid with child by him?

POMPEY No, but there's a woman with maid by him. You have not
heard of the proclamation, have you?

MISTRESS OVERDONE What proclamation, man?

POMPEY All houses in the suburbs of Vienna must be plucked down.   80

MISTRESS OVERDONE And what shall become of those in the city?

POMPEY They shall stand for seed. They had gone down too, but
that a wise burgher put in for them.

MISTRESS OVERDONE But shall all our houses of resort in the
suburbs be pulled down?   85

POMPEY To the ground, mistress.

MISTRESS OVERDONE Why, here's a change indeed in the commonwealth. What shall become of me?

POMPEY Come, fear not you: good counsellors lack no clients.
Though you change your place, you need not change your trade.   90
I'll be your tapster still. Courage, there will be pity taken on you,
you that have worn your eyes almost out in the service, you will
be considered.

MISTRESS OVERDONE What's to do here, Thomas Tapster? Let's
withdraw.   95

---

75 Groping 'A mode of catching trout by tickling them with the hands under rocks or banks' (Halliwell); with a bawdy innuendo. Eccles compares Marston, *Antonio and Mellida* (1602), 2.1.115–17, an instance earlier in date than the present one. The whole line means 'committing an act of seduction'.

75 peculiar private, i.e. where fishing is not allowed.

80 houses i.e. houses of prostitution, brothels.

80 suburbs Built-up areas outside the jurisdiction of the city where brothels were established. Lever notes a proclamation made on 16 September 1603 calling for the pulling down of houses in the suburbs as a protection against the spread of plague.

82 stand for seed i.e. like the grain left uncut to provide seeds for another season, remain standing to ensure the continuance (of prostitution). The idea of fertility in the image is ironic, when applied to prostitution.

83 put in made an offer, bid. Some commentators suggest 'intervened to defend' but

OED gives only one instance of the verb's use in this sense (*OED* Put v^1 44d).

87–8 commonwealth An ironic play on contrasted senses, one lofty (*OED sb* 2, 'the state of the body politic'), one down to earth (*OED sb* 5, 'persons united by some common interest', here, brothels). The word was associated with Puritan propaganda which harped on the dangers to the commonwealth of vice, especially sexual vice, and extremists advocated the death penalty for prostitutes. See pp. 2–6 above.

89 counsellors counselling lawyers (*OED* Counsellor *sb* 3).

92 worn . . . service 'The service' is an ironically dignified name for prostitution, whose presiding deity is blind Cupid (depicted on signs hung outside brothels). The cynical Surly, in Jonson's *The Alchemist*, describes some prostitutes in mock-heroic terms as 'the decayed vestals of Pickt-hatch . . . That keep the fire alive, there' (2.1.62–3).

94 Thomas Tapster A generic name, presumably, for any tapster.

POMPEY Here comes Signior Claudio, led by the provost to prison;
and there's Madam Juliet.

Exeunt

Enter PROVOST, CLAUDIO, JULIET, OFFICERS, LUCIO,
and two GENTLEMEN

CLAUDIO Fellow, why dost thou show me thus to th'world?
Bear me to prison, where I am committed.
PROVOST I do it not in evil disposition,   100
But from Lord Angelo by special charge.
CLAUDIO Thus can the demi-god, Authority,
Make us pay down for our offence by weight
The words of heaven; on whom it will, it will,
On whom it will not, so; yet still 'tis just.   105
LUCIO Why, how now, Claudio? Whence comes this restraint?
CLAUDIO From too much liberty, my Lucio, liberty.
As surfeit is the father of much fast,
So every scope by the immoderate use
Turns to restraint. Our natures do pursue   110

97 SD] *As Rowe; Exeunt. / Scena Tertia.* F   97 SD.3 *two* GENTLEMEN] F2 (*two Gent.*); 2. *Gent.* F   103 weight] F;
weight. *Warburton*

96–7 These lines indicate that Juliet enters
with Claudio, even though she is given nothing to
say (so that some commentators believe she is not
intended to be present), but her presence on
stage, a visibly pregnant woman, makes an
emphasis (compare *WT* 1.2, although there
Hermione's speaking role is a major one).
Shakespeare may have begun with the plan of
making Juliet's a speaking role in the present
scene, then decided on the present arrangement;
but it is also possible that he decided to remove
Juliet from the scene, but forgot to cancel the
reference to her in Pompey's speech and in this
SD. In *Ado* 1.1, there is the character Innogen
mentioned only in a SD, generally supposed a
'ghost' character whose name Shakespeare forgot
to cancel from the SD. See Textual Analysis,
pp. 198–9 below.

102 demi-god Possibly not sarcastic, since
divinity was represented in the judge and ruler in
Elizabethan and Jacobean doctrine; yet Claudio is
remarkable for the instability of his tone and his
attitude, and the line can certainly convince in a
bitter tone.

103–4 pay down ... words of heaven pay in
full the penalty. Warburton thinks the metaphor
taken from paying money by weight, which is

always exact, rather than by tale, counting the
number of coins. The grammar of 103–4 has
troubled editors, Johnson suspecting a line to be
missing, others making a break after 'weight' to
signal an elliptical construction with an implied
verb such as 'Remember' governing 'the words';
but F as it stands makes sense: 'The words of
heaven' are (with reference to 'offence') the
Commandments; but as he says the phrase
Claudio may think of other words, God's to
Moses quoted in Rom. 9.15, which he then
quotes: 'I will have mercy on him, to whom I will
show mercy'). 'The words of heaven' is then
transitional, referring back to 103 and on to
104–5.

106 restraint detention. Lucio's question
implies that he has not heard the cause of
Claudio's arrest at 59–60, 75–7 earlier: or we
may suppose his motive for asking is to see how
Claudio answers, possibly to enjoy his discom-
fiture. A cruel streak is apparent later when he
encounters Pompey newly arrested.

107 liberty Playing on the senses 'freedom'
and 'licentiousness'.

108 surfeit excessive eating or drinking,
gluttony.

109 scope liberty, licence.

> Like rats that ravin down their proper bane
> A thirsty evil, and when we drink, we die.

LUCIO If I could speak so wisely under an arrest, I would send for
certain of my creditors; and yet, to say the truth, I had as lief have
the foppery of freedom as the morality of imprisonment. What's   115
thy offence, Claudio?

CLAUDIO What but to speak of would offend again.

LUCIO What, is't murder?

CLAUDIO No.

LUCIO Lechery?   120

CLAUDIO Call it so.

PROVOST Away, sir, you must go.

CLAUDIO One word, good friend: Lucio, a word with you.

LUCIO A hundred, if they'll do you any good. Is lechery so looked
after?   125

CLAUDIO Thus stands it with me. Upon a true contract
> I got possession of Julietta's bed –
> You know the lady, she is fast my wife,
> Save that we do the denunciation lack
> Of outward order. This we came not to   130
> Only for propagation of a dower

---

115 morality] *Rowe*; mortality F   118–20] F; *as verse, Lever*   123 *One line, Pope*; One … friend: / *Lucio* … you.
F   124–5] *As prose, Pope; as verse*, F: *Luc.* A hundred: / If … after?; *as verse, Hanmer: Luc.* A … good: /
Is … after?   131 propagation] F2; propogation F; prorogation *conj. Malone*

---

111 **ravin down … bane** ravenously swallow
what is poison to them.

112 **thirsty** causing thirst.

113–14 **I would … creditors** Because they
would at once have him arrested.

115 **foppery** folly.

115 **morality** moral instruction. Shakespeare
never uses the word 'morality' elsewhere, but it
aptly serves as antithesis to 'foppery'. Defenders
of F's 'mortality' interpret it as 'dead earnest' or
'mortification'.

123 Line divided in two after a medial colon by
Compositor D or C. The same seems to have
been done by D or F in 4.6.12 and 15, and
5.1.32, 68.

124–5 **looked after** kept watch upon or
sought out (for punishment).

126 **true contract** The marriage was evidently
sworn by both parties but lacked the 'denunciation of outward order', which seems to mean 'was
not publicly announced' or 'was not followed by
a religious service as the Church required'. See
p. 35 above, n. 1.

129–30 Claudio's words can be paralleled in
a case of 1641 quoted by Martin Ingram (see
p. 35 above, n. 1): 'in 1641 a certain Thomas
Trepocke of Teffont Evias in Wiltshire confessed
how he and Elizabeth Macy "being … sure
together in marriage and man and wife save only
the outward solemnization thereof in the church
did since they were so contracted and sure the
one to the other lie together …" But it is notable
that, even in a case like this, the couple clearly
intended to marry in church when they could –
Trepocke had tried to obtain a licence, but could
not because some of Elizabeth's "friends" refused their consent.'

128 **fast** securely.

129 **denunciation** official, formal or public
announcement (*OED* sv *sb* 1). It is curious that
the word also meant 'public accusation' (*OED sb*
4) in view of the ambiguous attitude of Claudio to
his own conduct.

131 **propagation** increase (figuratively, gesta-
tion). Commentators note the prevalence of
metaphors of breeding generally in the play to

Remaining in the coffer of her friends,
From whom we thought it meet to hide our love
Till time had made them for us. But it chances
The stealth of our most mutual entertainment   135
With character too gross is writ on Juliet.

LUCIO With child, perhaps?

CLAUDIO   Unhappily, even so.
And the new deputy now for the Duke –
Whether it be the fault and glimpse of newness,
Or whether that the body public be   140
A horse whereon the governor doth ride,
Who, newly in the seat, that it may know
He can command, lets it straight feel the spur;
Whether the tyranny be in his place,
Or in his eminence that fills it up,   145
I stagger in – but this new governor
Awakes me all the enrollèd penalties
Which have, like unscoured armour, hung by th'wall

support this interpretation, and suppose that the speaker implies that his friends are unwilling at present to provide a dowry. This depends on the phrase in 134, 'made them for us'. Sisson supports Malone's conjecture 'prorogation' = 'delay'.

131 dower dowry.

132 friends i.e. people whose 'goodwill', though not legally necessary, was highly desirable: 'friends' was a conventional legal term; they might be either relatives or non-relatives of the couple, who had an interest in the marriage, including employers, guarantors or guardians. See Alan Macfarlane, *Marriage and Love in England*, 1986, p. 145.

134 made them for us won them over to us (?).

135 entertainment Perhaps from the verbal sense (*OED* Entertain *v* 1), 'to hold mutually, to hold intertwined'. *Per.* 4.2.56 has the noun in a context clearly signifying sexual embrace, a prostitute's reception of a male client. Other *OED* senses are associated with being socially agreeable or hospitable or amusing. It may be characteristic of Claudio that he applies this word, with its discordant associations, to the intimate relationship of newly wed husband and wife. 'Stealth' adds to the uneasiness.

136 character too gross writing, letters, too large or obvious. It may be that a trace of the sense of 'gross' = 'bloated with excess, repulsively fat' (*OED* Gross *adj* 2) is present, given Claudio's ambivalent tone generally here.

137 F has two short lines, possibly indicating that 137[b] should be presented as a new beginning, not linked to complete 137[a]. Since the two short lines constitute a single interruption in Claudio's long explanation, I arrange them as linked. See Textual Analysis, pp. 206–7 below.

139 fault and glimpse Malone suggests 'A fault arising from the mind being dazzled by a novel authority, of which the new governor has yet had only a glimpse'. *OED* Glimpse *sb* 3 gives 'a momentary and imperfect view'. Other commentators prefer 'the sudden brilliance (glimpse) of his new honour is to blame' (Evans). Although a hendiadys (two nouns used for adjective-plus-noun) for 'faulty glimpse', 'glimpse through a fault', the phrase has the effect of stressing 'fault', 'a deficiency' or a 'blameworthy act'.

143 straight straightway, immediately.

144–5 in … up inherent in his office or in the personal ambition of him who holds the office. *OED* Eminence *sb* 4a gives 'distinguished superiority, elevated rank', but also (*sb* 4 d) 'pride, ambition' which makes good sense in relation to the situation and gives an appropriately antithetical meaning to 'office' (although *OED* says it is rare in this sense).

146 stagger in am unable to decide.

147 enrolled i.e. recorded in the laws.

148 unscoured unpolished and hence rusty; compare *Tro.* 3.3.150–3, where the metaphor similarly conveys disapproval of inertia. Claudio seems to disapprove of a laxity which allowed

So long that nineteen zodiacs have gone round
And none of them been worn; and for a name   150
Now puts the drowsy and neglected Act
Freshly on me: 'tis surely for a name.

LUCIO I warrant it is; and thy head stands so tickle on thy shoulders
that a milkmaid, if she be in love, may sigh it off. Send after the
Duke and appeal to him.   155

CLAUDIO I have done so, but he's not to be found.

I prithee, Lucio, do me this kind service:
This day my sister should the cloister enter
And there receive her approbation.
Acquaint her with the danger of my state,   160
Implore her, in my voice, that she make friends
To the strict deputy: bid herself assay him.
I have great hope in that; for in her youth
There is a prone and speechless dialect
Such as move men; beside, she hath prosperous art   165
When she will play with reason and discourse,
And well she can persuade.

LUCIO I pray she may, as well for the encouragement of the like,

---

153–5] F; *as verse, Hanmer*   166 reason] *Pope;* reason, F   168–74] F; *as verse, Hanmer*

him to marry, and commends a severity which
condemns him to death. See 129, 135, 136 nn.
above.

149 nineteen zodiacs Possibly contradicting
1.3.22 where the Duke says he has let the laws
slip fourteen years; commentators suppose a
misreading of 4 for 9 or xiv for xix, or that
Shakespeare himself made a slip. Nathan (*SQ* 20
(1969), 83–4) points out that nineteen years is,
astronomically, a cycle, so that Claudio may in a
general way refer to the time it would take the sun
and moon to run their full cycle into realignment.

150 worn used (continuing the metaphor of
armour from 148) (Evans).

150, 152 for a name for the sake of reputation
(*OED* Name *sb* 6c).

151 drowsy half-asleep; compare 1.4.63–4.

151–2 puts . . . on imposes (*OED* Put *v* 46b),
also 'applies' (*OED* Put *v* 46k).

153 tickle insecurely.

154 milkmaid Proverbially prone to romantic
lovesickness. Some commentators detect a pun
on their easy loss of maiden *heads*.

158 should is supposed to.

159 approbation probation, period as a
novice.

162 assay address arguments to (*OED* sv *v* 15),
with allusion to the testing of precious metal
(*OED* sv *v²* 1, as in 1.1.48 and n.). Given that she
is told to 'make friends' with Angelo, the sense
'assail with words' seems inapposite.

164 prone Elsewhere in Shakespeare having
the sense 'quick, eager', not of a physical posture,
bending down or lying down. Yet the idea of
submissiveness, coupled with the unexpected
oxymoron 'speechless dialect', seems to suggest
that Isabella's physical femininity has an effect on
men, 'moves' their sexual feelings: compare *Tro.*
4.5.54–7, where Nestor says Cressida is a
'woman of quick sense' and Ulysses develops the
sense of wanton sensuality: 'There's language in
her eye, her cheek, her lip, / Nay, her foot
speaks . . .'

165 move The plural verb after the singular
subject is apparently influenced by the two preceding adjectives: compare 2.2.82 and 3.1.128.

165 prosperous consistently successful.

166 play with reason devise arguments.
'Reason' is here a noun, 'discourse' may be a
verb, but latent ambiguity remains because 'play'
may govern 'reason' and 'discourse' as two nouns.

168 the like similar behaviour or persons.

which else would stand under grievous imposition, as for the
enjoying of thy life, who I would be sorry should be thus foolishly   170
lost at a game of tick-tack. I'll to her.
CLAUDIO I thank you, good friend Lucio.
LUCIO Within two hours.
CLAUDIO Come, officer, away.

Exeunt

1.3   *Enter* DUKE *and* FRIAR THOMAS

DUKE No. Holy father, throw away that thought,
          Believe not that the dribbling dart of love
          Can pierce a complete bosom. Why I desire thee
          To give me secret harbour hath a purpose
          More grave and wrinkled than the aims and ends   5
          Of burning youth.
FRIAR May your grace speak of it?
DUKE My holy sir, none better knows than you
          How I have ever loved the life removed
          And held in idle price to haunt assemblies   10
          Where youth and cost witless bravery keeps.
          I have delivered to Lord Angelo,
          A man of stricture and firm abstinence,

Act 1, Scene 3   1.3] *Scena Quarta.* F   11 cost] *This edn;* cost, F; cost, and F2; cost, a NS

169 stand . . . imposition be subject to very
grave charges or accusations.
171 game of tick-tack A variety of back-
gammon played on a board with holes along the
edge, in which pegs were placed for scoring.
Lucio makes this procedure a bawdy synonym for
sexual intercourse. In modern slang 'score' can
mean 'have sexual intercourse'.

Act 1, Scene 3
2 dribbling dart arrow falling feebly. Compare *Rom.* 1.1.208–9: 'She'll not be hit / With
Cupid's arrow, she hath Dian's wit.'
3 complete with no weakness or defect, as if
clad in a complete armour. Compare *Rom.*
1.1.208–11, especially 'in strong proof of chastity
well arm'd'.
4 harbour shelter.
5 wrinkled i.e. befitting someone mature and
wise. The subsidiary suggestion 'formed in con-

volutions, sinuosities or windings' (*OED* sv *adj.* 1)
is very tempting in the present context of the
Duke's scheming and in relation to the Duke's
general character in the play as a whole.
6 burning youth Alluding both to the passionate hot-headedness and the sinful, hellish ten-
dencies of youth.
6–7 The Friar's opening line is short, but does
not constitute a direct link: rather, its abrupt
stress pattern signals that the Duke has made a
long pause and needs prompting. Contrast 34.
9 removed of retirement.
10 in idle price little worth ('it' is understood
before 'in').
11 cost extravagant expense.
11 witless bravery keeps Either 'maintains
foolish display' or 'is tied up by foolish display'
depending on which phrase is assumed to be the
subject of 'keeps'.
13 stricture strict self-discipline.

My absolute power and place here in Vienna,
And he supposes me travelled to Poland –   15
For so I have strewed it in the common ear,
And so it is received. Now, pious sir,
You will demand of me why I do this.

FRIAR Gladly, my lord.

DUKE We have strict statutes and most biting laws,   20
The needful bits and curbs to headstrong weeds,
Which for this fourteen years we have let slip,
Even like an o'er-grown lion in a cave
That goes not out to prey. Now, as fond fathers
Having bound up the threatening twigs of birch   25
Only to stick it in their children's sight
For terror, not to use – in time the rod
More mocked than feared – so our decrees,
Dead to infliction, to themselves are dead,
And Liberty plucks Justice by the nose,   30
The baby beats the nurse, and quite athwart
Goes all decorum.

---

15 travelled] trauaild F   21 weeds] F; Steeds *Theobald*   28 More] F; Becomes more *Pope*

---

15 **travelled** F's spelling puts the stress on the second syllable, giving a better rhythm.

16 **strewed** spread.

18 **demand** ask.

21 **weeds** Perhaps suggested by *Promos and Cassandra, Part 1* 2.3.8: 'Such wicked weedes', the same metaphor in the same situation. Stone notes how Shakespeare combines the idea of a well-bitted horse with the picture of a rank and noisome growth of weeds. Empson (*Seven Types of Ambiguity*, 1953, pp. 84–5) thinks the change of idea from steeds to weeds is accompanied 'with a twinge of disgust': 'biting' 'expresses both the effect of a *curb* on a "steed" and the effect of a scythe on a *weed*.' Compare 'weeds' and 'curb' in *Ham* 3.4.151–5. There may be a half-glimpsed play on 'slip' = cutting, a small branch bearing leaf buds used for horticultural propagation.

22 **fourteen** See 1.2.149, 'nineteen zodiacs', and n.

22 **let slip** Strictly, the subject is 'statutes' and 'laws', and these have not been enforced but allowed to slide into disuse. At the same time 'biting', 'bits and curbs', 'headstrong' suggest impatient steeds chafing, and with them (via 'biting') hounds ready to be 'let slip' to begin the chase. Hounds like steeds are associated with

sexual desire (as in the myth of Actaeon). Thus 'headstrong ... let slip' gives the impression of unleashed desire, when the Duke intended to say the laws had slipped into disuse (this was his fault or slip). See 1.3.33: 'unloose this tied-up justice' and, for 'let slip' as 'release hounds for the chase', see *1H4* 1.3.278.

23–4 **o'er-grown ... prey** Most commentators explain as referring to a lion grown too fat and hence inactive, but Schmidt thinks 'o'er grown' means 'too old' and Lever cites Horace, *Epist.* 1.i.73–5, through Camerarius, *Fabellae Aesiopicae*, explaining 'An old lion, pretending to be sick, invited the other animals to visit him in his cave, thus saving himself the trouble of going out to catch his prey.' The confusion about whether the prey are devoured or not perhaps inheres in the over-compressed imagery of steeds, hunting-dogs, weeds, lions.

24 **fond** foolish.

26 **it** i.e. the switch made of twigs, the 'rod'.

29 Completely unenforced, become as good as dead.

30 **Liberty** Licentiousness, licence.

30 **plucks ... nose** Expressing extreme contempt: see 5.1.334–5, and *Ham.* 2.2.574.

31 **athwart** awry.

FRIAR   It rested in your grace
        To unloose this tied-up justice when you pleased,
        And it in you more dreadful would have seemed
        Than in Lord Angelo.

DUKE   I do fear, too dreadful.   35
        Sith 'twas my fault to give the people scope,
        'Twould be my tyranny to strike and gall them
        For what I bid them do: for we bid this be done
        When evil deeds have their permissive pass
        And not the punishment. Therefore indeed, my father,   40
        I have on Angelo imposed the office,
        Who may in th'ambush of my name strike home,
        And yet my nature never in the fight
        To do in slander. And to behold his sway
        I will, as 'twere a brother of your order,   45
        Visit both prince and people. Therefore I prithee
        Supply me with the habit, and instruct me
        How I may formally in person bear
        Like a true friar. Moe reasons for this action
        At our more leisure shall I render you;   50
        Only this one: Lord Angelo is precise,
        Stands at a guard with envy, scarce confesses
        That his blood flows, or that his appetite
        Is more to bread than stone. Hence shall we see,
        If power change purpose, what our seemers be.   55

                                            Exeunt

---

55 SD] F2; *Exit.* F

35 **dreadful** inspiring with terror of punishment: compare 1.1.19.

37 **my tyranny** tyranny in me.

37 **strike and gall** To 'gall' was to make sore, especially by rubbing (*OED* sv *v* 1), associated with horses (see *Ham.* 3.2.242: 'galled jade'). Lever comments that the two previous figures, of the rod and the 'bits and curbs', are combined in 'strike and gall'.

42 **home** on target, to full effect.

43–4 **And yet . . . slander** i.e. while I myself am not directly the instrument of disgrace (with the possible ambiguity 'to do in slander' = to act discreditably, which gives the sense that he is guiltily devious rather than an upright dispenser of justice). *OED* explains 'slander' as disgrace, discredit (*sb* 3). Collier interprets 'to do what is necessary under an imputation, or slander, of too much severity', so clearing the Duke of guilt. Hanmer's emendation 'do it' clarifies the grammar, but perhaps too much so.

43 **nature** person, self (as opposed to 'name').

44 **behold his sway** observe his rule.

48 **formally** in outward appearance and manner.

49 **Moe** More in number.

52 **Stands at a guard** Keeps up his defence.

52 **envy** malice, especially calumny and depreciation (*OED* sv *sb* 1).

54 **bread than stone** See Matt. 4.3 and 7.9.

1.4 *Enter* ISABELL[A] *and* FRANCISCA *a nun*

ISABELLA And have you nuns no farther privileges?
NUN Are not these large enough?
ISABELLA Yes, truly; I speak not as desiring more,
    But rather wishing a more strict restraint
    Upon the sisterhood, the votarists of Saint Clare.   5
LUCIO (*Within*) Ho? Peace be in this place.
ISABELLA   Who's that which calls?
NUN It is a man's voice. Gentle Isabella,
    Turn you the key and know his business of him.
    You may, I may not; you are yet unsworn:
    When you have vowed, you must not speak with men   10
    But in the presence of the prioress;
    Then if you speak you must not show your face,
    Or if you show your face you must not speak.
    He calls again: I pray you answer him. [*Stands aside*]
ISABELLA Peace and prosperity. Who is't that calls?   15

[*Enter* LUCIO]

LUCIO Hail virgin, if you be – as those cheek-roses
    Proclaim you are no less – can you so stead me
    As bring me to the sight of Isabella,
    A novice of this place and the fair sister
    To her unhappy brother Claudio?   20
ISABELLA Why 'her unhappy brother'? Let me ask,
    The rather for I now must make you know
    I am that Isabella, and his sister.
LUCIO Gentle and fair: your brother kindly greets you.
    Not to be weary with you, he's in prison.   25

Act 1, Scene 4 1.4] *Scena Quinta.* F 0 SD ISABELLA] *Isabell* F 5 sisterhood] F2; *Sisterstood* F 14 SD] *Lever, subst., after Capell; Exit. / Rowe; not in* F 15 SD] *Rowe; not in* F 17 stead] *Rowe;* steed F

Act 1, Scene 4

4 restraint The word earlier used of Claudio's arrest is here used of the discipline of the holy order. Shakespeare indicates the link between brother and sister ironically in this dialogue about rules, restraint, licence, strict abstinence.

5 sisterhood F's spelling is probably a misreading of MS. 'h' as 'st'. See 2.2.22 for the correct reading.

5 votarist One given up by vow to a service or worship (*OED* quotes this line as its first example in this sense).

14 SD Lever supposes the nun would not leave the novice Isabella alone with Lucio: she will wait until the interview is over, and then the two women will make a joint exit. See 5.1.120 and n.

17 stead help (*OED* sv *v* 1c). F spells this verb 'steed' seven times, 'stead' twice, and 'sted' once.

25 weary tedious.

ISABELLA Woe me! For what?

LUCIO For that which, if myself might be his judge,
He should receive his punishment in thanks:
He hath got his friend with child.

ISABELLA Sir, make me not your story.

LUCIO   'Tis true.   30
I would not, though 'tis my familiar sin
With maids to seem the lapwing, and to jest
Tongue far from heart, play with all virgins so.
I hold you as a thing enskied and sainted,
By your renouncement an immortal spirit,   35
And to be talked with in sincerity
As with a saint.

ISABELLA You do blaspheme the good in mocking me.

LUCIO Do not believe it. Fewness and truth, 'tis thus:
Your brother and his lover have embraced;   40
As those that feed grow full, as blossoming time
That from the seedness the bare fallow brings
To teeming foison, even so her plenteous womb
Expresseth his full tilth and husbandry.

ISABELLA Someone with child by him? My cousin Juliet?   45

LUCIO Is she your cousin?

ISABELLA Adoptedly, as schoolmaids change their names
By vain though apt affection.

LUCIO   She it is.

ISABELLA O, let him marry her.

LUCIO   This is the point.
The Duke is very strangely gone from hence;   50

30–1] *Lines ending as Capell*; Sir . . . storie. / 'Tis . . . sin, F

29 **friend** lover.
31–3 I would not . . . virgins so The grammar is ambiguous: Lucio's 'I would not' can refer back to 'make me your story', so that in what follows he admits that his familiar sin is to play so with all virgins. Otherwise 'I would not' can be connected with 'play with all virgins' – he excepts Isabella.
31 **familiar** habitual.
32 **lapwing** The bird was proverbial for flying far from its nest to deceive predators. Compare *Err.* 4.2.27: 'Far from her nest the lapwing cries away'; and Tilley L68.
34 **enskied** placed in heaven.

38 **You blaspheme** against true saints in mockingly making me of their company.
39 **Fewness** In few words; compare 3.2.45.
42 **seedness** Action of sowing, or the state of having been sown.
43 **foison** abundance, harvest.
44 **Expresseth** Exhibits (*OED* Express *v* 7) (by pushing out her stomach).
44 **tilth** tilling.
44 **husbandry** cultivating (and a pun on 'husband').
47 **change** exchange.
48 **vain though apt affection** ineffectual love (they remain unrelated) but natural at their age.

Bore many gentlemen, myself being one,
In hand and hope of action: but we do learn,
By those that know the very nerves of state,
His givings-out were of an infinite distance
From his true meant design. Upon his place,   55
And with full line of his authority,
Governs Lord Angelo, a man whose blood
Is very snow-broth; one who never feels
The wanton stings and motions of the sense,
But doth rebate and blunt his natural edge   60
With profits of the mind: study and fast.
He, to give fear to use and liberty,
Which have for long run by the hideous law
As mice by lions, hath picked out an Act
Under whose heavy sense your brother's life   65
Falls into forfeit. He arrests him on it,
And follows close the rigour of the statute
To make him an example. All hope is gone,
Unless you have the grace by your fair prayer
To soften Angelo. And that's my pith of business   70
'Twixt you and your poor brother.

ISABELLA   Doth he so
    Seek his life?

LUCIO   Has censured him already,

54 givings-out] *Rowe*; giving out F   70 pith of] F; *omitted, Pope*   70–7] *Knight²*; To . . . businesse / 'Twixt . . . brother. / *Isa*. Doth he so, / seeke his life? / *Luc*. Has . . . already / And . . . warrant / For's execution. / *Isa*. Alas: What poore / Abilitie's . . . good. / *Luc*. Assay . . . haue. / *Isa*. My . . . doubt. / *Luc*. Our . . . traitors F   72 Has] F; H'as *Theobald*

51–2 **Bore . . . hand** An idiomatic expression meaning 'deluded'; but there is a separate, non-idiomatic phrase, 'bore in hope' = 'kept in hope', the suggestion of mixed construction giving an ambiguous sense to the second phrase, 'deceived with hope'.

52 **action** military action.

53 **nerves** Literally, 'sinews, tendons'; hence metaphorically, 'the means of acting, using strength'.

54 **givings-out** i.e. what he said publicly. Comparison with 3.2.125, 'bringings-forth', suggests that emendation is needed to F's 'giving out', although the singular form is possible if 'were' is taken as a subjunctive singular rather than an indicative plural verb.

58 **snow-broth** melted snow.

59 **motions** urges.

60 **rebate** reduce. The accent is on the second

syllable. For the metaphor of sexual desire as sharp as a dagger compare *Ham.* 3.2.250.

62 **use and liberty** licentiousness which has become customary.

65 **heavy sense** severe meaning.

66 **on it** In modern English, 'under it'.

70 **my pith of business** the essence of my errand.

70–2 F's lineation gives emphasis to a marked pause after Isabella's shocked and incredulous 'Doth he so', followed by the no less incredulous 'Seek his life?' Alternative lineation schemes blur this emphasis. Shakespeare may well have written the passage out as it is printed, 'pith of' being a first shot inadequately marked for deletion and included erroneously by the scribe.

72 **Has** Abbott 400 says 'He has' is frequently pronounced and sometimes written 'Has'.

And, as I hear, the provost hath a warrant
For's execution.
ISABELLA   Alas! What poor
        Ability's in me to do him good?   75
LUCIO Assay the power you have.
ISABELLA   My power? Alas, I doubt.
LUCIO Our doubts are traitors
        And makes us lose the good we oft might win,
        By fearing to attempt. Go to Lord Angelo
        And let him learn to know, when maidens sue   80
        Men give like gods, but when they weep and kneel
        All their petitions are as freely theirs
        As they themselves would owe them.
ISABELLA I'll see what I can do.
LUCIO But speedily.
ISABELLA   I will about it straight;   85
        No longer staying but to give the Mother
        Notice of my affair. I humbly thank you.
        Commend me to my brother: soon at night
        I'll send him certain word of my success.
LUCIO I take my leave of you.
ISABELLA   Good sir, adieu.   90

                                                Exeunt

2.1 *Enter* ANGELO, ESCALUS, *and* SERVANTS, [*and a*] JUSTICE

ANGELO We must not make a scarecrow of the law,
        Setting it up to fear the birds of prey,
        And let it keep one shape till custom make it
        Their perch and not their terror.
ESCALUS   Ay, but yet
        Let us be keen, and rather cut a little   5

78 makes] F; make *Rowe*³   **Act 2, Scene 1** 2.1] *Actus Secundus. Scæna Prima.* F

83 As As if
83 would owe would wish to have.
89 my success the result of my mediation,
good or bad.

Act 2, Scene 1
1 **scarecrow** The metaphor recalls those at
the beginning of the play on costume, and the

contrast between outer appearance and inner
reality – though here to grotesque effect, further
emphasised in the image of birds of prey, like
rats, unpleasant instances of animal appetite at its
most rapacious.
  2 **fear** scare, frighten away.
  3 **custom** i.e. their familiarity with it.
  5 **keen** sharp, perceptive.

Than fall and bruise to death. Alas, this gentleman
Whom I would save had a most noble father.
Let but your honour know,
Whom I believe to be most strait in virtue,
That in the working of your own affections,   10
Had time cohered with place, or place with wishing,
Or that the resolute acting of your blood
Could have attained th'effect of your own purpose,
Whether you had not sometime in your life
Erred in this point which now you censure him,   15
And pulled the law upon you.

ANGELO 'Tis one thing to be tempted, Escalus,
Another thing to fall. I not deny
The jury passing on the prisoner's life
May in the sworn twelve have a thief or two   20
Guiltier than him they try: what's open made to justice,
That justice seizes. What knows the laws
That thieves do pass on thieves? 'Tis very pregnant,
The jewel that we find, we stoop and take't,
Because we see it; but what we do not see   25
We tread upon and never think of it.
You may not so extenuate his offence
For I have had such faults; but rather tell me,
When I that censure him do so offend,

8–9] F; Let . . . believe / To . . . virtue *Steevens* 12 your] *Rowe, after Davenant;* our F 20 sworn twelve] *Rowe;*
sworne-twelue F 21–3] F; Guiltier . . . made / To . . . know / The . . . pregnant *Hanmer* 22 knows] F; know *Hanmer*

5–6 The idea is glimpsed of surgery as
opposed to brutal execution, or of the husband-
man's pruning as opposed to chopping down.

6 **fall** cause to fall, as of a tree, or sword of
justice.

8 A short line in which a change of subject is
evident. F's arrangement should therefore be
retained.

9 **strait** *OED* sv *adj* 7b, 'strict, rigorous',
with instances relating to the religious life,
laws and commandment, as well as character
and way of living.

10 **affections** desires.

12 **your blood** your passions. The rhetorical
design of the whole speech exploits the repetition
of 'your', making F 'our' in 12 an obvious
misprint.

13 **effect** achievement.

15 **censure** condemn.

19 **passing** passing judgement.

21–2 Lever speculates (p. xxix) that 'What's
. . . seizes' is an afterthought added in the MS.
margin which the scribe has faultily worked in.
'That' is also extrametrical. Hanmer's emendation corrects the metre of 21–2, not of 23.

22 **What knows** A plural subject with a
singular verb is frequent in Shakespeare (Abbott
333), but it is not clear whether 'laws' is object or
subject of 'knows': so either 'what knowledge has
the law of thieves judging thieves' or – more likely
– 'what do we know of the laws thieves apply to
their fellows'.

23 **pregnant** evident, obvious.

26 **tread upon** Half anticipating Isabella's
thought in 3.1.78–9.

28 **For** Because.

Let mine own judgement pattern out my death   30
And nothing come in partial. Sir, he must die.

Enter PROVOST

ESCALUS Be it as your wisdom will.
ANGELO   Where is the provost?
PROVOST Here, if it like your honour.
ANGELO   See that Claudio
Be executed by nine tomorrow morning.
Bring him his confessor, let him be prepared,   35
For that's the utmost of his pilgrimage.

                                                    [*Exit Provost*]
ESCALUS Well, heaven forgive him, and forgive us all.
Some rise by sin and some by virtue fall,
Some run from breaks of ice and answer none,
And some condemnèd for a fault alone.   40

Enter ELBOW [*and*] OFFICERS [*with*] FROTH [*and*] POMPEY

ELBOW Come, bring them away. If these be good people in a
commonweal, that do nothing but use their abuses in common
houses, I know no law. Bring them away.
ANGELO How now, sir, what's your name, and what's the matter?
ELBOW If it please your honour, I am the poor Duke's constable, and   45
my name is Elbow. I do lean upon justice, sir, and do bring in
here, before your good honour, two notorious benefactors.

---

31 SD] F; *after 32, Collier*   36 SD] *Rowe; not in* F   38] *Italic in* F   39] breaks of ice] *Collier, conj. Steevens;* brakes
of Ice F; brakes of vice *Rowe*

30 judgement sentence (on Claudio) (Evans).
31 come in partial extenuating be admitted on my behalf.
36 utmost . . . pilgrimage limit of his life's journey (Evans).
39 breaks of ice F's spelling 'brakes' has provoked much editorial speculation, but the simplest explanation of 39–40 seems preferable: 'some escape after breaking the ice many times, some are caught by the first fault'. 'answer none' = 'get away with it' (see *OED* Answer *v* 6). See *The Revenger's Tragedy*, ed. Brian Gibbons, 1990, 4.4.80–2: 'she first begins with one / Who afterward to thousand proves a whore: / "Break ice in one place, it will crack in more."' Sisson, in support of 'breaks', compares *Tro.* 3.3.215: 'The fool slides o'er the ice that you should break.'

Alternative suggestions are 'brake' = sharp bit, snaffle, or = thicket; both of these assume the emendation of 'ice' to 'vice'. Lever suggests 'brakes' = constrictions, and the whole phrase = hell pains. The key idea is the opposition of many crimes going unpunished to one crime fully punished.
42–3 use . . . houses carry on their corrupt activities in brothels.
45 poor Duke's i.e. Duke's poor (a comic reversal or hypallage).
46 lean upon Possibly 'depend on' (*OED* Lean *v*[1] 3, 'trust to'), possibly mistaken for 'uphold' (Evans), possibly an attempt at wit, playing on his name, 'Elbow'. The prolixity recalls Shakespeare's earlier constable Dogberry in *Ado*, also a gifted malapropist.

ANGELO Benefactors? Well, what benefactors are they? Are they not malefactors?

ELBOW If it please your honour, I know not well what they are: but   50
precise villains they are, that I am sure of, and void of all
profanation in the world that good Christians ought to have.

ESCALUS This comes off well: here's a wise officer.

ANGELO Go to. What quality are they of? Elbow is your name? Why
dost thou not speak, Elbow?   55

POMPEY He cannot, sir: he's out at elbow.

ANGELO What are you, sir?

ELBOW He, sir? A tapster, sir, parcel bawd, one that serves a bad
woman, whose house, sir, was, as they say, plucked down in the
suburbs; and now she professes a hot-house; which I think is a   60
very ill house too.

ESCALUS How know you that?

ELBOW My wife, sir, whom I detest before heaven and your honour –

ESCALUS How? Thy wife?

ELBOW Ay, sir: whom I thank heaven is an honest woman –   65

ESCALUS Dost thou detest her therefore?

ELBOW I say, sir, I will detest myself also, as well as she, that this
house, if it be not a bawd's house, it is pity of her life, for it is a
naughty house.

ESCALUS How dost thou know that, constable?   70

ELBOW Marry, sir, by my wife, who, if she had been a woman
cardinally given, might have been accused in fornication,
adultery, and all uncleanliness there.

63 sir,] F2; Sir? F

51 **precise** puritanical (*OED* sv *adj* 2 b), here
used mistakenly for 'decided' or 'precious',
'arrant', but see 3.1.93 and 96.

52 **profanation** Possibly 'profession' is meant,
possibly mistaken for 'fear of God'. As it is,
together with 'precise villain', unconsciously a
good descripion of Angelo. Through these verbal
echoes Shakespeare alerts the spectator to deeper
parallels and interconnections between ostensibly
separate dramatic actions and characters.

53 **comes off well** is well said.

56 Punning on (1) 'out', at a loss, speechless,
(2) 'out at elbow', impoverished in dress (and
intelligence).

58 **parcel** part-time.

60 **professes** Lever suspects an ironic allusion
to the sense 'make one's vows to a religious order

or house' (*OED* Profess *v* 1, citation of 1494 'to
be professed in an house of religion'); 'professes'
may also imply pretence or insincerity (*OED* sv *v*
3). Elbow intends to discredit but may nevertheless be making a malapropism; the irony then
being Shakespeare's.

60 **hot-house** bath-house. Jonson, *Epigrams*,
vii, says, 'hot-house' is another word for 'whore-
house'. See also 1.2.67 and n.

63 **detest** Mistake for 'attest' or 'protest'.

68 **pity of her life** a very sad thing for her.

69 **naughty** wicked.

72 **cardinally** Mistaken for 'carnally'. The
adjective 'cardinal' means 'chief', hence the
'cardinal virtues'.

72–3 Compare Gal. 5.19: 'adultery, fornication, uncleanness . . .'

ESCALUS By the woman's means?

ELBOW Ay, sir, by Mistress Overdone's means. But as she spit in his   75
face, so she defied him.

POMPEY Sir, if it please your honour, this is not so.

ELBOW Prove it before these varlets here, thou honourable man,
prove it!

ESCALUS Do you hear how he misplaces?   80

POMPEY Sir, she came in great with child; and longing, saving your
honours' reverence, for stewed prunes. Sir, we had but two in
the house, which at that very distant time stood, as it were, in a
fruit dish, a dish of some three pence; your honours have seen
such dishes, they are not china dishes, but very good dishes –   85

ESCALUS Go to, go to: no matter for the dish, sir.

POMPEY No indeed, sir, not of a pin; you are therein in the right –
but to the point: as I say, this Mistress Elbow, being, as I say,
with child, and being great-bellied, and longing, as I said, for
prunes, and having but two in the dish, as I said, Master Froth   90
here, this very man, having eaten the rest, as I said, and, as I say,
paying for them very honestly – for as you know, Master Froth, I
could not give you three pence again –

FROTH No indeed.

POMPEY Very well. You being then, if you be remembered, cracking   95
the stones of the foresaid prunes –

FROTH Ay, so I did indeed.

POMPEY Why, very well. I telling you then, if you be remembered,
that such a one, and such a one, were past cure of the thing you
wot of, unless they kept very good diet, as I told you –   100

FROTH All this is true.

POMPEY Why very well then –

---

82 honours'] *Capell;* honors F   82 prunes] prewyns F (*also at* 90, 96)

---

75 **his** i.e. Pompey's.
80 **misplaces** i.e. 'varlets' and 'honourable'.
82 **stewed prunes** A favourite dish in brothels
(a play on 'the stews' may be suspected, with
sexual innuendoes on 'two', 'stood' 'dish', 'pin',
'point', 'cracking the stones' and finally 'done'.
See Partridge and Colman for further analysis of
bawdy here). F's spelling 'prewyns' indicates the
required vulgar pronunciation.
83 **distant** It is possible to suspect Pompey of
parodying Elbow's malapropisms, 'distant' being
deliberately mistaken for 'instant', precise moment (see 141 n. below). *OED* gives no support
for 'distant' as 'remote in time', but the joke may

nevertheless be suspected. His further 'precise'
evidence (*two* prunes in a *three*penny dish, Froth
then cracking the stones) provides another joke,
this far 'distant' time being supposedly exactly
remembered by himself and by Froth. The
circumstantial details are of course all irrelevant
and deliberate red herrings.
99–100 **the thing you wot of** you-know-what:
here, venereal disease (Evans).
100 **diet** strict regimen, prescribed course of
food (*OED* sv *sb* 3). Recalling the comment of
Claudio at 1.2.108–10, another instance of ironic
parallel; see above, 2.1.52 n.

ESCALUS Come, you are a tedious fool, to the purpose: what was
      done to Elbow's wife, that he hath cause to complain of? Come
      me to what was done to her.   105
POMPEY Sir, your honour cannot come to that yet.
ESCALUS No, sir, nor I mean it not.
POMPEY Sir, but you shall come to it, by your honour's leave; and I
      beseech you, look into Master Froth here, sir; a man of four
      score pound a year; whose father died at Hallowmas – was't not   110
      at Hallowmas, Master Froth?
FROTH All-Hallond Eve.
POMPEY Why, very well: I hope here be truths. He, sir, sitting, as I
      say, in a lower chair, sir – 'twas in the Bunch of Grapes, where
      indeed you have a delight to sit, have you not?   115
FROTH I have so, because it is an open room, and good for winter.
POMPEY Why, very well then: I hope here be truths.
ANGELO This will last out a night in Russia
      When nights are longest there. I'll take my leave,
      And leave you to the hearing of the cause,   120
      Hoping you'll find good cause to whip them all.   *Exit*
ESCALUS I think no less: good morrow to your lordship.
      Now, sir, come on: what was done to Elbow's wife, once more?
POMPEY Once, sir? There was nothing done to her once.
ELBOW I beseech you, sir, ask him what this man did to my wife.   125
POMPEY I beseech your honour, ask me.
ESCALUS Well, sir, what did this gentleman to her?
POMPEY I beseech you, sir, look in this gentleman's face. Good
      Master Froth, look upon his honour; 'tis for a good purpose.
      Doth your honour mark his face?   130
ESCALUS Ay, sir, very well.

104–5 Come me i.e. come. See Abbott 220,
and 1.4.30, 1.2.147, for this redundant dative
form.

106 Pompey pretends to understand 'Come
me' as 'Let me come' (Evans), that is, 'Let me do
the same act.'

107 Escalus shows in this reply that he
recognises the bawdy quibbling on 'come' and
'done' in 104 and 105.

109–10 four score pound a year Eccles notes
that James I required all Englishmen in 1603 who
had land worth forty pounds a year to accept a
knighthood, or be fined, which shows that they
were considered well-to-do, and Froth had twice
that income. Yet we may wonder whether Pompey is not exaggerating.

110 Hallowmas All Saints' Day, 1 November.

112 All-Hallond Eve The eve of All Saints'.

114 lower chair Commentators note the
phrases 'chairs of ease' in *Tim.* 5.4.11 and
'drooping chair' in *1H6* 4.5.5, but the meaning is
obscure here; in any case Pompey is still striving
to appear exact and precise, and so 'lower'
indicates a particular chair. There may be some
obscure innuendo, too, via 'low'.

116 open public, where a fire was kept in
winter.

120 cause case, and reason.

122 think no less am of the same opinion,
expect I shall.

POMPEY Nay, I beseech you mark it well.

ESCALUS Well, I do so.

POMPEY Doth your honour see any harm in his face?

ESCALUS Why, no.   135

POMPEY I'll be supposed upon a book, his face is the worst thing about him: good then: if his face be the worst thing about him, how could Master Froth do the constable's wife any harm? I would know that of your honour.

ESCALUS He's in the right, constable, what say you to it?   140

ELBOW First, and it like you, the house is a respected house; next, this is a respected fellow; and his mistress is a respected woman.

POMPEY By this hand, sir, his wife is a more respected person than any of us all.

ELBOW Varlet, thou liest! Thou liest, wicked varlet! The time is yet   145
to come that she was ever respected with man, woman, or child.

POMPEY Sir, she was respected with him before he married with her.

ESCALUS Which is the wiser here, Justice or Iniquity? Is this true?

ELBOW Oh, thou caitiff! Oh, thou varlet! Oh, thou wicked Hannibal! I respected with her, before I was married to her? If ever I was   150
respected with her, or she with me, let not your worship think me the poor Duke's officer! Prove this, thou wicked Hannibal, or I'll have mine action of battery on thee.

ESCALUS If he took you a box o'th'ear, you might have your action of slander too.   155

ELBOW Marry, I thank your good worship for it. What is't your worship's pleasure I shall do with this wicked caitiff?

ESCALUS Truly, officer, because he hath some offences in him that thou wouldst discover, if thou couldst, let him continue in his courses till thou knowst what they are.   160

ELBOW Marry, I thank your worship for it. Thou seest, thou wicked varlet, now, what's come upon thee. Thou art to continue, now, thou varlet, thou art to continue.

---

136 supposed Mistake for 'deposed', i.e. sworn.

136 a book The Bible.

141, 142 respected Mistake for 'suspected'. Pompey uses the word in its correct sense at 143, knowing Elbow will misunderstand. This increases the likelihood that he parodies Elbow at 83, and Escalus at 106 above.

148 Justice or Iniquity Stock characters from Morality plays, here absurdly identified with Elbow and Pompey. Hal calls Falstaff 'that

reverent Vice, that grey Iniquity', *1H4* 2.4.453–4.

149 caitiff despicable knave (Johnson).

149 Hannibal Commentators suggest a mistake for 'cannibal', or confusion between the generals, Pompey and Hannibal. To Elbow Hannibal may just be a popular type of the hated foreign threat to the state.

159 discover expose.

162 continue Elbow assumes the word means some kind of punishment rather than the opposite.

ESCALUS Where were you born, friend?

FROTH Here in Vienna, sir.   165

ESCALUS Are you of four score pounds a year?

FROTH Yes, and't please you, sir.

ESCALUS So. [*To Pompey*] What trade are you of, sir?

POMPEY A tapster, a poor widow's tapster.

ESCALUS Your mistress' name?   170

POMPEY Mistress Overdone.

ESCALUS Hath she had any more than one husband?

POMPEY Nine, sir: Overdone by the last.

ESCALUS Nine? Come hither to me, Master Froth. Master Froth, I
      would not have you acquainted with tapsters; they will draw you,   175
      Master Froth, and you will hang them. Get you gone, and let me
      hear no more of you.

FROTH I thank your worship. For mine own part, I never come into
      any room in a taphouse, but I am drawn in.

ESCALUS Well, no more of it, Master Froth. Farewell.   180

                                                                    [*Exit Froth*]

      Come you hither to me, Master Tapster. What's your name,
      Master Tapster?

POMPEY Pompey.

ESCALUS What else?

POMPEY Bum, sir.   185

ESCALUS Troth, and your bum is the greatest thing about you, so
      that in the beastliest sense you are Pompey the Great. Pompey,
      you are partly a bawd, Pompey, howsoever you colour it in being
      a tapster, are you not? Come, tell me true, it shall be the better
      for you.   190

POMPEY Truly, sir, I am a poor fellow that would live.

180 SD] *Rowe; not in* F   181, 182 Master] Mr. F

---

173 **by the last** i.e. her surname is that of her
last husband (and with a bawdy quibble, treating
the surname as a verb meaning 'sexually worn
out': see 1.2.92).

175 **draw** (1) alluding to the drawing of ale
from the tap, hence 'drain away all your wealth',
(2) take in, deceive, (3) alluding to the punishment of hanging and drawing, disembowelling
(*OED* Draw *v* 50).

176 **hang** (1) be the cause of their hanging
(Hudson), (2) have cause to cry 'Hang them!'
(Evans).

179 **drawn in** (1) enticed in, (2) cheated, (3)

brought in by the drawer, who 'draws', i.e. fills
mugs from the barrel of ale. Excessive froth in a
tankard is still a way dishonest tapsters cheat
customers of their full measure of ale.

185 **Bum** The buttocks. Also applied opprob-
riously to a person (*OED* sv *sb* 2).

186 **the greatest thing** Probably alluding to
the padded breeches, round trunk-hose, he
wears, but also to his anatomy, resembling the
personification of gluttony.

188 **colour** disguise.

191 **would live** wishes to make a living.

ESCALUS How would you live, Pompey? By being a bawd? What do
you think of the trade, Pompey? Is it a lawful trade?

POMPEY If the law would allow it, sir.

ESCALUS But the law will not allow it, Pompey; nor it shall not be   195
allowed in Vienna.

POMPEY Does your worship mean to geld and splay all the youth of
the city?

ESCALUS No, Pompey.

POMPEY Truly, sir, in my poor opinion they will to't then. If your   200
worship will take order for the drabs and the knaves, you need
not to fear the bawds.

ESCALUS There is pretty orders beginning, I can tell you: it is but
heading and hanging.

POMPEY If you head and hang all that offend that way but for ten   205
year together, you'll be glad to give out a commission for more
heads. If this law hold in Vienna ten year, I'll rent the fairest
house in it after three pence a bay. If you live to see this come to
pass, say Pompey told you so.

ESCALUS Thank you, good Pompey; and in requital of your   210
prophecy, hark you: I advise you, let me not find you before me
again upon any complaint whatsoever; no, not for dwelling where
you do. If I do, Pompey, I shall beat you to your tent, and prove a
shrewd Caesar to you: in plain dealing, Pompey, I shall have you
whipped. So for this time, Pompey, fare you well.   215

POMPEY I thank your worship for your good counsel; [*Aside*] but I
shall follow it as the flesh and fortune shall better determine.
　　Whip me? No, no, let carman whip his jade,
　　The valiant heart's not whipped out of his trade.   　　　*Exit*

ESCALUS Come hither to me, Master Elbow, come hither, Master   220
Constable. How long have you been in this place of constable?

ELBOW Seven year, and a half, sir.

ESCALUS I thought, by the readiness in the office, you had continued

---

197 splay spay; synonym for 'castrate', but
referring specifically to female animals. Pompey
considers both sexes equally driven by sexual
appetite, whether 'knaves' or 'drabs'.

201 take order for take care of.

201 drabs prostitutes.

204 heading beheading.

206 commission order or authoritative demand (i.e. for begetting of children, with a play on
heads/maidenheads, and implying that the law
will in effect have to license illegitimacy and

lechery, an absurd result of extreme strictness).

208 three pence a bay i.e. dirt-cheap. The
bay being (*OED* Bay *sb³* 2) 'the space lying under
one gable, or included between two party walls'.

210 requital of return for.

213–14 beat...Caesar Alluding to Caesar's
defeat of Pompey the Great at Pharsalia in 48 BC.

214 shrewd severe.

218 carman carter.

218 jade worthless horse.

223 readiness proficiency.

in it some time. You say seven years together?
ELBOW And a half, sir.   225
ESCALUS Alas, it hath been great pains to you: they do you wrong to
    put you so oft upon't. Are there not men in your ward sufficient
    to serve it?
ELBOW Faith, sir, few of any wit in such matters. As they are chosen,
    they are glad to choose me for them; I do it for some piece of   230
    money, and go through with all.
ESCALUS Look you bring me in the names of some six or seven, the
    most sufficient of your parish.
ELBOW To your worship's house, sir?
ESCALUS To my house. Fare you well.   235

                                        [*Exit Elbow*]

    What's a clock, think you?
JUSTICE Eleven, sir.
ESCALUS I pray you home to dinner with me.
JUSTICE I humbly thank you.
ESCALUS It grieves me for the death of Claudio,   240
    But there's no remedy.
JUSTICE Lord Angelo is severe.
ESCALUS It is but needful.
    Mercy is not itself that oft looks so,
    Pardon is still the nurse of second woe.   245
    But yet, poor Claudio; there is no remedy. Come sir.

                                        Exeunt

2.2 *Enter* PROVOST [*and a*] SERVANT

SERVANT He's hearing of a cause, he will come straight,
    I'll tell him of you.
PROVOST   Pray you do.

                                        [*Exit Servant*]
                          I'll know

235 SD] *Rowe; not in* F   **Act 2, Scene 2** 2.2] *Scena Secunda.* F   2 SD] *Capell; not in* F

224 years Escalus is revealed as an educated
person in contrast to Elbow, who uses the
vernacular plural form 'year', like Pompey at 206.
227 put ... upon't make you undertake it so
often.
227 ward administrative district (of a city).
227 sufficient capable, competent enough.
229 chosen elected. Elbow, it seems, is also a

deputy, ironically reflecting Angelo's situation.
231 go through with all carry out all the
duties.
237 SH JUSTICE See Textual Analysis, p. 201
below.
244–5 Extending mercy is not always what it
seems, some commit further crimes after pardon.
Proverbial (Tilley P50). See *Rom.* 3.1.197.

His pleasure, may be he will relent. Alas,
He hath but as offended in a dream.
All sects, all ages smack of this vice, and he   5
To die for't?

Enter ANGELO

ANGELO   Now what's the matter, provost?
PROVOST Is it your will Claudio shall die tomorrow?
ANGELO Did not I tell thee yea? Hadst thou not order?
        Why dost thou ask again?
PROVOST   Lest I might be too rash:
        Under your good correction, I have seen   10
        When, after execution, judgement hath
        Repented o'er his doom.
ANGELO   Go to; let that be mine.
        Do you your office, or give up your place,
        And you shall well be spared.
PROVOST I crave your honour's pardon: 15
        What shall be done, sir, with the groaning Juliet?
        She's very near her hour.
ANGELO   Dispose of her
        To some more fitter place, and that with speed.

[*Enter* SERVANT]

SERVANT Here is the sister of the man condemned,
        Desires access to you.
ANGELO   Hath he a sister?   20
PROVOST Ay, my good lord, a very virtuous maid,
        And to be shortly of a sisterhood,

18 SD] *Capell; not in* F

Act 2, Scene 2
  4 **but as offended** offended only as if.
  4 **in a dream** i.e. without conscious intent
(Evans).
  5 **sects** classes.
  5 **smack** partake, possibly with a suggestion of
the sense 'relish' (*OED v*² 1 and 2).
  10 **Under** Subject to.
  12 **doom** sentence.
  12 **Go . . . mine** i.e. enough: that is for me to
decide, it is my responsibility.

  14 **you . . . spared** i.e. we shall easily manage
without you. Yet it was the Duke who appointed
both of them to temporary posts in his absence.
Angelo exceeds his brief, their relative authority
having been left ambiguous.
  16 **groaning** i.e. in labour.
  17 **hour** i.e. of giving birth.
  18 **more fitter** The doubled comparative form
is frequent in Shakespeare.

If not already.

ANGELO   Well. Let her be admitted.

[Exit Servant]

See you the fornicatress be removed.
Let her have needful, but not lavish, means.   25
There shall be order for't.

Enter LUCIO *and* ISABELLA

PROVOST   Save your honour. *[Going]*

ANGELO Stay a little while. *[To Isabella]* Y'are welcome: what's your
will?

ISABELLA I am a woeful suitor to your honour,
Please but your honour hear me.

ANGELO   Well; what's your suit?

ISABELLA There is a vice that most I do abhor,   30
And most desire should meet the blow of justice;
For which I would not plead, but that I must,
For which I must not plead, but that I am
At war 'twixt will and will not.

ANGELO   Well; the matter?

ISABELLA I have a brother is condemned to die.   35
I do beseech you, let it be his fault,
And not my brother.

PROVOST *[Aside]*   Heaven give thee moving graces!

ANGELO Condemn the fault, and not the actor of it?
Why, every fault's condemned ere it be done.
Mine were the very cipher of a function   40
To fine the faults, whose fine stands in record,
And let go by the actor.

ISABELLA   Oh just but severe law:
I had a brother then. Heaven keep your honour. *[Going]*

---

23 SD] *Theobald; not in* F   26 SD.2] *Malone; not in* F   27 SD] *Johnson; not in* F   43 SD] *Malone; not in* F

25 **needful** necessary.

26 **Save** i.e. God save. Thirlby conjectured that this is the first of several instances where the word 'God' has been purged from the text. A very plausible instance is 2.2.115 below.

36 **let...fault** i.e. that is condemned. Proverbial idea (Tilley P238).

37 **moving graces** gifts to persuade. See 1.2.164–5 and n.

38 **fault...actor** Compare the comment on

separating tongue and heart at 1.4.33 and 2.4.4.

41 **fine...fine** penalise...punishment.

41 **record** law, the statute books.

42 See the discussion of this line in the Textual Analysis, pp. 206–7 below. To link seems justified since her strong reaction constitutes a kind of completion to the thought. The resultant line is irregular, which may be an objection, although there are a number of irregular lines in the body of pentameter verse speeches in this play.

LUCIO [*To Isabella*] Give't not o'er so: to him again, entreat him,
    Kneel down before him, hang upon his gown.   45
    You are too cold. If you should need a pin,
    You could not with more tame a tongue desire it:
    To him, I say.
ISABELLA Must he needs die?
ANGELO   Maiden, no remedy.
ISABELLA Yes: I do think that you might pardon him,   50
    And neither heaven nor man grieve at the mercy.
ANGELO I will not do't.
ISABELLA   But can you if you would?
ANGELO Look what I will not, that I cannot do.
ISABELLA But might you do't, and do the world no wrong,
    If so your heart were touched with that remorse   55
    As mine is to him?
ANGELO   He's sentenced, 'tis too late.
LUCIO [*To Isabella*] You are too cold.
ISABELLA Too late? Why, no; I that do speak a word
    May call it again. Well, believe this:
    No ceremony that to great ones longs,   60
    Not the king's crown, nor the deputed sword,
    The marshal's truncheon, nor the judge's robe
    Become them with one half so good a grace
    As mercy does.
    If he had been as you, and you as he,   65
    You would have slipped like him, but he like you
    Would not have been so stern.
ANGELO   Pray you be gone.

44] SD *Collier, after Johnson; not in* F (*also at 57, 72, 92, etc.*).   59 again] F; back againe F2   64–5] *As Capell; one line in* F

46 pin i.e. the smallest thing, a trifle.

53 This very revealing assertion contradicts Angelo's claim at 82 that Claudio's fate is a matter of law, not Angelo's personal will.

55 remorse compassion.

59 again F2 corrects the metre which in F is deficient; but given the context I remain inclined to leave F as it stands. Sisson says 'There is in fact a marked and dramatic pause in the middle of the line and no irregularity is felt in speaking the passage.' Contrast 2.4.154.

60 ceremony External accessory or symbolic attribute of worship, state, or pomp (*OED* sv *sb* 64), such as the crown; but *not*, here, a formal act

expressing deference (*OED* sv *sb* 2), or sacred ritual (*OED* sv *sb* 1).

60 longs pertains to (*OED* Long v^2 1). Not a contracted form of 'belongs'.

61 deputed sword sword of justice; a symbol of divine authority in which kings and governors deputise.

62 marshal's truncheon i.e. field marshal's staff of military command.

63 grace appropriateness (and with an allusion to the divine influence and its effects, inspiring virtue and strength to resist evil).

66 slipped erred, sinned (*OED* Slip v^1 8c), and see 1.3.22 n., and 5.1.465.

ISABELLA   I would to heaven I had your potency,
                  And you were Isabel: should it then be thus?
                  No. I would tell what 'twere to be a judge,   70
                  And what a prisoner.
LUCIO   [*Aside*] Ay, touch him, there's the vein.
ANGELO   Your brother is a forfeit of the law,
                  And you but waste your words.
ISABELLA   Alas, alas!
                  Why all the souls that were, were forfeit once,   75
                  And he that might the vantage best have took
                  Found out the remedy. How would you be
                  If he, which is the top of judgement, should
                  But judge you as you are? Oh, think on that,
                  And mercy then will breathe within your lips   80
                  Like man new made.
ANGELO   Be you content, fair maid,
                  It is the law, not I, condemn your brother.
                  Were he my kinsman, brother, or my son,
                  It should be thus with him: he must die tomorrow.
ISABELLA   Tomorrow? Oh, that's sudden! Spare him, spare him!   85
                  He's not prepared for death. Even for our kitchens
                  We kill the fowl of season: shall we serve heaven
                  With less respect than we do minister
                  To our gross selves? Good, good my lord, bethink you.
                  Who is it that hath died for this offence?   90

71–2] F; *as one line, Hart*   85] *As Pope;* Tomorrow . . . sodaine. / Spare him, spare him: F

68 potency power, executive authority; but the whole thought shows that the sexual connotation of the word is also in play: Isabella identifies Angelo's use of power as an expression of his libidinous nature. See pp. 31–4 above.

72 touch him, there's the vein that's the way to have an effect on him; see *AYLI* 2.7.94: 'You touch'd my vein at first.' 'Vein' signifies 'style' of writing or speech, but taken with 'touch' alludes to finding a vein when blood-letting and hence 'move emotionally'. A direct literal sense may also be suspected: Lucio sees how emotion makes the veins stand out in Angelo's skin, and tells Isabella to reach out and touch him, to excite his pulse further.

73 forfeit i.e. his life is forfeited by his offence (Johnson).

75 See Rom. 3.23–6.

76 vantage advantage, profit (i.e. to punish mankind). See Matt. 25.27.

78 he . . . judgement the supreme judge, God.
78–81 See Matt. 7.1.
81 man new made 'as if a new man were formed within you' (Johnson). There is an allusion to the making of man in Gen. 2.7. Commentators explain as referring to the doctrine of redemption through Christ, 2 Cor. 5.17: 'Therefore if any man be in Christ, let him be a new creature.' Book of Common Prayer (1559), service for baptism: 'that the new man be raised up in them'.
82 condemn Possibly first-person singular, attracted by 'I', probably a plural influenced by preceding noun and pronoun; see 1.2.165.
85 Set as two lines by Compositor A or C. See 2.4.119 below.
87 of season in season, in the best state for eating (*OED* Season *sb* 5).

There's many have committed it.

LUCIO [*Aside*] Ay, well said.

ANGELO The law hath not been dead, though it hath slept.
Those many had not dared to do that evil
If the first that did th'edict infringe   95
Had answered for his deed. Now 'tis awake,
Takes note of what is done, and like a prophet
Looks in a glass that shows what future evils –
Either now, or by remissness new conceived,
And so in progress to be hatched and born –   100
Are now to have no successive degrees,
But here they live to end.

ISABELLA   Yet show some pity.

ANGELO I show it most of all when I show justice;
For then I pity those I do not know,
Which a dismissed offence would after gall,   105
And do him right, that answering one foul wrong
Lives not to act another. Be satisfied.
Your brother dies tomorrow. Be content.

ISABELLA So you must be the first that gives this sentence,
And he, that suffers. Oh, it is excellent   110
To have a giant's strength, but it is tyrannous
To use it like a giant.

LUCIO [*Aside*] That's well said.

ISABELLA Could great men thunder
As Jove himself does, Jove would ne'er be quiet,   115

99 now] F; new *Collier²*   102 here] F; ere *Hanmer*; where *Malone*   115 ne'er] F2; never F

96 answered paid the penalty.

98 glass The magic glass in which the future could be descried. A glass shows Britomart her future husband in Spenser, *The Faerie Queene*; this glass was devised by the 'great Magitian Merlin', and 'it round and hollow shaped was, / Like to the world it selfe, and seem'd a world of glas' (*FQ*, 3.2.18–9). See *Mac.* 4.1.119–20.

99–100 Either conceived already, or sinfully to be conceived in future. Pope's emendation seeks to create a balanced pattern, matching 'new' against 'new conceived', although it gives a less clear sense than if one read 'now' (already an embryo) and 'new conceived' (about to become an embryo). F's 'Either now, or by remissenesse' is an obscure expression, which no interpretation properly clarifies, but the NS conjecture of

'Egges' for 'Either' shows, as Ridley observes, 'more heroism than discretion'.

101 successive degrees further stages.

102 here...end here crimes live only that they may be brought to an end (Collier). Angelo is referring to the place of his own rule, 'here', in contrast to other places and times.

105 dismissed...gall forgiven offence would give trouble to later.

106 right justice.

110–12 it is...giant A proverbial idea, as in Tilley H170, or Sonnet 94.

115 Jove Perhaps the substitution of the classical deity for 'God' is the result of concern about censorship, as Thirlby conjectures.

115 be quiet have any peace.

For every pelting, petty officer
Would use his heaven for thunder –
Nothing but thunder. Merciful heaven,
Thou rather with thy sharp and sulphurous bolt
Splits the unwedgeable and gnarlèd oak   120
Than the soft myrtle; but man, proud man,
Dressed in a little brief authority,
Most ignorant of what he's most assured,
His glassy essence, like an angry ape
Plays such fantastic tricks before high heaven   125
As makes the angels weep; who, with our spleens,
Would all themselves laugh mortal.

LUCIO [*Aside*] Oh, to him, to him, wench, he will relent.
          He's coming: I perceive't.
PROVOST [*Aside*]   Pray heaven she win him!
ISABELLA We cannot weigh our brother with ourself.   130
          Great men may jest with saints: 'tis wit in them,
          But in the less foul profanation.

117–18] F; Would . . . but thunder: – / Merciful heaven *Capell, conj. Thirlby*   **129** SD] *Collier; not in* F

116 pelting paltry.

117–18 F's lineation gives strong rhetorical emphasis to 'thunder', whereas Thirlby's diminishes it a little, transferring emphasis to 'heaven'. Isabella's wrathful sarcasm seems to me uppermost and F's lineation expresses this.

119 bolt It was believed that lightning accompanied a bolt of brimstone (hence 'sulphurous') which caused the actual damage; see *Cym.* 5.5.240: 'The gods throw stones of sulphur on me.'

120 unwedgeable not to be cloven (Johnson). A metal wedge is driven into the wood with a sledgehammer to make it split. Oak is hard wood, the gnarls and knots in it much harder still. Perhaps recalling Marston; see p. 18 above, n. 1.

119–21 Thou . . . myrtle The idea was proverbial, and Hart cites Greene, *Mamillia* (1583), for an instance.

124 glassy essence If 'glass' means 'mirror', as in 2.4.126, 'the glasses where they view themselves', then the phrase may mean 'man's physical self, which he sees in his mirror'; yet the idea of the intellectual soul as an image or mirror of God is adduced by many commentators, some comparing 1 Cor. 13.12, where the metaphor exploits the transparent and opaque properties of glass (the intellectual soul is incorporeal, transparent, glassy essence, like the divinity); man is most assured of being made in the image of God, but *ignores* this truth and acts like a beast, satisfying physical promptings. As in 2.2.98 'glass' here seems to combine the senses of 'transparent' and 'mysterious' with the senses 'opaque' and 'corporeal'.

125 fantastic tricks See Lucio's comments at 3.2.82, 4.3.147, 5.1.497. 'fantastic' means 'extravagant, grotesque, incredible', and 'trick' 'capricious, foolish, stupid act'. Here man 'apes' the ape's grotesque similarity to man: so perverse is he, that man can grotesquely parody his own better nature.

126 with our spleens if they had spleens like us. The spleen was supposed the source of laughter as well as irascibility (Evans).

127 Would laugh themselves dead (?), would laugh themselves out of their state of immortality, so immoderately would they laugh (?), would laugh as much as men laugh at apes (?).

129 coming coming round.

130 We cannot use the same standard to judge ourselves and other men. But 'brother' may also refer directly to Claudio and reveal Isabella's unwitting arrogance.

131 jest trifle, treat with levity.

131–2 Great men may play tricks on saints to

LUCIO [*Aside*] Thou'rt i'th'right, girl, more o'that!
ISABELLA That in the captain's but a choleric word
    Which in the soldier is flat blasphemy.   135
LUCIO [*Aside*] Art avised o'that? More on't.
ANGELO Why do you put these sayings upon me?
ISABELLA Because authority, though it err like others,
    Hath yet a kind of medicine in itself
    That skins the vice o'th'top. Go to your bosom,   140
    Knock there, and ask your heart what it doth know
    That's like my brother's fault. If it confess
    A natural guiltiness, such as is his,
    Let it not sound a thought upon your tongue
    Against my brother's life.   145
ANGELO [*Aside*] She speaks, and 'tis such sense
    That my sense breeds with it. [*To Isabella*] Fare you well.
ISABELLA Gentle my lord, turn back.
ANGELO I will bethink me. Come again tomorrow.
ISABELLA Hark how I'll bribe you – good my lord, turn back.   150
ANGELO How? Bribe me?
ISABELLA Ay, with such gifts that heaven shall share with you.
LUCIO [*Aside*] You had marred all else.
ISABELLA Not with fond sickles of the tested gold,
    Or stones whose rate are either rich or poor   155
    As fancy values them; but with true prayers,

145–7] F; Against . . . 'tis / Such . . . well *Steevens*[3] 146, 147 SD] *Johnson; not in* F

test their virtue; such deviousness in a virtuous cause is commendable where in ordinary life it is to be condemned.

134–5 What might be seen simply as an expression of anger when uttered by an officer is held to be blasphemy if a common soldier says it.

136 Art . . . that? Have you discovered that?

137 put . . . upon me? apply . . . to me?

140 skins . . . top covers over the sore with a new skin.

144 sound utter.

145–6 Angelo's aside is a change in direction and of address, and should therefore stand as a short line and not be linked to 145.

146 sense meaning.

147 sense sensual desire.

147 breeds rises, grows. The verb's connotation of tumescence, sexual arousal, is to be noticed as well as that of fertility in a general sense; perhaps there is also the sense of rising as

in pregnancy – the associated senses of 'breed' all awakened in Angelo's turbulent mind.

149 bethink me consider.

154 fond foolishly valued.

154 sickles coins. Called 'sickles' in the Bishop's Bible (from Latin *siclus*), then 'sheckels' in the Geneva Bible, from Hebrew.

154 tested pure (see 1.1.48 n.). Can it be accidental that an acoustic pun on 'testicles' is latent in 'sickles . . . tested'? Compare 'stones' at 155.

155 stones i.e. precious stones; but the word could also mean 'testicles' (*OED* sv *sb* 11) which may be a sign of the subconscious pressure of the situation on Isabella, which thus betrays itself in her language.

155 are Plural verb with a singular subject; see also 1.2.165 and 3.1.128.

156 fancy caprice, individual taste.

That shall be up at heaven and enter there
Ere sun rise – prayers from preservèd souls,
From fasting maids whose minds are dedicate
To nothing temporal.

ANGELO   Well; come to me tomorrow.   160
LUCIO [*To Isabella*] Go to. 'Tis well. Away.
ISABELLA Heaven keep your honour safe.
ANGELO [*Aside*]   Amen.
For I am that way going to temptation
Where prayers cross.
ISABELLA   At what hour tomorrow
Shall I attend your lordship?
ANGELO   At any time 'fore noon.   165
ISABELLA Save your honour.

                    [*Exeunt Isabella, Lucio and Provost*]
ANGELO   From thee: even from thy virtue.
What's this? What's this? Is this her fault, or mine?
The tempter or the tempted, who sins most, ha?
Not she: nor doth she tempt: but it is I
That, lying by the violet in the sun,   170
Do as the carrion does, not as the flower,
Corrupt with virtuous season. Can it be
That modesty may more betray our sense
Than woman's lightness? Having waste ground enough
Shall we desire to raze the sanctuary   175
And pitch our evils there? Oh fie, fie, fie,

161, 162 SD] *Johnson; not in* F   166 SD] *Capell, after Rowe; Exeunt.* F2; *not in* F   168 most, ha?] *Kittredge;* most? ha? F

164 Where prayers cross Several senses are probably present: (1) referring to Angelo's corrupt hope of seducing her and so 'crossing' the pious prayer for his honour she has just uttered, (2) Angelo means that he is going towards evil where his daily prayers ask that he may *not* be led, (3) 'where prayers *thwart or impede* will'.

171 carrion corpse or carcass.

172 Corrupt with virtuous season Become more putrid in response to the sun's power. With complex play on senses; 'season' means 'time of the year, weather, when plant-life is stimulated by the sun to grow', and 'preservative'; 'virtue' = 'efficacious power' and 'moral goodness'. Hence the interpretation: because of his moral corruption Angelo reacts, unlike the healthy plant, by becoming putrescent. See the similar train of thought in *Ham.* 2.2.181–2: 'sun . . . breed . . .

carrion . . . daughter'. The syntax may produce ambiguity from the expectation that 169's 'nor doth she tempt: but it is I' implies a matching transitive verb, so that 'Corrupt' seems transitive (as if the carcass Angelo 'infected' the virtuous violet) rather than intransitive, itself going rotten while the flower grows more fragrant. The ambiguity testifies to Angelo's state of inner turbulent confusion.

173 betray our sense arouse our sensual desires (but 'betray' implies that senses are good, which is not Angelo's stated view).

174 lightness licentiousness.

175 raze the sanctuary pull down the holy building, leaving no trace.

176 pitch our evils As opposed to 'raze the sanctuary', the sense may be (*OED* Pitch *v*[1] 4) 'to fix and erect (a tent, pavilion, etc.) as a place of

What dost thou or what art thou, Angelo?
Dost thou desire her foully for those things
That make her good? Oh, let her brother live:
Thieves for their robbery have authority   180
When judges steal themselves. What, do I love her
That I desire to hear her speak again
And feast upon her eyes? What is't I dream on?
Oh cunning enemy that, to catch a saint,
With saints dost bait thy hook! Most dangerous   185
Is that temptation that doth goad us on
To sin in loving virtue. Never could the strumpet
With all her double vigour, art and nature,
Once stir my temper; but this virtuous maid
Subdues me quite. Ever till now   190
When men were fond, I smiled, and wondered how. *Exit*

2.3 *Enter* DUKE [*disguised as a friar*] *and* PROVOST

DUKE Hail to you, provost – so I think you are.
PROVOST I am the provost. What's your will, good friar?
DUKE Bound by my charity and my blessèd order
        I come to visit the afflicted spirits
        Here in the prison. Do me the common right   5
        To let me see them and to make me know

---

188 art] *Pope; Art, F*   **Act 2, Scene 3**   2.3] *Scena Tertia. F*   0 SD *disguised as a friar*] *Rowe, subst.; not in F*

lodgement', 'erect dwellings for evil purposes',
with a memory of the biblical phrase 'the tents of
the ungodly'. Some commentators suggest 'cast
our nasty refuse' or 'erect our privies' (recalling 2
Kings 10.27). The analogous line in *H8* 2.1.67,
'Nor build their evils on the graves of great
men', is inconclusive about the meaning of 'evils',
but the metaphor of destroying and erecting
buildings seems present. Marston, *The Malcontent*,
ed. Hunter, 1975, 2.5.125–32, offers a passage
Shakespeare may be half-remembering here:
MALEVOLE . . . I ha' seen oxen plough up altars.
        Et nunc seges ubi Sion fuit.
MENDOZA Strange!
MALEVOLE Nay, monstrous; I ha' seen a sump-
        tuous steeple turned to a stinking privy;
        more beastly, the sacredest place made a
        dog's kennel; nay, most inhuman, the stoned
        coffins of long-dead Christians burst up, and

made hogs' troughs: *Hic finis Priami.*

184 saint Angelo's overweening vanity is clear
whether the word is understood as 'Christian',
'one of the elect', or 'a person of extreme holiness
of life', all possible senses at the time. Isabella
also seems to refer to herself as a saint at 131.

188 double With a play on the sense 'false,
duplicitous'. Compare 3.1.240–1.

190 Subdues Overcomes, prevails over.

191 fond infatuated, foolishly doting.

Act 2, Scene 3

1 so I think you are The Duke suddenly
remembers that he is supposed to be a stranger in
Vienna.

3 charity i.e. the rule of the holy order to
perform charitable works.

5 Do Grant.

          The nature of their crimes, that I may minister
          To them accordingly.
PROVOST   I would do more than that, if more were needful.

                    Enter JULIET

          Look, here comes one, a gentlewoman of mine,   10
          Who, falling in the flaws of her own youth,
          Hath blistered her report. She is with child
          And he that got it, sentenced – a young man
          More fit to do another such offence
          Than die for this.   15
DUKE When must he die?
PROVOST   As I do think, tomorrow.
          [*To Juliet*] I have provided for you, stay awhile
          And you shall be conducted.
DUKE Repent you, fair one, of the sin you carry?
JULIET I do, and bear the shame most patiently.   20
DUKE I'll teach you how you shall arraign your conscience
          And try your penitence if it be sound
          Or hollowly put on.
JULIET   I'll gladly learn.
DUKE Love you the man that wronged you?
JULIET Yes, as I love the woman that wronged him.   25
DUKE So then it seems your most offenceful act
          Was mutually committed.
JULIET   Mutually.
DUKE Then was your sin of heavier kind than his.
JULIET I do confess it, and repent it, father.
DUKE 'Tis meet so, daughter, but lest you do repent   30

---

17 SD] *Theobald; not in* F

11–12 **falling . . . report** Taken with 'falling', 'flaws' can mean 'fissure' or 'breach' (as through a break in the ice). Taken with 12's 'blister', it can mean 'a sudden blast of wind of short duration', as in *Temp*. 1.2.323–4: 'A south-west blow on ye / And blister you all o'er!' Taken with 'report', 'reputation', 'flaws' means 'faults'. The metaphor begins with the idea of falling through a fissure or crack, then changes to the idea of a sudden wind causing soreness and unsightliness. A third sense of 'flaws', 'sudden onsets of passion', simply connects with the idea of blighting reputation. It may be that the image of the swollen womb is associated with 'blistered' in its more common sense of 'a swelling'. However uncomfortable the implied connection between pregnancy and disease, it is frequent in the play. A further link between 'report' and 'blister' may be unconscious memory of *Rom*. 3.2.90: 'Blistered be thy tongue.'

13 **got** fathered.

21 **arraign** bring to trial.

22–3 **sound . . . hollowly put on** genuine, healthy . . . spuriously, superficially assumed. Compare 1.2.42–5.

28 **heavier** more serious (with a play on the weight of the child she carries).

As that the sin hath brought you to this shame –
Which sorrow is always toward ourselves not heaven,
Showing we would not spare heaven as we love it,
But as we stand in fear –
JULIET I do repent me as it is an evil   35
And take the shame with joy.
DUKE   There rest.
Your partner, as I hear, must die tomorrow,
And I am going with instruction to him.
Grace go with you, *Benedicite*.   *Exit*
JULIET Must die tomorrow? Oh, injurious love   40
That respites me a life whose very comfort
Is still a dying horror!
PROVOST   'Tis pity of him.
                                                        Exeunt

2.4 *Enter* ANGELO

ANGELO When I would pray and think, I think and pray
To several subjects: heaven hath my empty words
Whilst my invention, hearing not my tongue,
Anchors on Isabel. Heaven in my mouth
As if I did but only chew his name,   5
And in my heart the strong and swelling evil
Of my conception. The state whereon I studied

40 love] F; law *Hanmer*   **Act 2, Scene 4**   2.4] *Scena Quarta.* F

35–6 Juliet acknowledges the dogmatic view, but her words affirm the supremacy of joy and gladness in the child and the love that made it.

36 **There rest** Keep yourself in this frame of mind.

37–8 The 'Friar''s abrupt announcement is a brutal shock to Juliet.

38 **instruction** spiritual advice.

40 **love** Juliet's pregnancy, the effect of love, saves her from execution, which she would prefer to share with Claudio. An alternative interpretation (Hanmer, Mason) reads 'law', supposing that the law affected the life of the man only, not the woman: to Juliet such a law is harsher than one condemning both partners. Angelo's reference to her as 'the fornicatress' does not decide the point (see 2.2.24). 'Injury' derives from Latin *jus* (= right) which would make of 'injurious law' a paradoxical conceit. Yet

the alternative paradox of love dealing injury goes to the heart of the situation. Being required to choose, I choose 'love'.

Act 2, Scene 4

2 **several** separate.

3 **invention** imagination.

4 **Heaven in my mouth** Commentators suggest that, possibly to accord with the 1606 Statute to Restrain the Abuses of Players, the word 'Heaven' has been substituted for 'God'; see Isa. 29.13, Matt. 15.8. Lever cites James I, *Basilikon Doron*: 'Keepe God more sparingly in your mouth, but aboundantly in your harte.'

5 **chew** 'taste without swallowing' (Johnson).

7 **conception** idea, thought (and forming, with 'swelling', a metaphor of pregnancy).

7 **state** statecraft (compare 3.2.126).

Is like a good thing being often read
Grown sere and tedious. Yea, my gravity,
Wherein – let no man hear me – I take pride,   10
Could I with boot change for an idle plume
Which the air beats for vain. Oh place, oh form,
How often dost thou with thy case, thy habit,
Wrench awe from fools and tie the wiser souls
To thy false seeming. Blood, thou art blood: 15
Let's write 'Good Angel' on the devil's horn,
'Tis not the devil's crest. How now, who's there?

Enter SERVANT

SERVANT   One Isabel, a sister, desires access to you.
ANGELO   Teach her the way.

                                                        [*Exit Servant*]
                         Oh, heavens,
Why does my blood thus muster to my heart,   20
Making both it unable for itself
And dispossessing all my other parts
Of necessary fitness?
So play the foolish throngs with one that swoons,

---

9 sere] *Hudson, conj. Heath;* feared F; sear'd *Hanmer*   19 SD] *Capell, after Johnson; not in* F

---

9 sere dry, withered. In collocation with 'tedious' a preferable reading to 'feard'. Hanmer suggests 'seard', which is plausible in the sense 'withered' (*OED* Sear *v* 2) and foul-case error is possible.

9 gravity dignified solemnity of manner.

11 boot advantage.

11 idle plume foolish feather, emblem of the prodigal gallant.

12 beats Grammatically ambiguous, with either 'air' or 'feather' as subject.

12 for vain Several meanings are possible: 'to no purpose', 'as expression of its vanity', 'as a weather-vane'; in view of the idea of folly and sloth, 'to no purpose' seems uppermost.

12 place . . . form rank . . . decorum, dignity.

13 case outward appearance, perhaps here associated with a mask, 'habit' disguising the rest of the body. In Jonson's play the fox, Volpone, finally puts off his disguise with the words 'The fox shall, here, uncase' (*Volpone* 5.12.85).

15 Blood . . . blood Possibly alluding to the sense 'high birth' as well as the bodily fluid, and

basic appetites and passions: hence, 'whatever rank or name he has, a man is subject to common basic instincts and emotions'. Angelo recognises that his blood is not 'snow-broth' (1.4.58).

16–17 Let's . . . crest i.e. however we try to disguise evil it remains evil still. The metaphor illustrates the idea since the whole heraldic device, the devil's horn, identifies the wearer, whatever the crest (a minor feature) may indicate. The motto is 'Good Angel', and the 'crest' (1) an excrescence on the top of an animal's head, (2) an ornament or device by which someone is recognised, placed in a coat-of-arms above the shield and helmet, or on items of clothing. The devil is recognised by his horns (at once natural and heraldic). The motto does not change his identity.

20 muster The metaphor is military, 'assemble in order to form an army', but the next line indicates a most unmilitary consequence, the rest of the body left unable to defend itself or function while the heart is too full to work.

24 foolish throngs Angelo shows the same attitude to crowds as the Duke does in 1.1.

Come all to help him and so stop the air   25
By which he should revive; and even so
The general subject to a well-wished king
Quit their own part and in obsequious fondness
Crowd to his presence, where their untaught love
Must needs appear offence.

Enter ISABELLA

                              How now, fair maid?   30
ISABELLA I am come to know your pleasure.
ANGELO That you might know it would much better please me
       Than to demand what 'tis. Your brother cannot live.
ISABELLA Even so. Heaven keep your honour.
ANGELO Yet may he live a while – and it may be   35
       As long as you or I – yet he must die.
ISABELLA Under your sentence?
ANGELO   Yea.
ISABELLA When, I beseech you? That, in his reprieve,
       Longer or shorter, he may be so fitted
       That his soul sicken not.   40
ANGELO Ha! Fie, these filthy vices! It were as good
       To pardon him that hath from nature stolen
       A man already made, as to remit
       Their saucy sweetness, that do coin heaven's image
       In stamps that are forbid. 'Tis all as easy   45
       Falsely to take away a life true made

---

30 SD] *As Johnson; after* Maid. F

27–30 **The general...offence** Perhaps
alluding to the visit of James I to the Royal
Exchange in March 1604, intending to watch the
merchants unobserved: news of his visit leaked
out and crowds pressed round so that the stair
door had to be closed against them. It was
reported in *The Time Triumphant*, 1604 (Lever).

27 **general subject** people under the dom-
inion of a sovereign (compare *Ham.* 1.2.33);
'subject' is a collective noun, singular.

28 **Quit...part** Break off their ordinary
business.

28 **obsequious fondness** foolishly expressed
loyalty.

29 **untaught** unconsidered, mindless.

32–3 Angelo would be pleased if she understood his desire as carnal (so quibbling on 'know

your pleasure', a polite formula) without his
having to state it explicitly.

39 **fitted** prepared.

42–3 **pardon ... made** pardon a man who has
killed another.

43 **remit** pardon.

44 **saucy sweetness** addiction to lascivious
pleasure (with a play on the culinary 'sauce' and
perhaps the proverb 'sweet meat will have sour
sauce'). See *Mac.* 3.4.35–6 for a metaphor of
sweet sauce to meat, and, for the idea of 'sweet' as
lascivious, *Ham.* 3.4.93: 'Stew'd in corruption,
honeying and making love'.

45 **stamps** The stamp and 'bed' used for
striking coins is called the 'matrix' (Latin for
womb or breeding-animal).

    As to put metal in restrainèd means
    To make a false one.
ISABELLA 'Tis set down so in heaven, but not in earth.
ANGELO Say you so? Then I shall pose you quickly.   50
    Which had you rather: that the most just law
    Now took your brother's life, or to redeem him
    Give up your body to such sweet uncleanness
    As she that he hath stained?
ISABELLA   Sir, believe this:
    I had rather give my body than my soul.   55
ANGELO I talk not of your soul. Our compelled sins
    Stand more for number than for accompt.
ISABELLA How say you?
ANGELO Nay, I'll not warrant that, for I can speak
    Against the thing I say. Answer to this: 60
    I, now the voice of the recorded law,
    Pronounce a sentence on your brother's life.
    Might there not be a charity in sin
    To save this brother's life?
ISABELLA   Please you to do't,
    I'll take it as a peril to my soul,   65
    It is no sin at all but charity.
ANGELO Pleased you to do't, at peril of your soul,
    Were equal poise of sin and charity.
ISABELLA That I do beg his life, if it be sin,
    Heaven let me bear it. You granting of my suit,   70
    If that be sin, I'll make it my morn-prayer
    To have it added to the faults of mine

---

47 metal] *Theobald;* mettle F   52 or] *Rowe, after Davenant;* and F

47 metal See 1.1.48 n. Angelo is a false coin because of his metal, not the stamp it bears.

47 restrainèd means forbidden means: minting counterfeit coins (see 'Good Angel' at 16) and begetting children illegitimately.

48 one i.e. coin or child.

50 pose question (with the additional sense 'place in difficulty, perplex with a question' *OED* sv v^2 2).

57 Are put on record but not held against us as crimes. Compare the proverb 'compelled sins are no sins' (Tilley s475). Halliwell cites *Promos and Cassandra, Part 1* 3.4: 'in forst faultes is no intent of yll'.

59–60 I'll . . . say I will not be held to that, for I can argue a case I don't actually believe in (to test you).

63 in sin in committing a sin.

64 Please . . . do't Isabella supposes Angelo means the sin involved in pardoning a guilty man.

67 do't i.e. surrender to my lust.

68 equal poise equilibrium, equal balance (as in the scales of Justice).

73 nothing . . . answer nothing to the account of sins you must personally be answerable for. (Continuing the metaphor of financial accounting from 44–5. See also 57 and the metaphor of scales at 68.)

And nothing of your answer.
ANGELO   Nay, but hear me,
Your sense pursues not mine: either you are ignorant
Or seem so crafty, and that's not good.   75
ISABELLA Let me be ignorant and in nothing good
But graciously to know I am no better.
ANGELO Thus wisdom wishes to appear most bright
When it doth tax itself, as these black masks
Proclaim an enshield beauty ten times louder   80
Than beauty could, displayed. But mark me.
To be received plain, I'll speak more gross:
Your brother is to die.
ISABELLA So.
ANGELO And his offence is so as it appears   85
Accountant to the law upon that pain.
ISABELLA True.
ANGELO Admit no other way to save his life –
As I subscribe not that, nor any other,
But in the loss of question – that you, his sister,   90
Finding yourself desired of such a person
Whose credit with the judge, or own great place,
Could fetch your brother from the manacles
Of the all-binding law, and that there were

---

75 crafty] F; *craftily Rowe, after Davenant*   76 Let me] F2; Let F   80 enshield] en-shield F; *enshell'd Keightley, conj.*
Tyrwhitt; enciel'd *Lever*   94 all-binding law] *Johnson, conj. Thirlby;* all-building-Law F

75 **crafty** Either an adjective or adverb. Emendation would improve the metre, but might efface Shakespeare's intention of a dramatic pause.

76–7 To be given, through the Grace of God, knowledge that one is sinful and ignorant, is the only goodness I pray for. (Isabella expresses orthodox Christian humility: men are sinful and do not understand or hold to virtue. Angelo answers that this is a crafty evasion of the issue.)

79 **these black masks** Generic use of 'these': 'the black masks that women wear' (Evans).

80 **enshield** guarded or screened by a shield (*OED*, but this is the only instance cited). Other suggestions recorded in the collation are possible, but in this case the difficult reading is to be preferred. There may be a link with the heraldic imagery of 16–17.

82 **received** understood.

89 **subscribe not** i.e. subscribe not to.

90 **loss of question** This phrase troubles many commentators, but the general sense is 'hypothetically'. Other suggestions include 'to avoid lack of matter for argument' (Evans), 'provided there is no dispute' (*OED*), 'as no better arguments present themselves' (Schmidt). Singer proposes changing 'losse' to 'loose', i.e. 'in the freedom of conversation'.

94 **all-binding** Law binds men together under common restraints. NS persuasively notes of the F reading: '"All-building" can hardly be right after "manacles".' Sisson supports Thirlby's emendation too, on orthographic grounds, though 'all-bridling' is also possible orthographically. Defenders of F explain it as meaning law that builds, maintains and repairs the social edifice. Lever notes a parallel from Webster, *The Duchess of Malfi* 1.1 (ed J.R. Brown, 1964, p. 37 n.), where the text has 'build' when 'bind' is evidently meant.

No earthly mean to save him, but that either 95
  You must lay down the treasures of your body
  To this supposed, or else to let him suffer:
  What would you do?
ISABELLA As much for my poor brother as myself:
  That is, were I under the terms of death, 100
  Th'impression of keen whips I'd wear as rubies,
  And strip myself to death as to a bed
  That longing have been sick for, ere I'd yield
  My body up to shame.
ANGELO Then must your brother die. 105
ISABELLA And 'twere the cheaper way:
  Better it were a brother died at once,
  Than that a sister by redeeming him
  Should die for ever.
ANGELO Were not you then as cruel as the sentence 110
  That you have slandered so?
ISABELLA Ignomy in ransom and free pardon
  Are of two houses: lawful mercy
  Is nothing kin to foul redemption.
ANGELO You seemed of late to make the law a tyrant, 115
  And rather proved the sliding of your brother
  A merriment than a vice.
ISABELLA Oh, pardon me my lord, it oft falls out

103 longing have] F; longing I've *Rowe;* long I have *Sisson, after Dyce* 104–5] F; *one line, Steevens*³ 105] F *has the catchword: / Ang.* That *on sig.* F5 *recto*

96 **treasures of your body** your chastity (see *Ham.* 1.3.31).
97 **him** i.e. your brother.
101 **rubies** Compare Chaucer, *Prioress's Tale* (609–10): 'This gemme of chastite . . . And eek of martirdom the ruby bright'. As one of the most precious stones, deep crimson in colour, the ruby could symbolise a martyr's blood or a secular woman's desirability. Unconsciously Isabella provokes Angelo's sadistic lust with the talk of whips . . . rubies . . . strip . . . bed . . . longing.
103 **longing** Omission of the personal pronoun possibly gives extra emphasis to this word, with its erotic connotation (something of which Isabella herself is not to be supposed to be conscious, but to which Shakespeare wishes to alert the audience).
104–6 F's lineation. A hexameter would be

created by combining either 104 and 105, or 105 and 106. F's arrangement of three short lines, if authorial, may be designed to stress the equal, opposed forces here. The catchword on F5ʳ is wrong, which could mean that half a line has dropped out of Angelo's speech.
107 **at once** immediately, at one stroke.
109 **die for ever** suffer eternal damnation.
111 **slandered** spoken out against.
112 **Ignomy** A contracted form of 'ignominy' in use up to the early nineteenth century (*OED*). Compare *Tro.* 5.10.33 in F.
113 **houses** families (i.e. they are quite different from each other).
116 **sliding** i.e. sin (compare 2.2.66).
117 **merriment** something inconsequential, light.

To have what we would have, we speak not what we mean.
I something do excuse the thing I hate   120
For his advantage that I dearly love.

ANGELO We are all frail.

ISABELLA   Else let my brother die,
If not a fedary but only he
Owe and succeed thy weakness.

ANGELO Nay, women are frail too.   125

ISABELLA Ay, as the glasses where they view themselves,
Which are as easy broke as they make forms.
Women? Help heaven, men their creation mar
In profiting by them. Nay, call us ten times frail,
For we are soft as our complexions are,   130
And credulous to false prints.

ANGELO   I think it well,
And from this testimony of your own sex –
Since I suppose we are made to be no stronger
Than faults may shake our frames – let me be bold;
I do arrest your words. Be that you are,   135
That is, a woman; if you be more, you're none.
If you be one, as you are well expressed
By all external warrants, show it now
By putting on the destined livery.

119] *As Rowe;* To...would haue, / We...meane; F   123 fedary] fedarie F; feodary F2; foedary *Mason, conj.*
Halliwell

119 This line was too long for Compositor B to get into one line in F.

120 **something** somewhat.

122 **frail** morally weak; compare the proverb, Tilley F363, Ecclesiastes 8.5.

123 **fedary** accomplice, confederate. Halliwell notes that 'feodary' is a different word, meaning one who owes feudal dues to his lord. (Shakespeare has 'federary' in *WT* 2.1.90. in the same sense of confederate.)

124 **Owe and succeed** Owns and inherits.

124 **thy weakness** this weakness you speak of (but with the unintended second meaning, 'this weakness of yours').

127 **forms** Assuming 'glasses' as the subject, 'reflect images', 'multiply shapes'; assuming 'women' as the subject, 'reproduce themselves, have children'. The broken mirror reflects as many times as there are fragments; virginity is proverbially as fragile as glass.

131 **credulous** Strictly, 'over-ready to believe', hence 'susceptible, over-ready to accept' taken with the metaphoric 'prints'.

131 **false prints** Alluding to the minting of coins, 'counterfeiting', hence, 'insincere persuasion' and 'seduction and illegitimate pregnancy'. Presumably the acoustic pun on 'prints/prince' is accidental or subconscious on Shakespeare's part.

134 **Than** Than that (giving the sense 'We are not made strong enough to avoid errors').

135 **arrest your words** take you at your word, hold you to that.

136 **if you be more, you're none** i.e. if you insist on remaining a virgin you are no woman (in terms of what you have just said of them) (Evans). Compare *Mac.* 1.7.46–7: 'I dare do all that may become a man; / Who dares do more is none.'

137 **expressed** shown to be.

139 **destined livery** role of woman which you

ISABELLA I have no tongue but one. Gentle my lord,   140
  Let me entreat you speak the former language.
ANGELO Plainly conceive, I love you.
ISABELLA My brother did love Juliet
  And you tell me that he shall die for't.
ANGELO He shall not, Isabel, if you give me love.   145
ISABELLA I know your virtue hath a licence in't
  Which seems a little fouler than it is
  To pluck on others.
ANGELO   Believe me on mine honour,
  My words express my purpose.
ISABELLA Ha! Little honour to be much believed,   150
  And most pernicious purpose. Seeming, seeming.
  I will proclaim thee, Angelo, look for't.
  Sign me a present pardon for my brother,
  Or with an outstretched throat I'll tell the world aloud
  What man thou art.
ANGELO   Who will believe thee, Isabel?   155
  My unsoiled name, th'austereness of my life,
  My vouch against you, and my place i'th'state,
  Will so your accusation overweigh
  That you shall stifle in your own report
  And smell of calumny. I have begun,   160
  And now I give my sensual race the rein.
  Fit thy consent to my sharp appetite,

143–4] F; My . . . me, / That . . . for't. *Steevens*[3]   154 world aloud] F; world *Hudson, conj. Dyce*

were born to (i.e. as opposed to the nun's rule of chastity). 'livery' carries the idea of 'distinctive badge or suit worn by a servant' (*OED*). According to Donne, on her wedding-day a virgin 'put[s] on perfection and a woman's name' (John Donne, 'Epithalamion made at Lincoln's Inn' in *Epithalamions* (1633)).

141 former language i.e. of debate about religion and law.

142–3 Two short lines, abruptly divided in content and rhythm.

142 conceive understand (Isabella quibbles in the following line on its more common sense 'become pregnant')

146 licence (1) licentiousness, (2) authority.

152 proclaim denounce.

153 present immediate.

154 world aloud The line is hypermetrical, and omission of 'aloud' would restore the metre: but Shakespeare may intend extra emphasis by giving Isabella an over-long line. Compare *Rom.* 4.3.58.

157 vouch formal statement or declaration.

159 you . . . report your narration will lead to your being silenced (because I shall discredit it); or, your reputation will be destroyed and you yourself silenced. 'Stifle' because your expense of breath will lead to your having no breath, like a candle or lamp going out, leaving a choking smell. 'Report' with the senses 'narration' and 'reputation'.

161 give . . . rein let my sensual desires gallop, give them free rein. Compare the metaphor of desires champing at the bit like steeds at 1.3.21.

Lay by all nicety and prolixious blushes
That banish what they sue for, redeem thy brother
By yielding up thy body to my will,   165
Or else he must not only die the death
But thy unkindness shall his death draw out
To lingering sufferance. Answer me tomorrow,
Or by th'affection that now guides me most
I'll prove a tyrant to him. As for you,   170
Say what you can, my false o'erweighs your true.   *Exit*

ISABELLA   To whom should I complain? Did I tell this
Who would believe me? Oh, perilous mouths
That bear in them one and the self-same tongue,
Either of condemnation or approof,   175
Bidding the law make curtsey to their will,
Hooking both right and wrong to th'appetite
To follow as it draws. I'll to my brother.
Though he hath fall'n by prompture of the blood
Yet hath he in him such a mind of honour   180
That had he twenty heads to tender down
On twenty bloody blocks he'd yield them up
Before his sister should her body stoop
To such abhorred pollution.
Then Isabel live chaste, and brother die: 185
More than our brother is our chastity.
I'll tell him yet of Angelo's request,
And fit his mind to death for his soul's rest.   *Exit*

186 More] "More F

163 **nicety** reserve, coyness.
163 **prolixious** lengthily circuitous in extent
and time. A coinage from 'prolix'.
163–4 **Lay by...sue for** Schanzer *The
Problem Plays of Shakespeare*, 1963, pp. 87–8,
suggests (1) blushes which banish all chance of a
change of heart in him, since they make her all
the more desirable, (2) the 'nicety' is a mere pose,
she is actually suing for what she pretends to
banish, his embrace (perhaps suggested to him by
her words at 101–3).
167–8 **draw...sufferance** i.e. extend his
death with added torture.
169 **affection** passion.
170 **tyrant** i.e. extremely cruel (with possible

allusion to the enraged massacring Herod in the
religious drama: see 3.2.167).
171 **o'erweighs** Compare the metaphor of
scales earlier at 68. Scales are an attribute of
Justice and also serve to weigh coins when testing
them to see whether they are genuine.
175 Either to condemn or approve.
179 **prompture** urging. Compare 'stricture'
(1.3.13) and 'razure' (5.1.13).
181 **tender down** lay down (of money, in pay-
ment: *OED* Tender v^1 1b). Compare 1.2.103, 'Pay
down by weight'.
186 F begins the line with inverted commas,
signalling it as a moral maxim; compare 2.1.38
which F prints in italics, so also 5.1.404 n.

3.1 *Enter* DUKE [*disguised as a friar*], CLAUDIO *and* PROVOST

DUKE So then you hope of pardon from Lord Angelo?
CLAUDIO The miserable have no other medicine
      But only hope.
      I have hope to live, and am prepared to die.
DUKE Be absolute for death: either death or life   5
      Shall thereby be the sweeter. Reason thus with life:
      If I do lose thee I do lose a thing
      That none but fools would keep; a breath thou art,
      Servile to all the skyey influences
      That dost this habitation where thou keepst   10
      Hourly afflict. Merely, thou art death's fool,
      For him thou labour'st by thy flight to shun
      And yet runn'st toward him still. Thou art not noble,
      For all th'accommodations that thou bear'st
      Are nursed by baseness; thou'rt by no means valiant,   15
      For thou dost fear the soft and tender fork
      Of a poor worm. Thy best of rest is sleep,
      And that thou oft provok'st, yet grossly fear'st
      Thy death, which is no more. Thou art not thyself,
      For thou exists on many a thousand grains   20
      That issue out of dust. Happy thou art not,
      For what thou hast not still thou striv'st to get,

Act 3, Scene 1 3.1] *Actus Tertius. Scena Prima.* F 0 SD *disguised as a friar*] Collier; *not in* F 3–4] *As* Capell; *prose in*
F 4 I have] Capell; I'haue F

Act 3, Scene 1

3 This short line may have been intended for cancellation but not clearly marked so by Shakespeare. It is not necessary to the sense.

5 absolute for completely decided on. The speech has parallels to Marston, *The Malcontent*, ed. Hunter, 1975, 4.5.110–21.

9 skyey influences i.e. influence of the stars (astrologically speaking).

10 dost Singular verb with plural subject, 'influences'.

11 Merely Absolutely.

11 death's fool Commentators have suspected allusion to traditional depictions of the Dance of Death: and although if personified as a king, Death might have a Fool, it is simpler to assume 'fool' means 'plaything, one made foolish'.

14 accommodations Judging by the use of 'unaccommodated' in *Lear* 3.4.106–8, this means apparel and all the advantages of civilised life.

14–15 bear'st … baseness The metaphor of clothing in 'accommodations' emerges in 'bear'st' (wear'st) but this transforms to the metaphor of bearing (giving birth to, carrying) a child ('nursed'). Man begins helplessly dependent upon his nurse for basic care: 'all the delicacies of the table may be traced back to the shambles and the dunghill, all magnificence of building was hewn from the quarry, and all the pomp of ornaments, dug from among the damps and darkness of the mine' (Johnson).

17 worm snake, as in *Ant.* 5.2.243. The idea in 14–15 memorably recurs earlier in the same scene, *Ant.* 5.2.7–8.

18 provok'st dost solicit (i.e. by prayer or narcotics).

20 exists Second-person singular: compare 'splits' at 2.2.120, and Abbott 340.

21 out of dust See Gen. 3.19: 'because thou art dust, and to dust shalt thou return'.

And what thou hast, forget'st. Thou art not certain,
For thy complexion shifts to strange effects
After the moon. If thou art rich thou'rt poor,   25
For like an ass whose back with ingots bows
Thou bear'st thy heavy riches but a journey
And death unloads thee. Friend hast thou none,
For thine own bowels which do call thee sire,
The mere effusion of thy proper loins,   30
Do curse the gout, serpigo, and the rheum
For ending thee no sooner. Thou hast nor youth nor age,
But as it were an after-dinner's sleep,
Dreaming on both: for all thy blessèd youth
Becomes as agèd and doth beg the alms   35
Of palsied eld; and when thou art old and rich,
Thou hast neither heat, affection, limb, nor beauty
To make thy riches pleasant. What's yet in this
That bears the name of life? Yet in this life
Lie hid moe thousand deaths; yet death we fear   40
That makes these odds all even.
CLAUDIO   I humbly thank you.
          To sue to live, I find I seek to die,
          And seeking death, find life: let it come on.
ISABELLA [*Within*] What ho, peace here; grace and good company.
PROVOST Who's there? Come in, the wish deserves a welcome.   45
DUKE [*To Claudio*] Dear sir, ere long I'll visit you again.
CLAUDIO Most holy sir, I thank you.

29 sire] F4; fire F   38 yet] F; *omitted, Pope*   44 SD] *Capell; Enter Isabella.* F (*after 43*)   46 SD] *This edn; not in* F
47 SD] *As Dyce; after 43,* F; *after 45, Capell*

23 **certain** constant.
24 **complexion** physical constitution, mental state.
25 **After the moon** Halliwell cites Bartholomaeus, *De Proprietatibus Rerum*: 'Vnder the moone is conteyned sykenesse, losse, fere and drede, and dommage. Therfore about the chaungynge of mans bodye, the vertue of the moone werketh principallye' (1535, 8.29, fol. cxxx).
29 **bowels** A biblical idiom for 'children'.
30 **mere** very.
30 **proper** own.
31 **serpigo** creeping or spreading skin disease (*OED*).
31 **rheum** catarrh; also, the supposed cause of rheumatism (Onions).
33 **after-dinner's** afternoon's. Dinner, the main meal of the day, being taken at noon in the early seventeenth century.
35–6 **Becomes . . . eld** Comes to be as if aged, having to beg an inadequate allowance from parents sunk into old age. Commentators also suggest that poverty makes youth covetous and haggard, or that their dependent status makes them resemble the old.
37 **heat, affection** vigour, passion.
37 **limb** i.e. the full use of the limbs.
38 **yet** The metre is irregular and 'yet' is thrice repeated. Pope omitted it.
40 **moe thousand** a thousand more.
42–3 Recalling Matt. 16.25. If life without Christ is death, then death is the gateway, for the Christian, to life: see also Matt. 10.39. The difficulty is in finding any trace of Christian,

Enter ISABELLA

ISABELLA My business is a word or two with Claudio.
PROVOST And very welcome. Look, signior, here's your sister.
DUKE Provost, a word with you.   50
PROVOST As many as you please.
DUKE Bring me to hear them speak where I may be concealed.
                 [*Duke and Provost conceal themselves*]
CLAUDIO Now, sister, what's the comfort?
ISABELLA Why,
            As all comforts are: most good, most good indeed.   55
            Lord Angelo, having affairs to heaven,
            Intends you for his swift ambassador,
            Where you shall be an everlasting lieger;
            Therefore your best appointment make with speed,
            Tomorrow you set on.
CLAUDIO   Is there no remedy?   60
ISABELLA None, but such remedy as, to save a head,
            To cleave a heart in twain.
CLAUDIO   But is there any?
ISABELLA Yes, brother, you may live;
            There is a devilish mercy in the judge,
            If you'll implore it, that will free your life,   65
            But fetter you till death.
CLAUDIO   Perpetual durance?
ISABELLA Ay, just, perpetual durance, a restraint,
            Though all the world's vastidity you had,

---

52 me to hear them] *Malone, conj. Steevens;* them to hear me F; *this line in* F2 *reads:* Bring them to speake, where I may be conceal'd, yet heare them.   52 SD] *This edn;* DUKE *and* PROVOST *retire / NS; Provost leads him aside / Winny; Exeunt Duke and Provost. / Rowe; Exeunt.* F2; *not in* F   53–5] F; Now . . . comfort? / Why . . . indeed: *Pope;* Now . . . Why, / As . . . indeed, *Dyce*   68 Though] *Rowe;* Through F

rather than Stoic, advice in what the Duke-as-Friar has said. It is as if Claudio is responding to what a friar ought to have said, not to what has actually been said here.

52 SD It is important that the audience remain aware of the observing but concealed presence of these two characters during the Claudio–Isabella encounter: see 151, 170. They should certainly not simply leave the stage.

53–4 F's lineation stresses the emphatic pause before and after Isabella's 'Why', as she collects herself before addressing Claudio.

56 **affairs to** business with.

58 **lieger** resident, permanent ambassador.

59 **appointment** preparation.

66 **durance** imprisonment.

66–9 **Perpetual . . . scope** I prefer the conditional clause beginning 'Though' since it gives emphasis to the spirit, the power of conscience. Claudio's sense of guilt would be inescapable however much scope he might have in other terms. F's 'Through' can be seen as possible if no comma follows 'restraint' but one is placed after 'had'. The sense could then be 'A restraint throughout all the world's vastidity which once was yours'.

68 **vastidity** vastness, immensity.

     To a determined scope.
CLAUDIO   But in what nature?
ISABELLA In such a one as you, consenting to't,   70
     Would bark your honour from that trunk you bear
     And leave you naked.
CLAUDIO   Let me know the point.
ISABELLA Oh, I do fear thee, Claudio, and I quake
     Lest thou a feverous life shouldst entertain
     And six or seven winters more respect   75
     Than a perpetual honour. Dar'st thou die?
     The sense of death is most in apprehension,
     And the poor beetle that we tread upon
     In corporal sufferance finds a pang as great
     As when a giant dies.
CLAUDIO   Why give you me this shame?   80
     Think you I can a resolution fetch
     From flowery tenderness? If I must die
     I will encounter darkness as a bride
     And hug it in mine arms.
ISABELLA There spake my brother, there my father's grave   85
     Did utter forth a voice. Yes, thou must die:
     Thou art too noble to conserve a life
     In base appliances. This outward-sainted deputy
     Whose settled visage and deliberate word
     Nips youth i'th'head and follies doth enew   90

---

88 outward-sainted] *Pope;* outward sainted F   90 enew] *Keightley;* emmew F

69 **determined scope** fixed and limited bounds (explained in 70–2: Claudio would be unable to escape his guilt).

71 **bark** Stripping its bark kills a tree. Compare *Cym.* 3.3.60–4, where this natural image is more fully developed in the metaphor of Belarius being stripped of honours as a tree is stripped of fruit and leaves.

74 **entertain** maintain (*OED* sv *v* 3), admit to consideration (*OED v* 14b).

75 **respect** value.

77 **apprehension** Ambiguous: (1) imagination, (2) anticipation of something fearful.

82 **flowery** Alluding to her femininity (a tender violet) and to her use of metaphor, flowers of rhetoric.

83–4 Compare *Rom.* 4.5.36–40 and elsewhere for the idea of death as a bridal partner. The grammar here is ambiguous but presumably

death is imagined as the bride rather than Claudio imagining himself the bride. Still, such identifications with the opposite sex seem suggested in the language of Isabella (2.2.68) and Angelo (2.2.147). See nn. to those lines.

85 **my . . . grave** the true spirit of my father.

88 **base appliances** ignoble remedies.

89 **settled** composed, grave.

90 **Nips . . . head** Strikes fatally at youth (from the falcon's strike at the neck of its prey with its deadly, sickle-shaped talons) (T.R. Henn, *The Living Image*, 1972, p. 31).

90 **enew** (of a hawk) to drive a fowl into the water (*OED*). F's spelling is either a misprint or a confusion with 'emmew', 'enmew', which means 'to cause to lie close or keep concealed, as a hawk in a mew'. 'Mews' are cages or coops. Henn, *The Living Image*, p. 31, cites *The Boke of St Albans* (1486): 'And if it happyn as it dooth ofttimes the

As falcon doth the fowl, is yet a devil:
His filth within being cast, he would appear
A pond as deep as hell.
CLAUDIO   The prenzie Angelo?
ISABELLA Oh 'tis the cunning livery of hell
The damned'st body to invest and cover   95
In prenzie guards. Dost thou think, Claudio,
If I would yield him my virginity
Thou might'st be freed!
CLAUDIO   Oh, heavens, it cannot be!
ISABELLA Yes, he would give't thee; from this rank offence
So to offend him still. This night's the time   100
That I should do what I abhor to name,
Or else thou diest tomorrow.
CLAUDIO   Thou shalt not do't.
ISABELLA Oh, were it but my life
I'd throw it down for your deliverance
As frankly as a pin.
CLAUDIO   Thanks, dear Isabel.   105
ISABELLA Be ready, Claudio, for your death tomorrow.
CLAUDIO Yes. Has he affections in him,
That thus can make him bite the law by th'nose

93, 96 prenzie] F; Princely F2; priestly *Hanmer;* precise *Knight, conj. Tieck*   95 damned'st] F2; damnest F

---

fowle for fere of yowre hawke woll spryng and fall ayen in to the Ryuer. or the hawke sees hir. and so lie styll and dare not arise. ye shall say then yowre hawke hath ennewed the fowle in to the Ryuer.'

92 cast Taken together with 'pond' (93), probably 'empty of mud', dug out. Other meanings of 'cast' which are interesting and also possible with 'pond' include 'sounded' or 'vomited'. For the idea of outer sanctity disguising inner uncleanness compare Matt. 23.27. Possibly the sense of 'cast' as 'diagnose' is present, as in 'casting urine'.

93, 96 prenzie This crux still resists solution; F2's emendation 'princely' and Tieck's 'precise' are possible, the latter orthographically more plausible, the former attractive for its irony: but Collier supposed Shakespeare introduced the Italian word for 'prince', 'prenze' and this, if unlikely, cannot be ruled out with certainty. 'Precise' was often applied to Puritans in the sense 'strict, scrupulous' (*OED*). Perhaps 'prenzie' is Shakespeare's coinage, fusing 'princely' and 'precise'?

94 livery Probably 'the action of distributing clothing to retainers or servants' (*OED* sv *v* 1a). The alternative (*OED* sb 2), 'the suit of clothes bestowed on retainers by which they may be recognised', or 'a badge or suit worn by a servant', though also a meaning in use at the time, does not so well fit the grammar and sense here, since the emphasis is on the act of concealing the devil's servants.

95 invest dress.

96 guards trimmings, facings, or other ornaments applied on clothing (*OED* Guard *sb* 11b).

96 Dost thou think Would you believe it possible.

100 So ... still To go on sinning in the same way.

105 frankly readily.

105 pin Recalling Lucio's reproof at 2.2.46, perhaps.

108 bite ... nose treat ... with contempt. Evans suggests 'an ironic reversal of the "biting laws" of 1.3.20'.

When he would force it? Sure it is no sin,
Or of the deadly seven it is the least.   110
ISABELLA Which is the least?
CLAUDIO If it were damnable, he, being so wise,
Why would he for the momentary trick
Be perdurably fined? Oh Isabel!
ISABELLA What says my brother?   115
CLAUDIO Death is a fearful thing.
ISABELLA And shamèd life a hateful.
CLAUDIO Ay, but to die and go we know not where,
To lie in cold obstruction and to rot,
This sensible warm motion to become   120
A kneaded clod, and the delighted spirit
To bathe in fiery floods or to reside
In thrilling region of thick-ribbed ice,
To be imprisoned in the viewless winds
And blown with restless violence round about   125
The pendent world, or to be worse than worst
Of those that lawless and incertain thought
Imagine howling; 'tis too horrible.

---

122 bathe] F2; bath F

113 **momentary trick** caprice of the moment, brief moment of folly. Partridge notes a bawdy sense which may be present.

114 **perdurably fined** everlastingly punished.

119 **obstruction** *OED* suggests 'stoppage or cessation of the vital functions, the condition of the body in death', which suits well with the next phrase, 'and to rot'. Claudio is horrified at the thought of lying close pent up in a coffin or grave: compare 'kneaded clod' (121), 'ice' (123), 'imprisoned' (124).

120 **sensible warm motion** warm organism capable of sensitive feeling. Some commentators suggest 'motion' signifies 'movement of the mind'; *OED* Motion *sb* 2c has the abstract sense 'power of movement', which, though implicit, does not go well with the direct physical adjectives 'sensible' and 'warm', and the contrast to 'spirit' (121).

121 **delighted** capable of delight, or now delighted (with a play on 'light'?).

122 **bathe** This could be either intransitive with 'spirit' as subject, or transitive, subject 'warm motion', object 'spirit'. Intransitive verbs predominate in the passage.

123 **thrilling** piercingly cold, causing shuddering.

124 **viewless** invisible. Compare 'sightless', *Mac.* 1.7.23.

125–6 **blown ... world** Possibly recalling Chaucer, *Parlement of Foules*, 78 ff. (itself echoing Cicero, *Dream of Scipio*): 'Shul whirle aboute th'erthe alwey in peyne'. In Cicero the lustful are thus punished. This is also the case in Dante, *Inferno*, v.

125 **restless** never resting.

126 **pendent** hanging or floating unsupported in the air or in space (*OED*).

127–8 The syntax is ambiguous or elliptical: is 'that ... thought' an interjection? And does 'imagine ... horrible' have a direct syntactic connection with the foregoing or is it exclamatory-incoherent? Certainly the speaker is becoming excited to the point of hysteria and the seeming breakdown of coherence here reinforces this impression. Editors who emend 'thought' to 'thoughts' perhaps seek to express emotional coherence. It is preferable to preserve F as it stands.

128 **Imagine** A plural verb with a singular subject, perhaps influenced by the two adjectives preceding as in 1.2.164.

128 **howling** Compare *Rom.* 3.3.47–8: 'the damned use that word in hell; / Howling attends it'.

The weariest and most loathèd worldly life
That age, ache, penury, and imprisonment   130
Can lay on nature, is a paradise
To what we fear of death.
ISABELLA   Alas, alas.
CLAUDIO Sweet sister, let me live.
What sin you do to save a brother's life,
Nature dispenses with the deed so far   135
That it becomes a virtue.
ISABELLA   Oh, you beast!
Oh faithless coward, oh dishonest wretch!
Wilt thou be made a man out of my vice?
Is't not a kind of incest to take life
From thine own sister's shame? What should I think?   140
Heaven shield my mother played my father fair,
For such a warpèd slip of wilderness
Ne'er issued from his blood. Take my defiance,
Die, perish. Might but my bending down
Reprieve thee from thy fate, it should proceed.   145
I'll pray a thousand prayers for thy death,
No word to save thee.
CLAUDIO Nay hear me, Isabel.
ISABELLA   Oh, fie, fie, fie!
Thy sin's not accidental, but a trade.
Mercy to thee would prove itself a bawd,   150
'Tis best that thou diest quickly.
CLAUDIO   Oh hear me, Isabella.
DUKE [*Coming from concealment*]
Vouchsafe a word, young sister, but one word.
ISABELLA What is your will?
DUKE Might you dispense with your leisure, I would by and by have
some speech with you: the satisfaction I would require is likewise   155
your own benefit.

---

130 penury] F2; perjury F   152 sd] *This edn; Duke steps in* F2; *The DUKE comes forward* / NS; *Enter the Duke disguised as a Friar* / Capell; *not in* F

132 **To** Compared to.
135 **dispenses with** pardons.
136 **beast** i.e. because unmanly, craven; also because devoid of soul.
138 **made a man** given life (possibly with a play on 'conceived, born' (Evans)).
141 **shield** ensure, grant that.
142 **warpèd** deformed, perverted.

142 **slip of wilderness** shoot of wild stock (metaphor from a cultivated fruit tree reverting to original wild stock).
143 **defiance** declaration of contempt, disownment.
150 Giving you mercy would only procure more sexual indulgence (Evans).
154 **dispense with** give up.

ISABELLA I have no superfluous leisure, my stay must be stolen out
of other affairs – but I will attend you a while.

DUKE [*To Claudio*] Son, I have overheard what hath passed between
you and your sister. Angelo had never the purpose to corrupt   160
her; only he hath made an assay of her virtue, to practise his
judgement with the disposition of natures. She, having the truth
of honour in her, hath made him that gracious denial which he is
most glad to receive. I am confessor to Angelo and I know this to
be true, therefore prepare yourself to death. Do not satisfy your   165
resolution with hopes that are fallible, tomorrow you must die:
go to your knees and make ready.

CLAUDIO Let me ask my sister pardon. I am so out of love with life
that I will sue to be rid of it.

DUKE Hold you there. Farewell. Provost, a word with you.   170

PROVOST [*Coming from concealment*] What's your will, father?

DUKE That now you are come, you will be gone: leave me a while
with the maid; my mind promises, with my habit, no loss shall
touch her by my company.

PROVOST In good time.   175

                        Exit Provost [*and Claudio*]

DUKE [*To Isabella*] The hand that hath made you fair hath made you
good: the goodness that is cheap in beauty makes beauty brief in
goodness; but grace, being the soul of your complexion, shall
keep the body of it ever fair. The assault that Angelo hath made
to you, fortune hath conveyed to my understanding, and but that   180

---

158 while] F; while. [*Walks apart*] / Capell 159 SD] *This edn; not in* F 169 it] F; it. *Exit.* F2; it. *Exit. Enter Provost /
Steevens²* 170 Farewell] F; farewell. *Exit* CLAUDIO *Malone;* farewell. – [*Claudio retires*] / *Lever* 171 SD] *Positioned
as Dyce; after* farewell *Capell; not in* F 175 SD *and Claudio*] *Lever, subst.; Exit.* F 176 SD] *This edn; not in* F

158 **attend** listen to (*OED* sv v 1a) or wait for.
Isabella retires to another part of the stage so that
the Duke and Claudio may converse.

161 **assay** test.

162 **disposition of natures** way people think
and behave.

163 **gracious** virtuous, expressing a state of
religious grace.

166 **fallible** liable to error.

171 **SD** F gives no entry direction for the
Provost. See 52 n. above. Lever supposes that the
exchange between the Duke and Provost leaves
the focal attention on Claudio and Isabella who
enact a 'mimed reconciliation', but this has no
support from the text here or later. There is no
indication of whether they communicate or not.

172 **be gone** The Duke needs the Provost to
take Claudio away.

173 **habit** friar's clothes.

175 **In good time** So be it.

177–8 **goodness . . . goodness** Commentators differ in interpreting this proverb-like saying:
if the sense of 'goodness' is modified by association with 'beauty' (presumably that beauty which
is of the body, short in duration) then the sense
might be 'those pleasing qualities which cost little
to be beautiful are the cause for beauty's soon
losing virtue'. On the other hand 'cheap in
beauty' might mean 'are held cheap by beauty',
giving the whole sense as 'goodness, which beauty
holds cheap, she will easily part with' (recalling
the proverb 'beauty and chastity seldom meet'
(Tilley B163)).

178 **complexion** disposition.

frailty hath examples for his falling, I should wonder at Angelo. How will you do to content this substitute and to save your brother?

ISABELLA I am now going to resolve him. I had rather my brother die by the law than my son should be unlawfully born; but oh, how   185 much is the good Duke deceived in Angelo! If ever he return and I can speak to him, I will open my lips in vain or discover his government.

DUKE That shall not be much amiss, yet as the matter now stands he will avoid your accusation: he made trial of you only. Therefore   190 fasten your ear on my advisings, to the love I have in doing good. A remedy presents itself. I do make myself believe that you may most uprighteously do a poor wronged lady a merited benefit, redeem your brother from the angry law, do no stain to your own gracious person, and much please the absent Duke, if peradven-   195 ture he shall ever return to have hearing of this business.

ISABELLA Let me hear you speak farther; I have spirit to do any thing that appears not foul in the truth of my spirit.

DUKE Virtue is bold, and goodness never fearful. Have you not heard speak of Mariana, the sister of Frederick the great soldier who   200 miscarried at sea?

ISABELLA I have heard of the lady, and good words went with her name.

DUKE She should this Angelo have married – was affianced to her oath, and the nuptial appointed; between which time of the   205 contract, and limit of the solemnity, her brother Frederick was wrecked at sea, having in that perished vessel the dowry of his sister. But mark how heavily this befell to the poor gentlewoman: there she lost a noble and renowned brother, in his love toward her ever most kind and natural; with him the portion and sinew   210

---

197 farther] F; father F2   204 her oath] F; her by oath F2

---

181 **examples** precedents.

181 **his** Angelo's or perhaps frailty's. The grammar is ambiguous. If the second is meant, then Angelo is seen as an instance of frailty's falling. Abbott 228 notes the rarity of 'its' at the time, though acknowledging 1.2.4.

184 **resolve him** inform him I am resolved.

190 **avoid** make void, refute (in law).

201 **miscarried** (1) failed in an enterprise, (2) was lost.

204–5 **affianced . . . oath** Betrothal is by oath, not to an oath, as Eccles notes, and F2 has 'by

oath'. Presumably what is meant is that Mariana had sworn (with Angelo) to a contract of future marriage, *sponsalia per verba de futuro*. See 5.1.207 n. and p. 35 above, n. 1.

205 **nuptial appointed** day set for the wedding.

206 **limit . . . solemnity** the day set for solemnising the marriage.

210 **natural** i.e. brotherly ('kind' means 're-lated by kinship', brotherly as well as loving).

210 **portion and sinew** Hendiadys for 'sinewy portion', the strongest effectual part.

of her fortune, her marriage dowry; with both, her combinate
husband, this well-seeming Angelo.

ISABELLA Can this be so? Did Angelo so leave her?

DUKE Left her in her tears, and dried not one of them with his comfort; swallowed his vows whole, pretending in her discoveries of   215
dishonour: in few, bestowed her on her own lamentation, which
she yet wears for his sake; and he, a marble to her tears, is
washed with them, but relents not.

ISABELLA What a merit were it in death to take this poor maid from
the world! What corruption in this life, that it will let this man   220
live? But how out of this can she avail?

DUKE It is a rupture that you may easily heal, and the cure of it not
only saves your brother but keeps you from dishonour in doing
it.

ISABELLA Show me how, good father.   225

DUKE This fore-named maid hath yet in her the continuance of her
first affection. His unjust unkindness, that in all reason should
have quenched her love, hath like an impediment in the current
made it more violent and unruly. Go you to Angelo, answer his
requiring with a plausible obedience, agree with his demands to   230
the point, only refer yourself to this advantage: first, that your
stay with him may not be long; that the time may have all shadow
and silence in it; and the place answer to convenience. This
being granted in course, and now follows all: we shall advise this
wronged maid to stead up your appointment, go in your place. If   235
the encounter acknowledge itself hereafter, it may compel him to
her recompense; and here, by this, is your brother saved, your
honour untainted, the poor Mariana advantaged, and the corrupt
deputy scaled. The maid will I frame and make fit for his
attempt; if you think well to carry this, as you may, the double-   240

235 stead] *Rowe;* steed F

211 **combinate** A coinage meaning 'promised on oath, betrothed'.

215–16 **in her . . . dishonour** to have discovered evidence of her unchastity.

216 **bestowed** committed (with play on the sense 'give in marriage').

226–7 **This . . . affection** This same maid is still in love.

230–1 **to the point** punctiliously.

231 **refer . . . advantage** insist on these – to you favourable – conditions (?), rely on these advantageous conditions (?).

235 **stead up . . . appointment** keep the appointment instead of you.

236 **acknowledge itself** make itself publicly known.

239 **scaled** weighed in the scales of Justice. Some commentators have suspected allusion to scaling a ladder (to reach him notwithstanding his high place), or to removing fish scales and hence 'to strip'. Johnson glosses 'to strip him and discover his nakednesss, though armed and concealed by the investments of authority'.

240–1 **doubleness** i.e. to you and to Mariana (with an unintentional play on 'double', 'deceive': benefit achieved through deceit).

ness of the benefit defends the deceit from reproof. What think
you of it?

ISABELLA The image of it gives me content already, and I trust it will
grow to a most prosperous perfection.

DUKE It lies much in your holding up. Haste you speedily to Angelo. 245
If for this night he entreat you to his bed, give him promise of
satisfaction. I will presently to Saint Luke's; there at the moated
grange resides this dejected Mariana; at that place call upon me,
and dispatch with Angelo, that it may be quickly.

ISABELLA I thank you for this comfort. Fare you well, good father. 250

Exit

[3.2] *Enter* ELBOW, POMPEY, *and* OFFICERS

ELBOW Nay, if there be no remedy for it, but that you will needs buy
and sell men and women like beasts, we shall have all the world
drink brown and white bastard.

DUKE Oh heavens, what stuff is here.

POMPEY 'Twas never merry world since, of two usuries, the merriest 5
was put down and the worser allowed by order of law – a furred
gown to keep him warm, and furred with fox and lamb-skins too,
to signify that craft, being richer than innocency, stands for the
facing.

ELBOW Come your way, sir – bless you, good father friar. 10

DUKE And you, good brother father. What offence hath this man
made you, sir?

Act 3, Scene 2   3.2] SCENE II *Capell; not in* F

247–8 **moated grange** A solitary farm house
surrounded by a ditch.

Act 3, Scene 2
0 SD The Duke remains on stage; a scene
division is marked purely for the reader's convenience of reference. Editors have questioned
F's simple stage directions, supposing a change
of fictional location from inside the prison to
the street outside, but Shakespeare's stagecraft
stresses the analogy between the plight of Claudio
and that of Pompey as two problems confronting
the Duke: the themes of the play take precedence
over realistic interest in precise location of the
action.
1–3 These words could be applied ironically

to the Duke in the scene which has just ended.
Compare the ironic appropriateness of Elbow's
first words, beginning 2.1, as a comment on
Angelo in the preceding scene, 1.4. Shakespeare's use of the sub-plot as parallel to the
main plot is thus lightly indicated.
3 **drink ... bastard** (1) drink a kind of sweet
wine, (2) procreate bastards of light and dark
complexions (Eccles).
5 **two usuries** i.e. lending money at usurious
interest and fornication. Perhaps a play on 'use'.
8–9 **stands ... facing** Playing on the senses
'represents', 'supports', for 'stands' and 'decorative surface', 'deceit' for 'facing'. There may also
be a bawdy pun on 'stands'.
11 **father** An appellation for any old man:

ELBOW Marry, sir, he hath offended the law; and, sir, we take him to
    be a thief, too, sir, for we have found upon him, sir, a strange
    pick-lock, which we have sent to the deputy.   15

DUKE Fie, sirrah, a bawd, a wicked bawd!
        The evil that thou causest to be done,
        That is thy means to live. Do thou but think
        What 'tis to cram a maw or clothe a back
        From such a filthy vice; say to thyself,   20
        'From their abominable and beastly touches
        I drink, I eat, array myself, and live.'
        Canst thou believe thy living is a life,
        So stinkingly depending? Go mend, go mend.

POMPEY Indeed, it does stink in some sort, sir, but yet, sir, I would   25
    prove –

DUKE Nay, if the devil have given thee proofs for sin
        Thou wilt prove his. Take him to prison, officer,
        Correction and instruction must both work
        Ere this rude beast will profit.   30

ELBOW He must before the deputy, sir, he has given him warning:
    the deputy cannot abide a whoremaster. If he be a whoremonger
    and comes before him, he were as good go a mile on his errand.

DUKE That we were all, as some would seem to be,
        From our faults, as faults from seeming, free.   35

---

22 eat, array] *Theobald, conj. Bishop;* eate away F   25–6] *As prose, Pope; as verse,* F: Indeed . . . Sir: / But . . . prouc.
31 has] ha's F   35 From] F; Free from F2

perhaps Elbow was imagined by Shakespeare as old. The Duke's reply responds humorously to Elbow's blundering address.

15 pick-lock Normally a skeleton key. This charge, forgotten as soon as uttered, seems to be a memory of the thief 'Deformed' who, Dogberry asserts (*Ado* 5.1.308–9), is said to wear a key in his ear and a lock hanging by it. A bawdy quibble is also to be suspected.

16 The harsh reproof may be fitting for a friar but the Duke's planning of the bed-trick moments before (3.1.229 ff.) puts him in an equivocal position – he is a kind of bawd, too. Anxiety perhaps informs his outburst, as with Angelo's outburst 'Fie, these filthy vices!' (2.4.41). Compare also Isabella's outburst at her brother's disconcerting instinct to live (3.1.148) which betrays her private anxieties as much as her professed principles.

19 maw stomach.

21 touches sexual contacts.

22 eat, array Eccles compares *Oth.* 4.1.94–5 and Jonson, *Epigrams*, xii, on Lieutenant Shift: 'By that one spell he liues, eates, drinkes, arrayes / Himselfe' to show the conventionality of the formula. F's 'eate away myselfe' would make sense but outside this context, in which all the emphasis is on being dependent on others and their vices. Compare 1.2.109–12.

25–6 Compositor D or B has occasional difficulty, setting prose as verse in this scene (see 199–200 and 218–20 below).

28 prove turn out to be.

29 Correction Punishment.

31 has F's spelling 'ha's' probably reveals the scribal habits of Ralph Crane; compare 5.1.356, 357, where F has 'Ha'st' and 'ha'st', and 1.2.16, 'was't'. See Textual Analysis, p. 196 below.

33 as . . . mile Proverbial: 'do anything rather than that' (Tilley M927).

35 Really free from our faults, as faults ought to be free from deceptive disguise. Compare *Oth.*

Enter LUCIO

ELBOW His neck will come to your waist, a cord, sir.

POMPEY I spy comfort, I cry bail: here's a gentleman and a friend of mine.

LUCIO How now, noble Pompey? What, at the wheels of Caesar? Art thou led in triumph? What, is there none of Pygmalion's images   40
newly made woman to be had now, for putting the hand in the pocket and extracting it clutched? What reply, ha? What say'st thou to this tune, matter, and method? Is't not drowned i'th'last rain, ha? What say'st thou, Trot? Is the world as it was, man? Which is the way? Is it sad and few words? Or how? The trick of   45
it?

DUKE Still thus, and thus: still worse.

LUCIO How doth my dear morsel, thy mistress? Procures she still, ha?

POMPEY Troth, sir, she hath eaten up all her beef, and she is herself   50
in the tub.

LUCIO Why, 'tis good; it is the right of it; it must be so. Ever your fresh whore and your powdered bawd, an unshunned consequence; it must be so. Art going to prison, Pompey?

POMPEY Yes, faith, sir.   55

LUCIO Why, 'tis not amiss, Pompey. Farewell. Go say I sent thee thither. For debt, Pompey? Or how?

42 it] *Rowe; not in* F

3.3.126–7: 'Men should be what they seem, / Or those that be not, would they might seem none!'

36 His ... cord His neck will be tied like your waist with a rope (Johnson, explaining that the Friar's garb includes a cord round the waist).

39 wheels ... Caesar It was the sons of Pompey who were, in history, led in triumph by Caesar after their defeat at Munda (Lever).

40–1 Pygmalion's ... woman Alluding to the mythical awakening to life of the female statue beloved by its sculptor Pygmalion, and to the indecent satiric poem *The Metamorphosis of Pygmalion's Image* by Marston (1598): hence, Malone suggests, 'Is there no courtezan, who being *newly made woman* (i.e. lately debauched) still retains the appearance of chastity, and looks as cold as a statue, to be had?' Contrast Donne, 'Epithalamion made at Lincoln's Inn', cited at 2.4.139 n.

42 clutched i.e. clutching coins to pay for them.

43–4 drowned ... rain An obscure expression. According to some commentators apparently alluding to Pompey's failure to reply, but it seems more likely to follow from the preceding question, which refers to the law's clamp-down on prostitution, and hence might mean 'is not the old style extinct, or out of use?' Compare 'Is the world as it was, man?' (44).

44 Trot Johnson says this was a familiar way of addressing a man among the poor common people.

45–6 The trick of it? i.e what is the style?

50–1 eaten ... tub Beef was salted down, or 'powdered' in a tub, and the treatment for venereal disease was the sweating-tub. Evans suggests 'eaten up all her beef' means worn out all her prostitutes.

53 fresh young, unsalted.

53 powdered Alluding to the treatment in the powder-tub for veneral disease, and also perhaps to face powder (to conceal the ravages of age and disease) and to the pickled, 'salted beef' appearance of the old woman's skin.

53 unshunned i.e. inevitable. Presumably the fresh whore turns into the old bawd, or, alternatively, is accompanied by the old bawd.

ELBOW For being a bawd, for being a bawd.

LUCIO Well then, imprison him: if imprisonment be the due of a
bawd, why, 'tis his right. Bawd is he, doubtless, and of antiquity   60
too. Bawd born. Farewell, good Pompey. Commend me to the
prison, Pompey; you will turn good husband now, Pompey, you
will keep the house.

POMPEY I hope, sir, your good worship will be my bail.

LUCIO No indeed will I not, Pompey, it is not the wear. I will pray,   65
Pompey, to increase your bondage: if you take it not patiently,
why, your mettle is the more. Adieu, trusty Pompey. – Bless you,
friar.

DUKE And you.

LUCIO Does Bridget paint still, Pompey, ha?   70

ELBOW Come your ways, sir, come.

POMPEY You will not bail me then, sir?

LUCIO Then, Pompey, nor now. – What news abroad, friar? What
news?

ELBOW Come your ways, sir, come.   75

LUCIO Go to kennel, Pompey, go. –
                    [*Exeunt Elbow, Pompey and Officers*]
What news, friar, of the Duke?

DUKE I know none. Can you tell me of any?

LUCIO Some say he is with the Emperor of Russia; other some he is
in Rome; but where is he, think you?   80

DUKE I know not where, but wheresoever, I wish him well.

LUCIO It was a mad fantastical trick of him to steal from the state and
usurp the beggary he was never born to. Lord Angelo dukes it
well in his absence: he puts transgression to't.

DUKE He does well in't.   85

LUCIO A little more lenity to lechery would do no harm in him:
something too crabbed that way, friar.

DUKE It is too general a vice, and severity must cure it.

66 bondage: if . . . patiently, why,] *Theobald, subst.;* bondage if . . . patiently: Why, F   76 SD] *Rowe; Exeunt.* F2; *not in* F

66 F's punctuation does not make sense: 'If . . .
patiently' is ambiguous.

67 **mettle** Lucio puns on the senses (1) spirit,
courage, (2) iron (a prisoner shackled is said to
be 'in irons').

73 **Then . . . now** Neither then nor now.

82 **steal from** leave surreptitiously.

83 **usurp** Ironically applied to the seizing of
the position, not of ruler, but of lowest rank in the
state. It is argued by Neville Coghill (*S.Sur.* 8
(1955), 25) that Lucio has penetrated the Duke's
disguise, and shows this by alluding to his disguise as a begging poor friar. Lucio does guess
very near the mark, but his intuitive sense clearly,
as the plot shows, does not take him all the way to
perceive the truth, and what matters here is the
comedy of his near miss.

84 **puts . . . to't** punishes offences.

LUCIO Yes, in good sooth, the vice is of a great kindred, it is well
  allied, but it is impossible to extirp it quite, friar, till eating and   90
  drinking be put down. They say this Angelo was not made by
  man and woman after this downright way of creation: is it true,
  think you?
DUKE How should he be made, then?
LUCIO Some report a sea-maid spawned him, some, that he was   95
  begot between two stock-fishes; but it is certain that when he
  makes water, his urine is congealed ice, that I know to be true;
  and he is a motion generative, that's infallible.
DUKE You are pleasant, sir, and speak apace.
LUCIO Why, what a ruthless thing is this in him, for the rebellion of a   100
  codpiece to take away the life of a man! Would the Duke that is
  absent have done this? Ere he would have hanged a man for the
  getting a hundred bastards, he would have paid for the nursing a
  thousand. He had some feeling of the sport, he knew the service,
  and that instructed him to mercy.   105
DUKE I never heard the absent Duke much detected for women, he
  was not inclined that way.
LUCIO Oh, sir, you are deceived.
DUKE 'Tis not possible.
LUCIO Who, not the Duke? Yes, your beggar of fifty: and his use   110
  was, to put a ducat in her clack-dish. The Duke had crotchets in
  him. He would be drunk too, that let me inform you.
DUKE You do him wrong, surely.
LUCIO Sir, I was an inward of his. A shy fellow was the Duke, and I
  believe I know the cause of his withdrawing.   115
DUKE What, I prithee, might be the cause?

92 after this] F; after the *Pope*

92 **this downright way** Compare 2.4.79, the
generic use of 'this', 'the way of creation that men
and women practise' (*OED* This *dem adj* 1d).
  95 **sea-maid** mermaid.
  96 **stock-fishes** dried cod (cold and blood-
lesss dead fish).
  98 **motion generative** puppet or automa-
ton, despite having the organs of generation.
Theobald proposes 'ungenerative', which gains
support from 148, 'This ungenitured agent'; but
F's reading, an oxymoronic phrase, is within
Lucio's capacity as an acute diagnosis of Angelo's
condition.
  99 **pleasant** full of jokes.
  99 **apace** rapidly (with the implication of
recklessly).

101 **codpiece** Close-fitting male breeches had
a 'bagged appendage to the front' (*OED* sv *sb* 1c).
Here signifying genitals.
  106 **detected for** accused of (meddling with).
It may be significant that the Duke-as-Friar uses
the modifying, perhaps conceding, 'much'.
  111 **put . . . clack-dish** put a coin (literally
'ducato', ducal coin) in her wooden begging
bowl (with a movable cover which the beggar
clacked to draw attention). The bawdy meaning
is 'copulate with her'.
  111 **crotchets** whims, strange fancies.
  114 **inward** intimate, confidant.

LUCIO No, pardon: 'tis a secret must be locked within the teeth and the lips; but this I can let you understand: the greater file of the subject held the Duke to be wise.

DUKE Wise? Why, no question but he was.   120

LUCIO A very superficial, ignorant, unweighing fellow.

DUKE Either this is envy in you, folly, or mistaking. The very stream of his life and the business he hath helmed must, upon a warranted need, give him a better proclamation. Let him be but testimonied in his own bringings-forth and he shall appear to the   125 envious a scholar, a statesman, and a soldier: therefore you speak unskilfully; or, if your knowledge be more, it is much darkened in your malice.

LUCIO Sir, I know him, and I love him.

DUKE Love talks with better knowledge, and knowledge with dearer   130 love.

LUCIO Come, sir, I know what I know.

DUKE I can hardly believe that, since you know not what you speak. But if ever the Duke return, as our prayers are he may, let me desire you to make your answer before him. If it be honest you   135 have spoke, you have courage to maintain it. I am bound to call upon you, and I pray you, your name?

LUCIO Sir, my name is Lucio, well known to the Duke.

DUKE He shall know you better, sir, if I may live to report you.

LUCIO I fear you not.   140

DUKE Oh, you hope the Duke will return no more? Or you imagine me too unhurtful an opposite? But indeed I can do you little harm: you'll forswear this again.

---

130 dearer] *Hanmer;* deare F

118 **greater file of the subject** majority of his subjects.

123 **helmed** steered (a nautical metaphor referring back to 'stream').

124 **warranted need** i.e. an occasion when a warrant or reference was needed.

125 **testimonied . . . bringings-forth** proved by evidence of his achievement. Compare Matt. 7.16–17: 'Ye shall know them by their fruits.'

126 **a scholar** educated, intelligent, well-informed.

126 **a statesman** one skilled in managing the affairs of a state. The term was associated at the time with the name and writings of Machiavelli, as in Jonson, *Every Man out of his Humour* 2.6.167–8: 'speaking of Machiavel, comprehend all statesmen'.

127 **unskilfully** ignorantly or foolishly.

130 The balanced construction opposes 'better' to 'dearer', two comparatives. Van Dam, *William Shakespeare, Prosody and Text*, Leyden, 1900, thinks F's 'deare' actually a form of comparative, like 'farre' in *WT* 4.4.431, where there is apocope of 'er'. Though *WT* was also set from one of Crane's transcripts, 'farre' occurs in *Shr.*, thought to be set from authorial MS., which would suggest van Dam is right. In a modernised text 'dearer' will be the preferred form.

135 **answer** Implying that the Friar intends to make a formal charge against him.

135–6 **If . . . spoke** If what you have said is true.

136 **I am bound** It is my duty.

LUCIO I'll be hanged first. Thou art deceived in me, friar. But no
more of this. Canst thou tell if Claudio die tomorrow, or no?   145
DUKE Why should he die, sir?
LUCIO Why? For filling a bottle with a tundish. I would the Duke
we talk of were returned again. This ungenitured agent will
unpeople the province with continency: sparrows must not build
in his house eaves, because they are lecherous! The Duke yet   150
would have dark deeds darkly answered, he would never bring
them to light. Would he were returned. Marry, this Claudio is
condemned for untrussing. Farewell, good friar, I prithee pray
for me. The Duke, I say to thee again, would eat mutton on
Fridays. He's now past it, yet – and I say to thee – he would   155
mouth with a beggar though she smelt brown bread and garlic –
say that I said so – farewell.   *Exit*
DUKE No might nor greatness in mortality
       Can censure 'scape: back-wounding calumny
       The whitest virtue strikes. What king so strong   160
       Can tie the gall up in the slanderous tongue?
       But who comes here?

Enter ESCALUS, PROVOST, MISTRESS OVERDONE [*and* OFFICERS]

ESCALUS Go, away with her to prison.
MISTRESS OVERDONE Good my lord, be good to me, your honour is
accounted a merciful man – good my lord.   165
ESCALUS Double and treble admonition, and still forfeit in the same
kind? This would make mercy swear and play the tyrant.
PROVOST A bawd of eleven years' continuance, may it please your
honour.

162 SD *and* OFFICERS] Theobald; not in F

147 tundish funnel (as used in brewing: tun =
cask). Here bawdy.
148 ungenitured (1) unendowed with effectual organs of generation, (2) not begotten, (3)
sterile.
148 agent deputy.
153 untrussing untying the tags which fasten-
ed hose to doublet (hence undressing).
154–5 mutton on Fridays The Catholic
Church forbade eating meat on Friday. 'Mutton'
was slang for prostitute; compare 'lac'd mutton',
TGV 1.1.97. The whole phrase means 'would
have his whores, law or no law'.
155 now Hanmer generously emends to 'not'

but Ridley persuasively prefers F: 'there is an
added insult in the picture of the now impotent
old lecher'.
156 brown bread Coarse rye or rye and wheat
bread, the food of the poor, which rapidly turned
musty and affected the breath.
158 mortality humanity, human affairs.
166 forfeit Either second-person plural, present tense, transitive, 'you transgress', or past,
passive, 'guilty, forfeit to the law'.
167 play the tyrant Compare 2.4.170; alluding to the Miracle-play tyrants of whom
Herod was most famous for raging and cruelty.
See *Ham.* 3.2.14.

MISTRESS OVERDONE My lord, this is one Lucio's information   170
  against me. Mistress Kate Keepdown was with child by him in
  the Duke's time, he promised her marriage, his child is a year
  and a quarter old come Philip and Jacob – I have kept it myself –
  and see how he goes about to abuse me.

ESCALUS That fellow is a fellow of much licence: let him be called   175
  before us. Away with her to prison, go to, no more words.
            [*Exeunt Officers with Mistress Overdone*]
  Provost, my brother Angelo will not be altered, Claudio must die
  tomorrow. Let him be furnished with divines, and have all
  charitable preparation. If my brother wrought by my pity, it
  should not be so with him.   180

PROVOST So please you, this friar hath been with him, and advised
  him for th'entertainment of death.

ESCALUS Good even, good father.

DUKE Bliss and goodness on you.

ESCALUS Of whence are you?   185

DUKE Not of this country, though my chance is now
         To use it for my time. I am a brother
         Of gracious order, late come from the See,
         In special business from his holiness.

ESCALUS What news abroad i'th'world?   190

DUKE None but that there is so great a fever on goodness that the
  dissolution of it must cure it. Novelty is only in request, and it is
  as dangerous to be aged in any kind of course, as it is virtuous to
  be constant in any undertaking. There is scarce truth enough
  alive to make societies secure, but security enough to make   195
  fellowships accursed. Much upon this riddle runs the wisdom of

176 SD] *Rome; not in* F   188 See] *Theobald*; Sea F   192–3 and it is as] F3; and as it is as F; and, as it is, as
Alexander

170 **information** accusation.

173 **Philip and Jacob** 1 May, feast of Saints
Philip and James, but also May Day, a popular
festival.

177 **brother** i.e. colleague in office.

179 **charitable** i.e. in Christian charity.

182 **entertainment** acceptance (*OED* sv *sb* 12
a).

187 **use . . . time** serve my particular occasion
(Evans).

188 **gracious order** i.e. of a holy order of
friars.

188 **See** Holy See, in Rome.

189 **his holiness** the Pope.

191–2 **that . . . it** that it can be cured only by
goodness itself dying.

192 **Novelty . . . request** People are only
interested in, or demand, what is novel.

193 **aged** constant, persevering.

194 **constant** Some commentators suppose
this should read 'inconstant' in the light of the
pattern of the preceding assertion, but 193–4
mean 'to be constant is as dangerous as it is
virtuous' (Bald).

195 **societies** associations.

195 **security** bonds, pledges in financial affairs.

195–6 **security . . . accursed** 'Endorsing
bonds has become the curse of friendship' (Bald).

the world. This news is old enough, yet it is every day's news. I
pray you, sir, of what disposition was the Duke?

ESCALUS One that above all other strifes contended especially to
know himself. 200

DUKE What pleasure was he given to?

ESCALUS Rather rejoicing to see another merry, than merry at
anything which professed to make him rejoice. A gentleman of
all temperance. But leave we him to his events, with a prayer they
may prove prosperous, and let me desire to know how you find 205
Claudio prepared. I am made to understand that you have lent
him visitation.

DUKE He professes to have received no sinister measure from his
judge, but most willingly humbles himself to the determination
of justice; yet had he framed to himself, by the instruction of his 210
frailty, many deceiving promises of life, which I by my good
leisure have discredited to him; and now is he resolved to die.

ESCALUS You have paid the heavens your function, and the prisoner
the very debt of your calling. I have laboured for the poor gentleman to the extremest shore of my modesty, but my brother 215
justice have I found so severe that he hath forced me to tell him
he is indeed Justice.

DUKE If his own life answer the straitness of his proceeding, it shall
become him well; wherein if he chance to fail, he hath sentenced
himself. 220

ESCALUS I am going to visit the prisoner. Fare you well.

DUKE Peace be with you.

[*Exeunt Escalus and Provost*]

He who the sword of heaven will bear

199–200] *As prose, Capell; as verse,* F: One . . . strifes, / Contended . . . himselfe.   218–20] *As prose, Pope; as verse,* F: If . . . life, / Answere . . . proceeding, / It . . . faile / he . . . himselfe.   **222** SD] *Capell; Exit.* F2 *(after 221); not in* F

Lever sees a play on 'fellowships', corporations formed by trading partners, balancing the simple and commercial senses of 'security'.

202–3 Rather . . . rejoice An obtrusively rhetorical use of the figure antimetabole, shaped to express balance, as befits the judicious Duke it describes.

203 professed attempted.

206–7 lent . . . visitation Escalus has become infected with the Duke-as-Friar's style; he simply means 'visited him'.

208 sinister unjust.

210–12 yet . . . him yet he had formed in his mind, prompted by his natural human weakness,

vain hopes of life, which as time gave me the chance I have disabused him of.

212 resolved prepared in mind, resolute.

217 indeed Justice the very embodiment of the principle of justice with no mingling of mercy (Rolfe).

218 answer correspond to.

218 straitness rigorous strictness.

223 sword of heaven The 'deputed sword', authority to execute justice.

223 (1) to recognise in himself heaven's pattern, (2) should be himself a pattern, of knowledge of grace and virtuous action, for others to follow. 'Pattern' means a perfect example and a model deserving imitation, a mould.

Should be as holy, as severe:
Pattern in himself to know,   225
Grace to stand, and virtue go:
More, nor less to others paying
Than by self-offences weighing.
Shame to him, whose cruel striking
Kills for faults of his own liking.   230
Twice treble shame on Angelo,
To weed my vice, and let his grow.
Oh, what may man within him hide,
Though angel on the outward side?
How may likeness made in crimes,   235
Making practice on the times,
To draw with idle spiders' strings
Most ponderous and substantial things?
Craft against vice I must apply.
With Angelo tonight shall lie   240
His old betrothèd but despised;
So disguise shall by th'disguised
Pay with falsehood false exacting
And perform an old contracting.   *Exit*

236 Making] F; Make a *Alexander*

226 i.e. grace goes with standing firm, virtue
with dynamic action. 'Stand' suggests 'withstand'
as well as 'stand fast'; 'virtue go' suggests walking
the straight path uprightly.
227 **paying** i.e. punishing (with the idea of
'paying out', a financial metaphor).
227–8 i.e. judging others neither more nor less
severely than he judges his own offences.
228 **self-offences** one's own offences.
232 **weed** Compare 1.3.21.
232 **my vice** The Duke's vice is laxity, but
commentators are reluctant to see this meaning
here, suggesting rather that he means the vice of
other persons in contrast to Angelo's own.
(Jenkins, in Lever, explains that 'the Duke speaks
chorically as an "everyman"'.)
235 **likeness** seeming (i.e. outward) likeness to
an angel, but false.
236 i.e. practising deception on the world. Is
the Duke referring to himself, or to such as
Angelo? 'Making practice' = using stratagems
(*OED* Practise *v* 6c), following on, perhaps from
'likeness' (235) = disguise (of virtue), false
seeming. Lever supposes a couplet to have been
omitted after this line.

235–6 How may criminal seeming practise
deception on the world, and thereby get control
and possession of important matters by a deceptive appearance of lightness and triviality. The
Duke as puppeteer manipulating the characters
by pulling strings, making them play his game, is
certainly how the Duke himself likes to think of
his own role (though Shakespeare ensures that
he is less than omnipotent), but I suppose the
three lines lament how great criminals commit
great crimes and escape punishment by employing deception (like Angelo). Smith, recorded by
Eccles, supposes an allusion to a proverb – that
laws are like spiders' webs which catch the small
flies but let big insects break through. 'Draw' =
'pull towards' but also 'entice, deceive, dupe'
(see 2.1.175). 'To-draw', with 'To-draw',
as one word, an archaic form (as in 'to-burst':
see *OED*), with the meaning 'pull to pieces' (so
NS, Nosworthy).
243 **Pay with** deception what is exacted
through deception. Angelo's guise of righteous-
ness is 'seeming', morally false; Mariana's substituting for Isabella is a kind of disguise too, but
in a just cause.

4.1 *Enter* MARIANA, *and* BOY *singing*

BOY [*Sings*] Take, oh take those lips away,
　　　　That so sweetly were forsworn,
　　　　And those eyes, the break of day,
　　　　Lights that do mislead the morn;
　　　　But my kisses bring again, bring again,　　　　　　　　　　5
　　　　Seals of love, but sealed in vain, sealed in vain.

Enter DUKE [*disguised as a friar*]

MARIANA Break off thy song and haste thee quick away.
　　　　Here comes a man of comfort, whose advice
　　　　Hath often stilled my brawling discontent. –

　　　　　　　　　　　　　　　　　　　　　　　　　[*Exit Boy*]

　　　　I cry you mercy, sir, and well could wish　　　　　　　　10
　　　　You had not found me here so musical.
　　　　Let me excuse me, and believe me so,
　　　　My mirth it much displeased, but pleased my woe.
DUKE 'Tis good; though music oft hath such a charm
　　　　To make bad good and good provoke to harm.　　　　　15
　　　　I pray you tell me, hath anybody enquired for me here today?

Act 4, Scene 1   4.1] *Actus Quartus. Scæna Prima.* F   6 but] F; though *Rollo Duke of Normandy* 5.2   9 SD] *Capell; not in* F

Act 4, Scene 1

1–22 Some commentators believe that the opening of the scene is non-Shakespearean and that a second stanza of the song should be printed. I am content with F and consider the second stanza very inferior; nor do I find convincing the argument that the song at this point in the play is a blunder. Alice Walker (*RES* (1983), 3–5) revives the suggestion that the opening of the scene is a non-Shakespearean interpolation, and that the scene Shakespeare wrote began with the Duke's speech at 23; she argues that 'in a consistently ironic comedy, which makes no concession to the sentimental or romantic, the song is an artistic blunder and the following dialogue is clearly the work of an inexpert hand'. The assertion about romance is wrong, though doubts of the authorship of the song go back to the eighteenth century. The song appears with a second stanza in Beaumont and Fletcher's *Rollo Duke of Normandy* (1639), 5.2:
　　Hide ô hide those hills of Snow,
　　That thy frozen bosome beares,
　　On whose tops the pincks that grow,

Are yet of those that Aprill wears,
But first set my poore heart free,
Bound in those Icy chaines by thee.
Capell, and many later commentators, consider the second verse too inferior to be Shakespearean. Warburton included the second stanza in the text. Some commentators suppose Mariana's remark at 7 leads the audience to infer that the song is not complete.

3–4 The idea of eyes so bright that morning takes them for the rising sun may be directly remembered from Marlowe, *Hero and Leander*, 2.321–2: 'this false morne / Brought foorth the day before the day was borne'.

6 The variant reading occurs in the version of this stanza which appears in *Rollo Duke of Normandy*.

9 **brawling** clamorous.

13 Some commentators suppose Mariana is not indulging her melancholy, and explain that she is tempering her grief; yet in explaining that she is not committing one fault, unseemly merriment, she admits another, as the plain sense 'pleased my woe' indicates.

Much upon this time have I promised here to meet.

MARIANA You have not been enquired after: I have sat here all day.

Enter ISABELLA

DUKE I do constantly believe you. The time is come even now. I shall
crave your forbearance a little, may be I will call upon you anon   20
for some advantage to yourself.

MARIANA I am always bound to you.   *Exit*

DUKE Very well met, and welcome.
        What is the news from this good deputy?

ISABELLA He hath a garden circummured with brick,   25
        Whose western side is with a vineyard backed;
        And to that vineyard is a planchèd gate
        That makes his opening with this bigger key.
        This other doth command a little door
        Which from the vineyard to the garden leads;   30
        There have I made my promise, upon the heavy
        Middle of the night to call upon him.

DUKE But shall you on your knowledge find this way?

ISABELLA I have tane a due and wary note upon't.
        With whispering and most guilty diligence   35
        In action all of precept, he did show me
        The way twice o'er.

DUKE   Are there no other tokens
        Between you 'greed, concerning her observance?

ISABELLA No, none, but only a repair i'th'dark
        And that I have possessed him my most stay   40
        Can be but brief: for I have made him know
        I have a servant comes with me along
        That stays upon me, whose persuasion is

31–2] *As Collier;* There . . . the / Heauy . . . him. F.

17 **Much upon** Just about.

19 **constantly** firmly.

20 **crave . . . little** i.e. impose upon you by
asking you to leave the room for a moment.

25 **circummured** walled round.

27 **planchèd** made of planks.

31–2 **upon . . . night** 'heavy' can mean
'drowsy', 'weary', but its physical sense is present
in the personification of 'night', also, and half
suggests the act of love. Compare *Rom.* 2.5.76:
'you shall bear the burthen soon at night'; and
Ant. 1.5.21: 'bear the weight'. F's lineation is
unsatisfactory, the metre defective. Collier offers

a rearrangement with minimal disturbance to F.
Lever suggests 'to call on him' belonged to 31,
and 'The heavy . . . night' was a later addition in
the MS., wrongly placed by the scribe.

36 **In . . . precept** With instructive gestures.

38 **concerning her observance** which it is
important for her to observe.

39 **a repair** going to the place.

40 **possessed** explained to.

40 **most stay** longest possible stay.

43 **stays upon** waits for.

43 **persuasion** belief.

I come about my brother.

DUKE   'Tis well borne up.
I have not yet made known to Mariana   45
A word of this. What ho, within, come forth.

Enter MARIANA

I pray you be acquainted with this maid,
She comes to do you good.

ISABELLA   I do desire the like.

DUKE Do you persuade yourself that I respect you?

MARIANA Good friar, I know you do, and have found it.   50

DUKE Take then this your companion by the hand,
Who hath a story ready for your ear.
I shall attend your leisure, but make haste:
The vaporous night approaches.

MARIANA *[To Isabella]* Will't please you walk aside?   55
[Mariana and Isabella walk aside]

DUKE Oh place and greatness, millions of false eyes
Are stuck upon thee; volumes of report
Run with these false and most contrarious quest
Upon thy doings; thousand escapes of wit
Make thee the father of their idle dream   60

46 SD] *As Rowe; after 45* F **55** SD.1] *This edn; not in* F **55** Will't] *Hanmer;* Wilt F **55** SD.2] *Lever, subst.; Exit.* F

44 borne up sustained (i.e. the scheme of deception is generally well thought out).

49 Do . . . respect you Are you persuaded I have your best interests at heart? The Duke's deviousness, and the apparent impropriety of the bed-trick, are acknowledged in his 'persuade yourself'.

55 SD.2 Many editors accept F's *Exit* here. The problem is discussed in the Textual Analysis, p. 198 below. Here it may be briefly noted that with the Duke's short speech, 56–61, it seems clumsy for the women to exit and enter, when they need only draw apart for a moment; moreover this staging 'rhymes' with other episodes in which certain characters are visible, but apart, while others carry on dialogue. See 1.2, 1.4, 3.1.52 ff., 3.1.158.

56–61 Warburton thinks this speech should be placed at 3.2.158, referring specifically to Lucio's scandals there. Kellner and A.P. Rossiter (cited by Winny) suppose on the contrary that the Duke's couplets from the end of 3.2 could be placed here.

56 false treacherous. Yet taken with 'stuck' (57) there is the additional idea that these are artificial eyes on the robes of a pageant or emblem figure, like Fame described in Jonson, *Poetaster* 5.2.85: 'Looke, how many plumes are plac't / On her huge corps, how many waking eyes / Sticke vnderneath.' Lever notes that Ripa, *Iconologia* (1603), depicts Gelosia as a woman whose robe is covered with eyes and ears. The Duke begins by complaining about false eyes directed at himself and ends thinking about the false eyes on his own robes directed against others.

57 report rumour.

58 Follow a false scent and hunt counter (i.e. in the opposite direction) (Onions); 'false' qualifies 'run' and 'contrarious' qualifies 'quest'.

58 quest give tongue (of hunting-dogs scenting game).

60 Make you the source of their foolish fantasies.

And rack thee in their fancies.
      MARIANA *and* ISABELLA [*approach the Duke*]
      Welcome, how agreed?
ISABELLA She'll take the enterprise upon her, father,
      If you advise it.
DUKE   It is not my consent,
      But my entreaty too.
ISABELLA   Little have you to say   65
      When you depart from him but, soft and low,
      'Remember now my brother.'
MARIANA   Fear me not.
DUKE Nor, gentle daughter, fear you not at all.
      He is your husband on a pre-contract:
      To bring you thus together 'tis no sin,   70
      Sith that the justice of your title to him
      Doth flourish the deceit. Come, let us go,
      Our corn's to reap, for yet our tithe's to sow.
                                        Exeunt

4.2 *Enter* PROVOST *and* POMPEY

PROVOST Come hither, sirrah; can you cut off a man's head?
POMPEY If the man be a bachelor, sir, I can; but if he be a married
    man, he's his wife's head, and I can never cut off a woman's
    head.
PROVOST Come, sir, leave me your snatches and yield me a direct   5

---

61 SD] *Lever, subst.; Enter Mariana and Isabella* F (*after* agreed)   Act 4, Scene 2   4.2] *Scena Secunda.* F   2–4] *As prose, Pope; as verse,* F: *If . . . can: / But . . . head, / And . . . head.*

61 rack distort, tear apart (as if stretched out on the rack).
64 not not only.
72 flourish The term is taken from embroidery and decorative penmanship on documents, and has the connotation of giving decorative finish; but here, as Warburton notes, with somewhat equivocal sense: in embroidery 'a coarse ground is filled up and covered with figures of rich materials and elegant workmanship'.
73 Taking 'tithe' as loosely meaning 'seed' (literally it means the tenth part of income, due to the Church), this means 'our corn is yet to be harvested for we have still to sow the seed'. The

obtrusive metaphor repetitiously conveys the simple idea: that there is much to be done before success is assured.

Act 4, Scene 2
2–4 Compositor B sets prose as verse several times in this scene: see 88–91, 100–2, 112–13, 148–51. Compositor A or C sets 2–4 as verse too, however, which could indicate the scribe's or author's layout.
3 he's his wife's head see Eph. 5.23: 'For the husband is the wife's head, even as Christ is the head of the Church . . .'
5 snatches quibbles.

answer. Tomorrow morning are to die Claudio and Barnardine. Here is in our prison a common executioner, who in his office lacks a helper. If you will take it on you to assist him, it shall redeem you from your gyves. If not, you shall have your full time of imprisonment, and your deliverance with an unpitied whipping;   10
for you have been a notorious bawd.

POMPEY Sir, I have been an unlawful bawd time out of mind, but yet I will be content to be a lawful hangman: I would be glad to receive some instruction from my fellow partner.

PROVOST What ho, Abhorson! Where's Abhorson, there?   15

Enter ABHORSON

ABHORSON Do you call, sir?

PROVOST Sirrah, here's a fellow will help you tomorrow in your execution. If you think it meet, compound with him by the year and let him abide here with you; if not, use him for the present and dismiss him, he cannot plead his estimation with you: he   20
hath been a bawd.

ABHORSON A bawd, sir? Fie upon him, he will discredit our mystery!

PROVOST Go to, sir, you weigh equally: a feather will turn the scale.

Exit

POMPEY Pray, sir, by your good favour – for surely, sir, a good favour you have, but that you have a hanging look – do you call, sir, your   25
occupation a mystery?

ABHORSON Ay, sir, a mystery.

POMPEY Painting, sir, I have heard say, is a mystery; and your whores, sir, being members of my occupation, using painting, do prove my occupation a mystery; but what mystery there should   30
be in hanging, if I should be hanged, I cannot imagine.

ABHORSON Sir, it is a mystery.

POMPEY Proof.

ABHORSON Every true man's apparel fits your thief. If it be too little

34 If] *Capell; Clo.* If F

7 **common** public.
7 **office** duties.
9 **gyves** shackles, i.e. imprisonment.
10 **deliverance** release.
18 **compound** make an agreement.
20 **plead ... estimation** make claims for his worthiness (i.e. you need not pay him much).
22 **mystery** skilled trade (from Latin *ministerium*), distinct from the word meaning 'secret

rite' (which derives from Greek *mysterion*) which is played on equivocally here.
24 **favour** leave.
24 **favour** face.
25 **hanging look** downcast expression (with a quibble on his being a hangman, and another on the sense 'foreboding death by the halter').
29 **using painting** i.e painting their faces.
34–7 Capell is surely right to ascribe the rest of

for your thief, your true man thinks it big enough. If it be too big   35
for your thief, your thief thinks it little enough: so every true
man's apparel fits your thief.

Enter PROVOST

PROVOST Are you agreed?
POMPEY Sir, I will serve him, for I do find your hangman is a more
    penitent trade than your bawd: he doth oftener ask forgiveness.   40
PROVOST You, sirrah, provide your block and your axe tomorrow,
    four a clock.
ABHORSON Come on, bawd, I will instruct thee in my trade. Follow.
POMPEY I do desire to learn, sir, and I hope, if you have occasion to
    use me for your own turn, you shall find me yare. For truly, sir,   45
    for your kindness, I owe you a good turn.
PROVOST Call hither Barnardine and Claudio.

                      Exeunt [*Abhorson and Pompey*]
    Th'one has my pity; not a jot the other,
    Being a murderer, though he were my brother.

Enter CLAUDIO

    Look, here's the warrant, Claudio, for thy death.   50
    'Tis now dead midnight, and by eight tomorrow
    Thou must be made immortal. Where's Barnardine?
CLAUDIO As fast locked up in sleep as guiltless labour
    When it lies starkly in the traveller's bones.
    He will not wake.
PROVOST   Who can do good on him?   55

---

45 yare] *Theobald*; y'are F   47 SD] *Capell; Exit.* F (*after 46*)

---

this speech to Abhorson, though F gives it to
Pompey. Perhaps the compositor found the copy
confusing here. Abhorson needs the opportunity
to establish himself as a character in the scene. It
is not clear why Abhorson says 'thief' when he is
supposed to be talking about the hangman.
Perhaps the 'proof' applies to the hangman as
well as to the thief. The executioner received the
clothes of the executed man as part of his due.
Presumably he either wore them or, if they were
the wrong size, sold them.
  40 he . . . forgiveness the executioner always
asks forgiveness of the criminal.
  42 four Taken together with 51, presumably it
is Barnardine who is to be executed at four and
Claudio at eight (so Lever); yet this is the kind of
trivial slip that Shakespeare sometimes makes,
and which is rarely noticed in the theatre.
  45 your own turn Punning on the senses 'your

own purpose' and 'your own hanging' (turning
off).
  45 yare ready, nimble, dextrous.
  46 a good turn Alluding to the proverb 'one
good turn deserves another'. Evans sees an
allusion to other senses – sexual satisfaction
(Pompey being a bawd) and hanging, as at 45.
  51 dead profound (*OED* sv *adj* 26), absolute,
full (*OED* sv *adj* 31). Hart further suggests 'still as
death'. Compare *Ham.* 1.2.198.
  54 starkly stiffly. Compare Jonson, *Catiline*
4.73: 'a sleepe, as starke, as death'.
  54 traveller's Both he who journeys and he
who labours heavily. Commentators compare
Ecclesiastes 5.12: 'The sleep of him that trauel-
leth, is sweete' (1595 Geneva). The 1560 and the
1583 Geneva versions read 'trauaileth'.
  55 do good on produce an effect on.

Well, go, prepare yourself –
              [*Knocking within*]
                          But hark, what noise?
Heaven give your spirits comfort.

                                          [*Exit Claudio*]
              [*Knocking within*]
                          By and by!
I hope it is some pardon or reprieve
For the most gentle Claudio.

              Enter DUKE [*disguised as a friar*]

                          Welcome, father.
DUKE The best and wholesom'st spirits of the night   60
              Envelop you, good provost: who called here of late?
PROVOST None since the curfew rung.
DUKE Not Isabel?
PROVOST   No.
DUKE   They will then, ere't be long.
PROVOST What comfort is for Claudio?
DUKE There's some in hope.
PROVOST   It is a bitter deputy.   65
DUKE Not so, not so: his life is paralleled
              Even with the stroke and line of his great justice:
              He doth with holy abstinence subdue
              That in himself which he spurs on his power
              To qualify in others. Were he mealed with that   70
              Which he corrects, then were he tyrannous;

---

56 SD] *Rowe, subst.; not in* F   **57** SD.1] *Capell; not in* F   **57** SD.2] *NS; not in* F   **59** SD] *As Dyce; after* father F
62–5] *As Cam.; Pro.* None . . . rung. / *Duke.* Not *Isabell*? / *Pro.* No. / *Duke.* They . . . long. / *Pro.* What . . . *Claudio*? /
Duke. There's . . . hope. / *Pro.* It . . . Deputie. F

57 By and by Just a minute (called out to the person who knocks) (Evans).

60 Contrast the reference at 4.1.54 to the unhealthy 'vaporous night'. The Duke's greeting also serves to add emphasis to the time, the middle of the night, which is important to the atmosphere of this part of the play. Such direct allusions in the dialogue would have been reinforced by staging conventions for night scenes.

62–5 Lineation is difficult here, any arrangement other than short lines being open to some objection; yet the Cam. arrangement seems to find verse rhythms.

67 stroke and line stroke of a pen or a line (Johnson); but NS sees a quibble on the executioner's axe-stroke and the line of the hangman's rope. Perhaps 'paralleled' implies italic calligraphy or geometry's dry abstractions. The fluidity of the imagery is characteristic of the Duke.

70 qualify abate. The effect is almost bathetic coming after the urgent energy of 'spurs on his power'. The metaphor recalls Claudio's referring to Angelo at 1.2.141–3.

70 mealed spotted, stained (*OED* Meal v^3); NS suggests 'moaled', i.e. marked by a blemish or mole.

But this being so, he's just.

[*Knocking within*]

[*Exit Provost*]

Now are they come.

This is a gentle provost; seldom when

The steelèd gaoler is the friend of men.

[*Knocking within*]

How now, what noise? That spirit's possessed with haste   75

That wounds th'unsisting postern with these strokes.

[*Enter* PROVOST]

PROVOST There he must stay until the officer

Arrives to let him in: he is called up.

DUKE Have you no countermand for Claudio yet

But he must die tomorrow?

PROVOST   None, sir, none.   80

DUKE As near the dawning, provost, as it is,

You shall hear more ere morning.

PROVOST   Happily

You something know; yet I believe there comes

No countermand. No such example have we.

Besides, upon the very siege of justice   85

Lord Angelo hath to the public ear

Professed the contrary.

Enter a MESSENGER

This is his lordship's man.

72 SD.1] *Rowe, subst.; not in* F   72 SD.2] *Theobald, subst.; not in* F   74 SD] *Dyce, after Collier; not in* F   76 unsisting] F;
unassisting *Rowe;* unshifting *Capell;* resisting *Collier*   76 SD] *Theobald, subst.; not in* F   87–8 This . . . / DUKE And]
Rann, conj. Tyrrwhitt; Duke. This . . . / *Pro.* And F   87 lordship's] *Rowe;* Lords F

72 **this** i.e. his state of 'holy abstinence'.

72 SD.1 Compare the dramatic use of off-stage knocking in *Rom.* 3.3.70 ff. and *R2* 5.3.

73 **gentle** kindly.

74 **steelèd** hardened.

75 **spirit's . . . haste** An extravagant way of saying 'in a frantic hurry'; 'possessed' means inhabited or controlled by a demon (*OED* sv *ppl adj* 2). Presumably the Duke hopes such language will make his impersonation of a friar more plausible.

76 **unsisting** Probably a shortened form of 'unassisting' (Rowe) but 'resisting' is attractive.

The figure of speech is a little over-strained, being applied merely to a stout door.

81–2 **As . . . morning** i.e. even though it is near dawn you will hear news before dawn breaks. This seems to imply that a considerable time has elapsed since 51. By 92 we learn that 'it is almost day'. Shakespeare manipulates fictional narrative time for dramatic effect.

84 **No such . . . we** We have no other instances of such lenity.

85 **siege of justice** seat (*OED* Siege *sb* 1) of judgement. The phrase presumably carries no anticipatory allusion to the way Angelo will suffer

DUKE And here comes Claudio's pardon.

MESSENGER My lord hath sent you this note, and by me this further
charge – that you swerve not from the smallest article of it,   90
neither in time, matter, or other circumstance. Good morrow:
for, as I take it, it is almost day.

PROVOST I shall obey him.

[*Exit Messenger*]

DUKE [*Aside*] This is his pardon, purchased by such sin
For which the pardoner himself is in.   95
Hence hath offence his quick celerity,
When it is borne in high authority.
When vice makes mercy, mercy's so extended
That for the fault's love is th'offender friended.
Now, sir, what news?   100

PROVOST I told you: Lord Angelo, belike, thinking me remiss in
mine office, awakens me with this unwonted putting on,
methinks strangely: for he hath not used it before.

DUKE Pray you, let's hear.

PROVOST [*Reading*] *the letter* 'Whatsoever you may hear to the   105
contrary, let Claudio be executed by four of the clock, and in the
afternoon, Barnardine. For my better satisfaction let me have
Claudio's head sent me by five. Let this be duly performed with
a thought that more depends on it than we must yet deliver.
Thus fail not to do your office, as you will answer it at your peril.'   110
– What say you to this, sir?

DUKE What is that Barnardine who is to be executed in th'afternoon?

89–92] *As prose, Pope; as verse, F:* My . . . note, / And . . . charge; / That . . . it, / Neither . . . circumstance. /
Good . . . day. **93** SD] *Rowe; not in F* **94** SD] *Johnson; not in F* **101–3**] *As prose, Pope; as verse, F:* I . . . you: /
Lord . . . remisse / In . . . mee / With . . . strangely: / For . . . before. **105** SD] *Rowe, subst.; The Letter. F (as centred
SD)* **105–10** Whatsoever . . . peril] *Italic in F*

siege (*OED* sv *sb* 6) by just claimants in the final
scene.

88 The Provost has just declared his conviction
that the execution will not be counter-manded,
yet in F he at once guesses that the messenger
brings a pardon. Rann makes good sense locally,
but the F text may indicate revision during composition, Shakespeare seeing that focus must be
on the Duke, not the Provost. The Provost's
expectation of a pardon could be a first version,
replaced by 83–4 and by the Duke's expression
of confidence in a pardon.

94–5 i.e. the pardoner is as guilty as the one
pardoned.

96 quick celerity A tautologous phrase. Evans
compares 'swift celerity' at 5.1.387.

98 extended widened in scope (*OED* Extend
v 4c), stretched forcibly, strained (*OED* sv *v* 1).

99 That the offender is treated in a friendly
way because his fault is loved.

99 friended *OED* cites Camden (1605): 'As a
man is friended, so is the law ended.'

101 belike I suppose.

102 awakens . . . on puts this unwonted
pressure on me to act.

107 For . . . satisfaction To keep me better
informed (and with the further sense 'the better
to gratify my desire').

109 deliver make known.

110 as otherwise.

PROVOST A Bohemian born, but here nursed up and bred; one that is a prisoner nine years old.

DUKE How came it that the absent Duke had not either delivered 115 him to his liberty or executed him? I have heard it was ever his manner to do so.

PROVOST His friends still wrought reprieves for him: and indeed his fact, till now in the government of Lord Angelo, came not to an undoubtful proof. 120

DUKE It is now apparent?

PROVOST Most manifest, and not denied by himself.

DUKE Hath he borne himself penitently in prison? How seems he to be touched?

PROVOST A man that apprehends death no more dreadfully but as a 125 drunken sleep: careless, reckless, and fearless of what's past, present, or to come: insensible of mortality and desperately mortal.

DUKE He wants advice.

PROVOST He will hear none. He hath evermore had the liberty of the 130 prison: give him leave to escape hence, he would not. Drunk many times a day, if not many days entirely drunk. We have very oft awaked him, as if to carry him to execution, and showed him a seeming warrant for it. It hath not moved him at all.

DUKE More of him anon. There is written in your brow, provost, 135

113–14] *As prose, Pope; as verse,* F: A . . . bred, / One . . . old.   126 reckless] *Theobald;* wreaklesse F

113 **Bohemian** Bohemia was part of the Holy Roman Empire. In *Promos and Cassandra, Part 2* 2.3 Corvinus is styled 'King of *Hungarie* and *Boemia*'. Compare the dialogue at 1.2.1–5.
113 **here** i.e. in Vienna.
114 **nine years old** for nine years.
118 **His** i.e. Barnardine's.
119 **fact** crime.
124 **touched** affected. Compare 2.2.55.
125 **apprehends** imagines, anticipates (chiefly things adverse). Compare 3.1.77.
126 **sleep** Ironically recalling the Duke's observations to Claudio 3.1.17–19, 32–3.
126 **careless** without anxiety.
127–8 **insensible . . . mortal** (1) unconscious of his own imminent death and hopelessly committed to this world, (2) indifferent to the full meaning of death and in a state entailing spiritual death. A complex play is made upon different senses of 'mortal': (1) alive, pertaining to man as a creature of this earth (*OED* sv *adj* 7), (2) subject to or doomed to die (*OED* *adj* 1, 2), (3) of sin,

entailing spiritual death (*OED* *adj* 5). Here 'desperately' means 'enough to make one despair because so extreme' as well as 'hopelessly'. A further play may be supposed on 'insensible' as 'incapable of physical or mental feeling' – compare 54 and n.
129 **wants advice** needs (lacks) spiritual counsel.
130–1 **He . . . prison** He has always been permitted to go anywhere in the prison. Though in part ironic, the phrase 'liberty of' has a legal sense – 'privilege, immunity or right enjoyed by prescription or grant' – and *OED* (Liberty *sb* 7a) cites Fulbecke (1602): 'The Heluetians did bestow the liberties of their citie vpon Lewis the eleuenth.' English cities still bestow the honour of Freeman of the City (*OED* Freeman *sb* 2). Applying the term 'liberty' to Barnardine and prison stresses the thematic function of the prison scenes in the play as an ironic mirror of the whole society of Vienna.

honesty and constancy; if I read it not truly, my ancient skill beguiles me; but in the boldness of my cunning, I will lay myself in hazard. Claudio, whom here you have warrant to execute, is no greater forfeit to the law than Angelo who hath sentenced him. To make you understand this in a manifested effect, I crave but four days' respite: for the which, you are to do me both a present and a dangerous courtesy. 140

PROVOST Pray, sir, in what?

DUKE In the delaying death.

PROVOST Alack, how may I do it? Having the hour limited, and an express command, under penalty, to deliver his head in the view of Angelo? I may make my case as Claudio's to cross this in the smallest. 145

DUKE By the vow of mine order I warrant you. If my instructions may be your guide, let this Barnardine be this morning executed and his head borne to Angelo. 150

PROVOST Angelo hath seen them both and will discover the favour.

DUKE Oh, death's a great disguiser, and you may add to it: shave the head and tie the beard, and say it was the desire of the penitent to be so bared before his death. You know the course is common. If anything fall to you upon this, more than thanks and good fortune, by the saint whom I profess I will plead against it with my life. 155

PROVOST Pardon me, good father, it is against my oath.

149–51] *As prose, Pope; as verse,* F: By…you, / If…guide, / Let…executed, / And…Angelo. / Pro….both, / And…fauour. 154 tie] F; dye *White, conj. Thirlby; not in Collier, conj. Thirlby* 155 bared] *Malone;* bar'de F; barb'd F4

136–7 my ancient…me my long experience deceives me.
137–8 in the boldness…hazard I will be bold and on the basis of my skill take a risk.
139 no greater…than no worse a criminal than. Compare 2.2.73.
140 manifested effect clear demonstration.
141 four days' Compare 'two days' in 174. As Evans notes, 'it is difficult to account for *four*'. Compare 4.2.42 and n.
142 present immediate.
142 courtesy service, favour (*OED* sv *sb* 6).
145 limited fixed.
146–7 in…Angelo before the very eyes of Angelo.
147–8 I may…smallest I may be condemned like Claudio if I make the slightest contravention of this.

149 warrant you guarantee your safety.
152 discover the favour recognise the features.
154 tie Taken with 'bared' (155), Collier's suggestion (1875) that the compositor saw double ('tie the') is attractive. Omit 'tie' and 'no more is required: to shave head and beard would completely disguise'. If 'tie' is retained it must mean 'tie up short and tidy'. Johnson supposes this would give 'a very new air to that face, which had never been seen but with the beard loose, long and squalid'.
155 bared F4's reading might be related to 'tie' (154), making the beard as unobtrusive and tidy as possible.
155 course practice.
156 fall to befall.

DUKE Were you sworn to the Duke or to the deputy?   160
PROVOST To him, and to his substitutes.
DUKE You will think you have made no offence, if the Duke avouch
    the justice of your dealing?
PROVOST But what likelihood is in that?
DUKE Not a resemblance, but a certainty; yet since I see you fearful,   165
    that neither my coat, integrity, nor persuasion, can with ease
    attempt you, I will go further than I meant, to pluck all fears out
    of you: look you, sir, here is the hand and seal of the Duke. You
    know the character I doubt not, and the signet is not strange to
    you.   170
PROVOST I know them both.
DUKE The contents of this is the return of the Duke; you shall anon
    over-read it at your pleasure, where you shall find within these
    two days he will be here. This is a thing that Angelo knows not,
    for he this very day receives letters of strange tenor, perchance of   175
    the Duke's death, perchance entering into some monastery, but
    by chance nothing of what is writ. Look, th'unfolding star calls
    up the shepherd. Put not yourself into amazement how these
    things should be: all difficulties are but easy when they are
    known. Call your executioner, and off with Barnardine's head. I   180
    will give him a present shrift, and advise him for a better place.
    Yet you are amazed, but this shall absolutely resolve you. Come
    away, it is almost clear dawn.

                                                        [*Exeunt*]

183 SD] *Pope; Exit.* F

162 **avouch** uphold.

165 **resemblance** likelihood.

166 **coat** friar's robes.

166 **persuasion** i.e. the efforts I have made to persuade.

167 **attempt** tempt (*OED* sv *v* 5).

169 **character** handwriting; compare 1.1.27.

175 **strange** Perhaps, as in 3.1.24, 'new', or 'extraordinary' (*OED* sv *adj* 9), or 'obscure'.

175 **tenor** The general sense or meaning of a document.

177 **what is writ** direct authoritative commands. *OED* notes the legal sense of 'writ' as 'a written command . . . issued by a court in the name of the sovereign . . . enjoining the person or persons to whom it is addressed to do or refrain from doing some act specified therein'. (The

indirect obscure communication recalls that given to Angelo and Escalus by the Duke in the first scene.) Other interpretations of 'writ' include Hanmer's supposing that the letter is indicated by the Duke-as-Friar: 'writ here'. Collier proposed 'right' as emendation for 'writ'. Lever suggests that Shakespeare wrote 'writ is right' but the scribe mistook it for dittography, 'writ is writ', and hence emended.

177 **unfolding star** The star whose appearance bids the shepherd release his sheep from the fold (*OED* Unfolding *ppl adj*[2] 1).

179–80 **all . . . known** Proverbial; see Tilley D418.

181 **shrift** confession (made to a priest).

182 **resolve you** clear your doubts.

4.3 *Enter* POMPEY

POMPEY I am as well acquainted here as I was in our house of profession. One would think it were Mistress Overdone's own house, for here be many of her old customers. First, here's young Master Rash, he's in for a commodity of brown paper and old ginger, nine score and seventeen pounds, of which he made 5 five marks ready money: marry, then ginger was not much in request, for the old women were all dead. Then is there here one Master Caper, at the suit of Master Threepile the mercer, for some four suits of peach-coloured satin, which now 'peaches him a beggar. Then have we here young Dizie, and 10 young Master Deepvow, and Master Copperspur, and Master Starvelackey the rapier and dagger man, and young Dropheir that killed lusty Pudding, and Master Forthright the tilter, and

Act 4, Scene 3   4.3] *Scena Tertia.* F   13 Forthright] *Warburton; Forthlight* F

Act 4, Scene 3

1 am as well acquainted have as wide an acquaintance.

1–2 house of profession house of trade, i.e. prostitution. Ironically echoing the phrase 'house of correction' (*OED* Correction 4d). An Act of 1575–6 provided for the establishment of houses of correction to set to work and punish those taken as rogues. No doubt there is further ironic allusion in 'profession' to its senses: (1) a vocation in which professed knowlege of learning or science is used, as in divinity, law, medicine or the military (*OED* Profession *sb* 6a), (2) the fact of being professed in a religious order (*OED* sv *sb* 1).

4 Rash His name implies imprudent haste, and the terms he accepted when borrowing money are extortionate. Evans explains that 'a moneylender could circumvent the statute limiting interest on loans to ten percent by forcing a borrower to take a substantial part of the loan in some "commodity" at a valuation determined by the lender. Rash has had to agree to a valuation of 197 pounds on merchandise which on resale has brought little more than three pounds (a mark was two-thirds of a pound).'

6–7 ginger...women 'Candied, greene, or condited' ginger was considered to be an aphrodisiac according to Gerard's *Herball* (1633 edn), p. 62. Compare *TN* 2.3.117–18.

8 Threepile Velvet. See 1.2.27 and n.

10 'peaches denounces (with a pun on 'peach' (9)).

10 Dizie Either 'giddy, thoughtless', or corrupted from 'dicey', i.e. a dice-player, a gambler.

The '-zie' difficulty recalls 'prenzie', 3.1.93, 96.

11 Deepvow One who vows or swears deeply. Eccles compares Chapman, *All Fools* (1605), where a prodigal in prison for debt 'deeply swears' he will repay 40 crowns next week.

11 Copperspur Simulating gold, like Falstaff's grandfather's seal-ring (Hart).

12 Starvelackey He cannot or will not pay his menial servant or footman.

12 rapier and dagger man These are the weapons worn by the young gentlemen in *Rom*. They fight with rapiers; Juliet kills herself with Romeo's dagger.

12 Dropheir 'Drop' has the sense 'cause to droop or pine' as well as 'cause to die'. Hart supposed a usurer to be meant, and the conventional gaunt appearance of the usurer seen to contrast with the fat and lusty 'Pudding', embodiment of good living. Although the image of gaunt Usury piercing lusty Pudding is a telling one, it should be noted that 'pudding' also has the sense 'dull, stupid person' (*OED* sv *sb* 11 cites G. Harvey (1593): 'the bag pudding of fooles') and there may be quibble on hair/heir, loss of hair being a side effect of treatment for venereal disease (see 1.2.28 n.). Lever thinks 'Dropheir' to be like the 'bawd-gallant' in Middleton, *Father Hubberd's Tales*, 'a most glorious-spangled gallant ...that fed upon young landlords, riotous sons and heirs ...and would not stick to be a bawd or pandar to such'.

13 Forthright Alluding to the handling of a lance at tilt, a horizontal thrust. The word is a noun in *Tro*. 3.3.158 and *Temp*. 3.3.3.

brave Master Shoetie the great traveller, and wild Halfcan that
stabbed Pots, and I think forty more, all great doers in our trade,   15
and are now 'for the Lord's sake'.

Enter ABHORSON

ABHORSON Sirrah, bring Barnardine hither.

POMPEY Master Barnardine, you must rise and be hanged, Master
    Barnardine!

ABHORSON What ho, Barnardine!   20

BARNARDINE [*Within*] A pox o'your throats, who makes that noise
    there? What are you?

POMPEY Your friends, sir, the hangman: You must be so good, sir, to
    rise and be put to death.

BARNARDINE [*Within*] Away, you rogue, away, I am sleepy.   25

ABHORSON Tell him he must awake, and that quickly, too.

POMPEY Pray, Master Barnardine, awake till you are executed, and
    sleep afterwards.

ABHORSON Go in to him, and fetch him out.

POMPEY He is coming, sir, he is coming, I hear his straw rustle.   30

Enter BARNARDINE

ABHORSON Is the axe upon the block, sirrah?

POMPEY Very ready, sir.

14 Shoetie] *Capell, subst.; Shootie* F 15 Pots] *Treated as a proper name by Rowe; as an unitalicised plural noun in* F   16
'for . . . sake'] *Rann;* for . . . sake F   18–19] *As prose, Pope;* Mr . . . hang'd, / Mr *Barnardine.* F   21 SD] *Barnardine
within* F (*as centred SD*)   23–4] *As prose, Pope; as verse,* F: Your . . . Hangman: / You . . . death.   25 SD] *Theobald; not in*
F   26] *As prose, Pope; as verse,* F: Tell . . . awake, / And . . . too.

14 Shoetie The long ribbons with which shoes
were tied (a yard and a quarter each) developed
into rosettes, ornamental and sometimes concealing small ties beneath them (Linthicum).

14 Halfcan Jonson, *Every Man in his Humour*
2.2.49–50, has a reference to 'two cannes of
beere'. Presumably the can was the larger measure, as with today's pint measure of beer. In *Oth.*
2.3 the terms cup and canikin (a small can) are
used interchangeably as terms for drinking-
vessels (in *Oth.* for wine). It seems that a half-can
might have had the colloquial sense of the
modern English 'half-pint', applied to a person of
diminutive size. 'Halfcan' may also imply that he
is unable to take his liquor, becoming quarrel-
some after only one drink.

15 Pots Some commentators suppose this not
to be a proper name but simply referring to the
drinking-vessels which the drunken Halfcan
attacked. Yet we may suspect nevertheless that
'Pots' = pot-boy, one employed at a public house

to attend to pots and serve liquor. Compare
'boots' (*OED* Boots[1] 1), one employed to clean
the boots.

15 doers fornicators. See note to Mistress
Overdone in the List of Characters, p. 78 above.

16 'for . . . sake' The cry of prisoners begging
for charity.

18 rise and be hanged 'rise' = (1) get up, (2)
mount the scaffold. Also, 'be hanged' is an
imprecation (*OED* Hang *v* 3c). The joke is varied
at 24, 'rise and be put to death'.

30 straw Either sewn into a primitive mattress
or loose, as a cheap aid to repose. Rushes were
also strewn on the stage in the theatres, and on
the floors of houses (see *Rom.* 1.4.36). A humorous analogy between Barnardine and a stabled
or caged animal (where straw would also be
provided) is often emphasised in stage productions by giving Barnardine an outrageously wild
appearance.

31 axe Pompey has been speaking of hanging

BARNARDINE How now, Abhorson, what's the news with you?

ABHORSON Truly, sir, I would desire you to clap into your prayers; for look you, the warrant's come. 35

BARNARDINE You rogue, I have been drinking all night, I am not fitted for't.

POMPEY Oh, the better, sir; for he that drinks all night, and is hanged betimes in the morning, may sleep the sounder all the next day. 40

Enter DUKE [*disguised as a friar*]

ABHORSON Look you, sir, here comes your ghostly father, do we jest now, think you?

DUKE Sir, induced by my charity, and hearing how hastily you are to depart, I am come to advise you, comfort you, and pray with you.

BARNARDINE Friar, not I. I have been drinking hard all night, and I 45 will have more time to prepare me, or they shall beat out my brains with billets. I will not consent to die this day, that's certain.

DUKE Oh, sir, you must; and therefore I beseech you
    Look forward on the journey you shall go. 50

BARNARDINE I swear I will not die today for any man's persuasion.

DUKE But hear you –

BARNARDINE Not a word. If you have anything to say to me, come to my ward, for thence will not I today. *Exit*

Enter PROVOST

33] *As Pope; How . . . Abhorson? / What's . . . you?* F   36–7] *As prose, Pope; as verse,* F*: You . . . night, / I . . . for't.*
44] *As prose,* F3*; as verse,* F*: Comfort . . . you*   49–50] F*; as prose,* F3

yet here the mode of execution is beheading. Possibly the confusion is meant as a deliberate comic effect by Shakespeare. Escalus associates the two modes of execution in 2.1.204. Hanging was the penalty for common felons; beheading was for gentlemen (Lever).

34 clap into 'to enter with alacrity and briskness upon anything' (Johnson).

39–40 hanged . . . next day These sentiments are echoed by the gaoler in *Cym.* 5.4. Compare the proverb 'He rises over soon who is hanged ere noon' (Tilley N208).

41 ghostly spiritual (as in *Rom* 2.3.45). Possibly also an instance of black humour, in view of Barnardine's imminent death. Hamlet threatens to 'make a ghost' of anyone who tries to restrain him from following the ghost in 1.4. Compare 5.1.126 and n.

47 billets small wooden logs.

50 journey i.e. out of the world. Hamlet refers to death as 'The undiscovered country from whose bourn / No traveller returns' (*Ham* 3.1.78–9).

51 persuasion faith, conviction (with reference to the Duke-as-Friar) as well as 'the act of persuading'.

54 ward section of a prison (like the section of a hospital: *OED* Ward *sb*² 17b). Barnardine has the 'liberty' of the prison (4.2.130–1) and roams it at will, so he stipulates where he may be found. There is perhaps irony in a prisoner thus choosing to spend some time in his own cell, almost as if it were his club, but Barnardine's sense of dignity is apparent.

DUKE Unfit to live or die: oh gravel heart!   55
    After him, fellows, bring him to the block.
                 [Exeunt Abhorson and Pompey]
PROVOST Now, sir, how do you find the prisoner?
DUKE A creature unprepared, unmeet for death,
    And to transport him, in the mind he is,
    Were damnable.
PROVOST   Here in the prison, father,   60
    There died this morning of a cruel fever
    One Ragozine, a most notorious pirate,
    A man of Claudio's years, his beard and head
    Just of his colour. What if we do omit
    This reprobate till he were well inclined,   65
    And satisfy the deputy with the visage
    Of Ragozine, more like to Claudio?
DUKE Oh, 'tis an accident that heaven provides:
    Dispatch it presently, the hour draws on
    Prefixed by Angelo. See this be done   70
    And sent according to command, whiles I
    Persuade this rude wretch willingly to die.
PROVOST This shall be done, good father, presently:
    But Barnardine must die this afternoon,
    And how shall we continue Claudio,   75
    To save me from the danger that might come
    If he were known alive?
DUKE   Let this be done:

56 SD] *Capell; not in* F 77–80] *Knight;* If … aliue? / *Duke.* Let … done, / Put … *Claudio,* / Ere … greeting /
To … finde F

55 **gravel heart** flint heart (Schmidt). Religious teaching falls on stony ground in the case of
Barnardine.
  56 Johnson believed the line to be the Provost's
and the SH may have been incorrectly placed by
the compositor at 57 instead of 56.
  59 **transport** i.e. execute (death imagined as a
journey, as at 50).
  62 **Ragozine** Ragusa, a port on the Adriatic,
gave its name to the character often found in
sixteenth-century Italian comedy, where he is
Raguseo, usually a seafarer.
  63–4 **his beard … colour** Hence there
would be no need for shaving.
  64 **omit** leave disregarded.
  65 **well inclined** Presumably the Provost

means 'well-prepared spiritually' but an audience
may recall the common usage of 'inclined',
'disposed in favour of', 'in the mood for', which
corresponds to Barnardine's attitude of insisting
on determining for himself as the mood takes
him when or if he is to be executed. This topsy-
turvy or Carnivalesque principle in the play is
discussed at pp. 28–30, 38–9 above.
  70 **Prefixed** Fixed in advance.
  73 **presently** at once.
  75 **continue** i.e. retain alive (a rare use of the
verb in a transitive sense).
  76 In 5.1.450–9 the Duke interrogates the
Provost with apparent severity (only for Angelo's
benefit) about the warrant for execution.

Put them in secret holds, both Barnardine and Claudio.
Ere twice the sun hath made his journal greeting
To yonder generation you shall find   80
Your safety manifested.
PROVOST I am your free dependant.
DUKE Quick, dispatch, and send the head to Angelo.

Exit [Provost]

Now will I write letters to Angelo,
The provost he shall bear them, whose contents   85
Shall witness to him I am near at home
And that by great injunctions I am bound
To enter publicly. Him I'll desire
To meet me at the consecrated fount
A league below the city; and from thence,   90
By cold gradation and well-balanced form
We shall proceed with Angelo.

Enter PROVOST [with a head]

PROVOST Here is the head, I'll carry it myself.
DUKE Convenient is it. Make a swift return,
For I would commune with you of such things   95
That want no ear but yours.
PROVOST   I'll make all speed.   *Exit*
ISABELLA [*Within*] Peace, ho, be here.
DUKE The tongue of Isabel. She's come to know
If yet her brother's pardon be come hither:
But I will keep her ignorant of her good   100

---

80 yonder] *Rowe;* yond F; th'under *Hanmer* 83 SD] *Pope; Exit.* F (*after 82*) 91 well-balanced] weale-ballanc'd F
92 SD *with a head*] *Dyce, subst.; not in* F 97 SD] *Isabell within* F (*as centred* SD)

---

78 **holds** cells.

80 **yonder generation** Malone explains 'yonder' as meaning that the sun greets only those outside the gaol. Johnson, assuming 'generation' to mean 'those now living on earth', supported Hanmer's reading 'th'under generation', all mankind under the sun. In support of Malone, Howard-Hill notes that Crane, the scribe, 'who was apt to omit terminal letters, is as likely as Compositor B to have truncated "yonder"'.

82 **free dependant** willing servant.

84 **Angelo** Lever believes 'Varrius' was intended.

84–90 Lever notes that the Provost bears no letters, does not in fact return, and Angelo meets

the Duke at the city gates, not the consecrated fount. See the Textual Analysis, pp. 202–3 below.

91 **By cold gradation** Coolly, step by step.

91 **well-balanced form** due observance of proper forms. Some commentators suppose F's spelling 'weale' signifies 'the public good'.

95 **commune** talk. The verb has religious overtones, possibly meant as part of a distinctive idiolect for the 'Friar'.

96 **That . . . yours** Fit for your ears only.

100–2 Johnson rightly comments 'A better reason might have been given. It was necessary to keep Isabella in ignorance, that she might with more keenness accuse the Deputy.' The Duke's explanation offers virtually a playwright's view of

To make her heavenly comforts of despair
When it is least expected.

Enter ISABELLA

ISABELLA Ho, by your leave.
DUKE Good morning to you, fair and gracious daughter.
ISABELLA The better given me by so holy a man.   105
    Hath yet the deputy sent my brother's pardon?
DUKE He hath released him, Isabel, from the world:
    His head is off, and sent to Angelo.
ISABELLA Nay, but it is not so!
DUKE   It is no other.
    Show your wisdom, daughter, in your close patience.   110
ISABELLA Oh, I will to him and pluck out his eyes!
DUKE You shall not be admitted to his sight.
ISABELLA Unhappy Claudio, wretched Isabel,
    Injurious world, most damnèd Angelo!
DUKE This nor hurts him nor profits you a jot.   115
    Forbear it therefore, give your cause to heaven.
    Mark what I say, which you shall find
    By every syllable a faithful verity:
    The Duke comes home tomorrow – nay, dry your eyes –
    One of our covent, and his confessor,   120
    Gives me this instance. Already he hath carried
    Notice to Escalus and Angelo,
    Who do prepare to meet him at the gates,
    There to give up their power. If you can pace your wisdom
    In that good path that I would wish it go,   125
    And you shall have your bosom on this wretch,
    Grace of the Duke, revenges to your heart,

102–3] F; *as one line, Dyce* 109–10] *As Steevens*[3]; *Isa.* Nay . . . so. / *Duke.* It . . . other, / Shew . . . patience. F
120 covent] F

---

the supreme importance of surprise reversal from
despair to comfort.
  103 F gives Isabella a short line to announce
herself at 97 and so it seems appropriate that her
repetition at 103 should also interrupt the verse.
  105 Isabella's simple trust in the 'Friar' ironically contrasts with his calculating speech at
98–102.
  108 His head is off Hart (1905) notes that the
Duke 'spurs on' Isabella's vengeance with this
cruelly direct statement.

110 close uncommunicative.
111 Lever notes parallels to Cinthio's play
Epitia, 3.2 and 3.5.
112 shall will.
120 covent An earlier form of 'convent'.
121 instance proof.
124 pace train to pace (as of a horse), proceed
with measured pace (*OED* sv *v* 4).
126 bosom heart's desire.

                    And general honour.
ISABELLA   I am directed by you.
DUKE This letter then to Friar Peter give,
        'Tis that he sent me of the Duke's return.   130
        Say by this token I desire his company
        At Mariana's house tonight. Her cause and yours
        I'll perfect him withal, and he shall bring you
        Before the Duke; and to the head of Angelo
        Accuse him home and home. For my poor self,   135
        I am combinèd by a sacred vow
        And shall be absent. Wend you with this letter:
        Command these fretting waters from your eyes
        With a light heart; trust not my holy order
        If I pervert your course. Who's here?   140

Enter LUCIO

LUCIO Good even; friar, where's the provost?
DUKE Not within, sir.
LUCIO Oh pretty Isabella, I am pale at mine heart to see thine eyes so
        red: thou must be patient. I am fain to dine and sup with water
        and bran; I dare not for my head fill my belly, one fruitful meal   145
        would set me to't. But they say the Duke will be here tomorrow.
        By my troth, Isabel, I loved thy brother; if the old fantastical
        Duke of dark corners had been at home, he had lived.
                                                        [*Exit Isabella*]

141] *As prose, Hudson; as verse,* F: Good'euen; / Frier . . . Prouost?   148 SD] *Theobald; not in* F

130 **of** about.
133 **perfect** fully inform.
134 **to . . . Angelo** without any reserve or fear
of Angelo's person or power (see *Ado* 5.1.62);
directly to his face (*OED* Head *sb* 38).
135 **home and home** The repetition acts as an
intensifier: 'up to the hilt', 'right to the heart'.
136 **combinèd** bound by oath (see 3.1.211).
The language is slightly strange – perhaps
Shakespeare fuses 'combine' and 'bind' – possibly representing the 'Friar''s idiolect, or calling
attention to the element of blurring or obscuring
inherent in the Duke-as-Friar's role.
137 **Wend** Go.
138 **fretting** corroding (figurative, as in *Lear*
1.4.285: 'tears fret channels in her cheeks').

141 **Good even** This conflicts with the Duke's
'morning' at 104. See the Textual Analysis,
pp. 202–3 below.
144 **fain** compelled.
144–5 **water and bran** Thirlby compares *LLL*
1.1.301 where this is the punishment for lechery.
145 **for** to save.
146 **set . . . to't** prompt me to commit lechery.
147–8 **old fantastical . . . corners** (1) 'old'
implies familiarity rather than age. (2) Lever
thinks the phrase might have been suggested by
Whetstone, *A Mirror for Magistrates of Cities*
(1584), sig. A3ᵛ, 'visible Lightes in obscure
Corners'. Eccles compares Jonson, *Discoveries* 59:
'making a little winter-love in a darke corner'.
148 **had lived** would have lived.

DUKE Sir, the Duke is marvellous little beholding to your reports,
but the best is, he lives not in them.   150
LUCIO Friar, thou knowest not the Duke so well as I do: he's a better
woodman than thou tak'st him for.
DUKE Well; you'll answer this one day. Fare ye well.
LUCIO Nay, tarry, I'll go along with thee. I can tell thee pretty tales of
the Duke.   155
DUKE You have told me too many of him already, sir, if they be true;
if not true, none were enough.
LUCIO I was once before him for getting a wench with child.
DUKE Did you such a thing?
LUCIO Yes, marry, did I; but I was fain to forswear it, they would else   160
have married me to the rotten medlar.
DUKE Sir, your company is fairer than honest, rest you well.
LUCIO By my troth, I'll go with thee to the lane's end. If bawdy talk
offend you, we'll have very little of it. Nay, friar, I am a kind of
burr, I shall stick.   165

Exeunt

4.4 *Enter* ANGELO *and* ESCALUS

ESCALUS Every letter he hath writ hath disvouched other.
ANGELO In most uneven and distracted manner. His actions show
much like to madness; pray heaven his wisdom be not tainted.
And why meet him at the gates, and redeliver our authorities
there?   5

154–5] *As prose, Pope; as verse,* F: Nay...thee, / I...Duke.   160–1] *As prose, Pope; as verse,* F: Yes...it, / They...Medlar.   Act 4, Scene 4   4.4] *Scena Quarta.* F   4 redeliver] *Capell;* re- / liver F

149 **beholding** obliged.
150 **he lives not in them** his life is not as you report it.
152 **woodman** hunter of women.
161 **rotten medlar** i.e. prostitute. A 'medlar' was a fruit like a small brown-skinned apple, eaten when decayed to a soft, pulpy state. There was a usual quibble on 'meddler', one who indulges in sexual activity. The proverb (Tilley M863) 'medlars are never good till they be rotten' conveys the equivocal sense.
162 **rest you well** farewell to you.
165 **burr ... stick** A proverbial phrase (Tilley B724): 'to stick like a burr'.

Act 4, Scene 4
1 Hart (1905) noted a parallel to the last act of Jonson's *Sejanus*, where the sending of letters immediately leads to the catastrophe of the play, and also that the Duke's public profession of honour to Angelo parallels that of Tiberius (via Macro) to Sejanus. For a fuller exploration of the significance of parallels to *Sejanus*, see pp. 23–4, 44–7 above.
1 **disvouched** contradicted, disavowed.
3 **tainted** infected with (mental) disease.
4 **redeliver our authorities** give back the power conferred on us. Eccles notes 'reliver' to be a legal term (*OED* sv *v*, 'to give up again,

ESCALUS I guess not.

ANGELO And why should we proclaim it in an hour before his
entering, that if any crave redress of injustice they should exhibit
their petitions in the street?

ESCALUS He shows his reason for that: to have a dispatch of   10
complaints, and to deliver us from devices hereafter, which shall
then have no power to stand against us.

ANGELO Well; I beseech you let it be proclaimed betimes i'th'morn.
I'll call you at your house. Give notice to such men of sort and
suit as are to meet him.   15

ESCALUS I shall, sir. Fare you well.

ANGELO Good night.

Exit [Escalus]

    This deed unshapes me quite, makes me unpregnant
And dull to all proceedings. A deflowered maid,
And by an eminent body that enforced   20
The law against it? But that her tender shame
Will not proclaim against her maiden loss,

---

17 SD] Capell; *Exit*. F (*after 16*)

restore'). Cotgrave explains the French *relivrer* as
'To redeliver'. F nevertheless may be an error, a
syllable being omitted by oversight induced by
the line-break: on the other hand, elsewhere are
the forms 'disvouched' for 'disavouched' and
'ignomy' for 'ignominy'. Could all three be com-
positorial misreadings of the manuscript?

  7 in an hour leaving a clear hour (Lever).

  8 exhibit officially present.

  10 dispatch prompt settlement.

  11 devices contrived plots.

  14–15 sort and suit men of rank (*OED* Sort
*sb*² 2b) with a retinue (*OED* Suit *sb* 16).

  18 unshapes confounds, destroys (figurative).

  18–32 Angelo's guilt for the death of Claudio
(as he supposes) and the rape of Isabella,
repressed during his discussion with Escalus, is
here confessed in a tightly strained soliloquy.
This is the only occasion on which he speaks of
his personal reaction to the 'bed-trick' in which,
it should be recalled, he loses his own virginity
while committing (in his own mind) rape. The
speech expresses his sense of the inseparability of
his political potency, as Deputy, and his sexual
potency, both no sooner discovered than lost
through the crime of the ransom and the betrayal.
The 'deed' which he says 'unshapes' him is both
the killing of Claudio and the rape (as public
betrayals of his duty as Deputy they are in-

separable in his mind). At the same time the
'deed' is the personal sexual act (so Pompey uses
the verb 'done' in 1.2.72–3). After coitus comes
male detumescence ('unshapes') and proverbial
post-coital dullness ('makes me unpregnant').
Guilt too leaves him bereft of resource, dull of
wit, in confronting the crisis of the Duke's return.
The strong awareness of his own body and
physiology is further apparent in the unconscious
ambiguity of the syntax in 'A deflowered maid /
And by an eminent body that enforced /' (where
the line-end seems also to make 'enforced' relate
back to 'maid'), and in the words 'eminent body',
'enforced', 'tender shame', 'credent bulk',
'touch', 'dangerous sense', and the collocation of
'tane' and 'receiving'. The unconsciousness of
the sexual play in the language witnesses to
Angelo's deep disturbance.

  18 unpregnant The negative form of 'pregnant', which can mean 'quick of wit, full of ideas,
apt', here having the primary sense 'dull', as in
Ham 2.2.568.

  20 eminent exalted, dignified in rank or
station (*OED* says this is the first instance of the
word applied to a person).

  20 body person (with a quibble, as discussed in
18–32 n. above).

  21 it i.e. fornication.

  22 maiden loss loss of virginity.

How might she tongue me? Yet reason dares her no;
For my authority bears of a credent bulk,
That no particular scandal once can touch   25
But it confounds the breather. He should have lived,
Save that his riotous youth with dangerous sense
Might in the times to come have tane revenge
By so receiving a dishonoured life
With ransom of such shame. Would yet he had lived.   30
Alack, when once our grace we have forgot,
Nothing goes right: we would, and we would not.   *Exit*

4.5 *Enter* DUKE [*in his own robes*] *and* FRIAR PETER

DUKE These letters at fit time deliver me.
The provost knows our purpose and our plot.
The matter being afoot, keep your instruction
And hold you ever to our special drift,
Though sometimes you do blench from this to that   5

---

24 bears of] F; bears a *Theobald*   **Act 4, Scene 5**   4.5] *Scena Quinta.* F   **0** SD *in his own robes*] *Rowe, subst.; not in*
F   1] *Johnson adds* SD *Giving letters.*

---

23 tongue assail with words, denounce.

23 dares her no frightens her into saying nothing; 'dare' = 'to daze, paralyse' (*OED* Dare v^2 5), as (in fowling) 'to dare larks'.

24 bears of a Theobald seeks to correct the grammar, but Shakespeare conflates (perhaps) 'bears' and 'consists of', and in any case the sense is clear. Lever proposes 'bears so', assuming a slip of the pen in the MS. and a compositor's addition of 'a'.

24 credent bulk great size having unquestionable credit; 'bulk' connotes especial largeness of the body, 'credent' recurs in *WT* 1.2 in the sense 'plausible'.

26 breather person who speaks it.

27 sense Johnson suggests 'quickness or keenness of perception'; Empson thinks 'sensuality is the idea that comes first in his mind'. Certainly Angelo is thinking about Claudio's sensuality, which infringed the edict, but he is also preoccupied with his own sensuality which motivated the ransom. The uppermost sense is surely, as Johnson says, 'keen perception', since this could in time to come have enabled Claudio to see the need for vengeance and to carry it out (to summarise 27–30).

32 we would . . . not Echoing Rom. 7.19: 'For

I do not the good thing, which I would, but the evil, which I would not, that do I.'

Act 4, Scene 5

1 These letters Commentators offer conflicting explanations, Johnson objecting that 'Peter never delivers the letters, but tells his story without any credentials. The poet forgot the plot which he had formed.' Lever supposes the letters to be credentials to be presented to Flavius, Valencius, and the rest, and NS points out that 'deliver me' may mean 'deliver for me', not 'to me'. At all events the reference to the letters suggests busy preparations and so arouses audience expectation, and more specifically may serve to alert knowing members of an audience to a parallel with Act 5 of *Sejanus* where the Deputy is destroyed by letters.

4 drift aim or intention.

5 blench swerve (*OED* sv v^1 2); Johnson suggests 'shrink', the present day's surviving sense, which at least corresponds to the shocks Act 5 has in store. Since the audience here does not learn what 'our special drift' is, they are not given the reassurance necessary to view the Duke's behaviour in Act 5 without real anxiety, until his unhooding by Lucio.

> As cause doth minister. Go call at Flavius' house,
> And tell him where I stay; give the like notice
> To Valencius, Rowland, and to Crassus,
> And bid them bring the trumpets to the gate.
> But send me Flavius first.

FRIAR PETER It shall be speeded well. [*Exit*] 10

Enter VARRIUS

DUKE I thank thee, Varrius, thou hast made good haste.
  Come, we will walk, there's other of our friends
  Will greet us here anon, my gentle Varrius.

Exeunt

4.6 *Enter* ISABELLA *and* MARIANA

ISABELLA To speak so indirectly I am loath;
  I would say the truth, but to accuse him so
  That is your part, yet I am advised to do it:
  He says, to veil full purpose.

MARIANA   Be ruled by him.

ISABELLA Besides, he tells me that if peradventure 5
  He speak against me on the adverse side

6 Flavius'] *Rowe; Flavia's* F **10**] *As one line, Steevens*[3]; But . . . first. / Peter. It . . . well. F **10** SD.1] *Theobald; not in* F **Act 4, Scene 6 4.6**] *Scena Sexta.* F **4** veil] vaile F

6 As . . . minister As events suggest.

6 Flavius' Evidently, as 7 shows, male. Law comments that Shakespeare is remembering North's Plutarch: Flavius is a tribune in *JC* and a steward in *Tim.*; the life of Crassus is in Plutarch, and there too Varrius is a drinking companion of Antony. These figures who have no speaking parts give an impression of a social context; nevertheless their Latin form of names is odd. Admittedly, none of the names in the play strikes a typically Viennese note; possibly the Latin form has some connection with Shakespeare's conscious use of Jonson's *Sejanus* at this point. There may have been revision to the text affecting these characters; see my discussion in the Textual Analysis, pp. 202–3 below.

9 trumpets i.e. trumpeters; compare *Tro.* 4.5.6. The preparations for the Royal Entry to the city in Whetstone's play are highly elaborate (see pp. 11 above) and Shakespeare may have expected the staging at the King's Men's performance at the Globe to be more complex than what seems suggested here. The actual Royal Entry to the city of London by James I was elaborate, and most of the original audience could have witnessed it.

Act 4, Scene 6

1 indirectly far from the truth. Isabella is to maintain the deception that it was she, not Mariana, who gave herself to Angelo.

4 veil conceal. Mariana enters wearing an actual veil over her face in 5.1.167, as the dialogue shows.

5–6 Thirlby acutely notices that 'he' should refer to 'Friar Lodowick' who is not rough with Isabella, whereas the Duke in his own person is so; thus the warning would only make sense coming from the Duke *in propria persona*. Shakespeare appears to have made a slip, unless Friar Peter is meant by 'he'.

I should not think it strange, for 'tis a physic
That's bitter to sweet end.

        Enter FRIAR PETER

MARIANA I would Friar Peter –
ISABELLA   Oh peace, the friar is come.
FRIAR PETER Come, I have found you out a stand most fit,   10
    Where you may have such vantage on the Duke
    He shall not pass you. Twice have the trumpets sounded.
    The generous and gravest citizens
    Have hent the gates, and very near upon
    The Duke is ent'ring; therefore hence, away.   15

                                Exeunt

5.1 *Enter* DUKE [*in his own robes*], VARRIUS, LORDS, ANGELO,
ESCALUS, LUCIO, [PROVOST, OFFICERS,] CITIZENS, *at several doors*

DUKE My very worthy cousin, fairly met.
    Our old and faithful friend, we are glad to see you.
ANGELO *and* ESCALUS Happy return be to your royal grace.
DUKE Many and hearty thankings to you both:
    We have made enquiry of you, and we hear   5
    Such goodness of your justice that our soul
    Cannot but yield you forth to public thanks
    Forerunning more requital.
ANGELO   You make my bonds still greater.

8–9] *As Steevens*³; That's . . . end. / *Enter Peter.* / *Mar.* I . . . *Peter* F; That's . . . Peter – / *Isa.* Oh . . . come. *Lever*
12] *One line, Pope;* He . . . you: / Twice . . . sounded. F 15] *One line, Pope;* The . . . entring: / Therefore . . . away. F
Act 5, Scene 1 5.1] *Actus Quintus. Scæna Prima.* F 0 SD.2 ESCALUS] F2; *Esculus* F 0 SD.2 PROVOST, OFFICERS]
Capell, subst.; not in F 8] *One line, Steevens*³; Forerunning . . . requital. / *Ang.* You . . . greater. F

10 stand place to stand.
11 have such vantage on be so advantageously placed (to intercept).
13 generous Abbott 398 shows that the
superlative governs both 'generous' and 'gravest',
hence 'most high-born and dignified'.
14 hent arrived at, taken up position at (*OED*
Hent *v* 3b).
14 near upon soon (i.e. close on their arrival).

Act 5 Scene 1
0 SD The direction *at several doors* is conventional and may here indicate some differences
between the timing of entry of different groups,
especially if some attempt is made to represent a
crowd, with Isabella advantageously placed to
make her appeal, and if the Duke's formal entry is
to be marked by formal dignity, with trumpets
and ceremonial involving the Deputies Angelo
and Escalus, who greet him in unison.
1 cousin Used by a sovereign in addressing a
nobleman: flattery of Angelo?
2 friend The Duke greets Escalus as of lesser
dignity but warmer intimacy.
7–8 Contorted expression presumably meaning 'cannot but concede to public demand by
handing you over to be thanked by them, before I
myself give you further reward'.
8 bonds obligation.

DUKE Oh, your desert speaks loud, and I should wrong it
    To lock it in the wards of covert bosom   10
    When it deserves with characters of brass
    A forted residence 'gainst the tooth of time
    And razure of oblivion. Give me your hand
    And let the subject see, to make them know
    That outward courtesies would fain proclaim   15
    Favours that keep within. Come, Escalus,
    You must walk by us on our other hand:
    And good supporters are you.

Enter FRIAR PETER *and* ISABELLA

FRIAR PETER Now is your time. Speak loud, and kneel before him.
ISABELLA Justice, oh royal Duke! Vail your regard   20
    Upon a wronged – I would fain have said a maid.
    Oh worthy prince, dishonour not your eye
    By throwing it on any other object
    Till you have heard me in my true complaint
    And given me justice, justice, justice, justice!   25
DUKE Relate your wrongs: in what? By whom? Be brief.

13 me] F3; we F 18–19] *As Pope*; And . . . you. / *Enter Peter and Isabella.* / *Peter.* Now . . . time / Speake . . . him.
F 26] *As Pope*; Relate . . . wrongs; / In . . . briefe: F

10 **lock . . . bosom** The figurative use of 'lock'
and 'wards' presents the metaphor of the heart as
a prison in which Angelo's virtue is locked away
from public view.
  11–13 deserves . . . oblivion deserves to be
fortified against the assaults of time and fallible
human memory by being recorded in engraved
brass (with allusions to Horace, *Odes* III.30, Ovid,
Metamorphoses XV.871 ff.).
  11 characters See 1.1.27 n.
  12 forted A word possibly invented by Shakespeare, from the noun 'fort', with the same sense
as 'fortified' (*OED* Fort *sb*). See Sonnet 16.3.
  13 razure act of effacement or obliteration.
See Sonnet 122.7.
  14 the subject A collective plural noun for 'the
subjects', citizens of Vienna; compare 2.4.27.
  15 outward courtesies Eccles compares 'outward showes' in *Promos and Cassandra, Part 2,*
1.9. An ironic inversion of the idea that 'external
warrants' are betrayed by what is false within.
  16 Favours The Duke's slightly odd choice of
word implies an irony, since though ostensibly
'Favours' means 'approval, love' it could also
mean a badge, an external sign (see *Ado* 2.1.94).

18 supporters *OED* aptly suggests an allusion
to the heraldic figures represented as holding up
or standing beside a shield, and called 'supporters'. This corresponds to other allusions to the
deceptiveness of external show, as with 'favours'
(16 above); compare also the heraldic metaphor
in 2.4.16–17, 'Let's write "Good Angel" on the
devil's horn, / 'Tis not the devil's crest.' The
Duke calls explicit attention to the stage image of
harmony and upright authority which he, Angelo
and Escalus constitute. In what follows both
Angelo and Escalus independently will be seen to
betray justice, and the Duke himself will be its
sole supporter, finally bringing external show and
inward substance into harmony.
  18–19 It is possible to link Friar Peter's 'Now
. . . time' to the end of the Duke's speech, but the
Friar makes a clear break in addressing Isabella,
so an independent line is preferable.
  20 Lever notes how in Kyd, *The Spanish
Tragedy* 3.12, Hieronimo seeks to intercept the
king and three times repeats the cry 'Iustice,
O iustice'.
  20 Vail your regard Look down.

Here is Lord Angelo shall give you justice;
Reveal yourself to him.
ISABELLA   Oh worthy Duke,
You bid me seek redemption of the devil.
Hear me yourself: for that which I must speak   30
Must either punish me, not being believed,
Or wring redress from you. Hear me, oh hear me, here!
ANGELO My lord, her wits I fear me are not firm;
She hath been a suitor to me for her brother
Cut off by course of justice.
ISABELLA   By course of justice!   35
ANGELO And she will speak most bitterly and strange.
ISABELLA Most strange, but yet most truly will I speak.
That Angelo's forsworn, is it not strange?
That Angelo's a murderer, is't not strange?
That Angelo is an adulterous thief,   40
An hypocrite, a virgin-violator,
Is it not strange, and strange?
DUKE   Nay, it is ten times strange.
ISABELLA It is not truer he is Angelo
Than this is all as true as it is strange;
Nay, it is ten times true, for truth is truth   45
To th'end of reck'ning.
DUKE   Away with her: poor soul,
She speaks this in th'infirmity of sense.
ISABELLA Oh prince, I conjure thee as thou believ'st
There is another comfort than this world,
That thou neglect me not with that opinion   50
That I am touched with madness: make not impossible
That which but seems unlike. 'Tis not impossible

32] *As* Pope; Or . . . you: / Heare . . . heere. F   32 here] heere F; hear *Chambers, conj. Keightley*   42 *One line, Steevens*³;
Is . . . strange? / *Duke.* Nay . . . strange? F

---

28 Reveal . . . him Disclose your complaint to him.

32 hear me, here Keightley's conjecture makes a more conventional rhetorical plea than F (which there are no grounds to question). Isabella stresses 'here' because she wants judgement on the spot.

35 By course of According to the customary procedure of.

45–6 it . . . reck'ning Johnson comments 'That is, Truth has no gradations . . . if a pro-position be true there can be none more true'.

47 infirmity of sense irrational state (with a play on the meaning of 'sense' as 'strong feeling', i.e. 'exaggerated terms of strong feeling'). Empson supposes the Duke to be ironic (*The Structure of Complex Words*, 1951, pp. 277–8).

48 conjure appeal earnestly to.

51 touched . . . madness mentally deranged to a slight degree.

51 make consider.

52 unlike unlikely, improbable.

But one, the wicked'st caitiff on the ground,
May seem as shy, as grave, as just, as absolute
As Angelo; even so may Angelo   55
In all his dressings, characts, titles, forms,
Be an arch-villain. Believe it, royal prince,
If he be less, he's nothing, but he's more,
Had I more name for badness.

DUKE   By mine honesty,
If she be mad – as I believe no other –   60
Her madness hath the oddest frame of sense,
Such a dependency of thing on thing,
As e'er I heard in madness.

ISABELLA   Oh, gracious Duke,
Harp not on that; nor do not banish reason
For inequality, but let your reason serve   65
To make the truth appear where it seems hid,
And hide the false seems true.

DUKE   Many that are not mad
Have sure more lack of reason. What would you say?

ISABELLA I am the sister of one Claudio,
Condemned upon the act of fornication   70
To lose his head, condemned by Angelo.
I, in probation of a sisterhood,
Was sent to by my brother; one Lucio
As then the messenger –

LUCIO   That's I, an't like your grace.

68] *One line, Hanmer;* Haue . . . reason: / What . . . say? F

53 **But** But that.
53 **caitiff** villain.
54 **shy** reserved.
54 **absolute** free from all imperfection (*OED* sv *adj* 4).
56 **dressings** robes of office.
56 **characts** insignia of office.
56 **forms** ceremonies.
57 **arch-villain** chief villain (first use in this sense recorded in *OED*).
61 **frame of sense** rational structure.
62 Such a logical structure, drawing consequences from premises. The Duke's air of uncertainty gives Angelo the opportunity either to deepen his guilt or come clean and admit everything: on the other hand, to Isabella the Duke appears an unsympathetic, possibly unjust

ruler, 'Friar Lodowick''s scheme seems in deep trouble and she herself in danger of prison.
64 **Harp** Dwell, insist.
65 **For inequality** Johnson suggests 'because of the high quality of my adversary' but Mason supposes 'because of apparent inconsistency'. Perhaps both are equally acceptable.
67 **hide** Isabella may be confused. Her meaning must be 'dismiss the false from your mind': it is *the false* which hides truth by seeming to be it.
70 **upon** as a result of.
72 **probation** trial.
74 **As** Abbott 114 comments: 'Perhaps it means *as far as regards* that occasion.' Lever refers to *OED* 34a, 'as' with an adverb of time signifying 'being at that time'.
74 **an't like** if it please.

I came to her from Claudio, and desired her   75
To try her gracious fortune with Lord Angelo
For her poor brother's pardon.
ISABELLA   That's he indeed.
DUKE [*To Lucio*] You were not bid to speak.
LUCIO   No, my good lord,
Nor wished to hold my peace.
DUKE   I wish you now then.
Pray you take note of it; and when you have   80
A business for yourself, pray heaven you then
Be perfect.
LUCIO   I warrant your honour.
DUKE The warrant's for yourself: take heed to't.
ISABELLA This gentleman told somewhat of my tale.
LUCIO Right.   85
DUKE It may be right, but you are i'th'wrong
To speak before your time. Proceed.
ISABELLA   I went
To this pernicious caitiff deputy –
DUKE That's somewhat madly spoken.
ISABELLA   Pardon it,
The phrase is to the matter.   90
DUKE Mended again: the matter: proceed.
ISABELLA In brief, to set the needless process by.
How I persuaded, how I prayed, and kneeled,

---

78 SD] *Rowe; not in* F   78–9] *As Steevens*[3]; You . . . speake. / *Luc.* No . . . Lord, / Nor . . . peace. / *Duk.* I . . . then,
F   80–2] *As Steevens*[3]; Pray . . . haue / A . . . then / Be perfect. / *Luc.* I . . . honor. F

78 The Duke's attempt to silence Lucio indicates his nervousness that Lucio's unpredictability may upset his complex scheme. Lucio's intervention recalls his intervention in Isabella's first appeal to Angelo in 2.2.

79 wished The grammatical form is ambiguous, which affects meaning. If Lucio's 'wished' is taken with the Duke's previous 'You were' (78) it must be a past participle with the strong sense 'bidden', 'commanded'. Alternatively Lucio can be understood to say 'Nor wished I to hold my peace' where 'wished' is active imperfect, first-person singular, meaning 'desired'. At any rate, Lucio is impudent.

82 perfect With a suggestion of the sense 'thoroughly learned, as of a lesson or part', implying the Duke's preoccupation with seeing

this secret play-within-a-play work out just as he has planned it. Lucio, being unaware, will understand the straightforward sense of 'perfect' = 'correct in stating your case'.

83 warrant's The Duke quibbles on the sense of the noun, a legal order of arrest, whereas Lucio uses the verb to mean 'assure, guarantee'.

87 speak . . . time Again the Duke is secretly thinking of his plan in which Lucio is, unknowingly, to play a part. Later, when Escalus takes charge, Lucio disrupts his authority just as the Duke anticipated.

90 to the matter directly relevant.

91 Mended Set right. Isabella's testimony is again rational.

92 to . . . by to cut a long story short (Lever); 'process' = narration (*OED* sv *sb* 4).

How he refelled me, and how I replied –
For this was of much length – the vild conclusion   95
I now begin with grief and shame to utter.
He would not but by gift of my chaste body
To his concupiscible intemperate lust,
Release my brother; and after much debatement
My sisterly remorse confutes mine honour   100
And I did yield to him. But the next morn betimes,
His purpose surfeiting, he sends a warrant
For my poor brother's head.

DUKE   This is most likely!

ISABELLA Oh, that it were as like as it is true.

DUKE By heaven, fond wretch, thou know'st not what thou speak'st,   105
Or else thou art suborned against his honour
In hateful practice. First, his integrity
Stands without blemish; next, it imports no reason
That with such vehemency he should pursue
Faults proper to himself. If he had so offended,   110
He would have weighed thy brother by himself
And not have cut him off. Some one hath set you on:
Confess the truth and say by whose advice
Thou cam'st here to complain.

ISABELLA   And is this all?
Then, oh you blessèd ministers above,   115
Keep me in patience, and with ripened time
Unfold the evil which is here wrapped up
In countenance. Heaven shield your grace from woe,
As I, thus wronged, hence unbelievèd go.

DUKE I know you'ld fain be gone. An officer!   120

---

105 thou know'st] ᵘ/ᵧ knowst F

94 **refelled** refused, rejected.
95 **vild** A common variant form of 'vile'.
101 **betimes** early.
104 Isabella wishes it were as probable as it is true because then the Duke would believe her.
105 **fond** foolish, deranged.
106 **suborned** bribed or induced to give false testimony.
107 **practice** scheme, plot.
108 **imports** has within it.
109 **pursue** seek out and punish.
110 **Faults ... himself** Crimes of which he is himself guilty.

112 **set you on** incited you.
115 **ministers** angels (see *Ham.* 1.4.39).
118 **countenance** privilege (as in *1H4* 1.2.29: 'under whose countenance we steal' (Lever)). NS suggests 'confident facial expression', 'hypocrisy', 'worldly credit' as all possible, and that Isabella points at Angelo as she says the word.
120 It is essential for the Duke's plan that he be able to call Isabella back when the time comes: imprisoning her also deepens her misery and encourages Angelo to more open arrogance, and his continuing bravado deepens his guilt. F gives no exit for Isabella though the Duke at 240 says

To prison with her! Shall we thus permit
A blasting and a scandalous breath to fall
On him so near us? This needs must be a practice.
Who knew of your intent and coming hither?
ISABELLA One that I would were here, Friar Lodowick.   125
DUKE A ghostly father, belike. Who knows that Lodowick?
LUCIO My lord, I know him, 'tis a meddling friar.
          I do not like the man: had he been lay, my lord,
          For certain words he spake against your grace
          In your retirement, I had swinged him soundly.   130
DUKE Words against me? This' a good friar, belike;
          And to set on this wretched woman here
          Against our substitute! Let this friar be found.
LUCIO But yesternight, my lord, she and that friar,
          I saw them at the prison: a saucy friar,   135
          A very scurvy fellow.
FRIAR PETER Blessèd be your royal grace.
          I have stood by, my lord, and I have heard
          Your royal ear abused. First hath this woman
          Most wrongfully accused your substitute,   140
          Who is as free from touch or soil with her
          As she from one ungot.
DUKE   We did believe no less.
          Know you that Friar Lodowick that she speaks of?
FRIAR PETER I know him for a man divine and holy,

126] *One line, Hanmer;* A . . . belike: / Who . . . *Lodowicke?* F   136–7] F; *as one line, Steevens*[3]

she has 'gone' and she enters the action again at 274. NS thinks it 'absurd' to take her off immediately after Peter says she shall be disproved 'to her eyes' at 161. This phrase may not be literally meant; it could mean 'flatly, incontrovertibly' as in 4.3.134, 'to the head of Angelo' (see also 132 n. below). I believe that 274–378 repeats a staging effect of keeping in view a figure who is the focus of moral debate, like Juliet in 2.1. NS has the SD *the officer and* ISABELLA *withdraw to a distance* and omits Isabella from F's SD at 274. See also the Textual Analysis, p. 198 below.

126 **ghostly** Quibbling on 'spiritual' and 'insubstantial, non-existent'. The irony is that 'Lodowick' is of course the Duke-in-disguise.

127 **meddling** Lucio may intend the common bawdy quibble on this word (see 4.3.161).

130 **retirement** absence.

130 **swinged** beaten (Lucio does attack the 'Friar' at 345 ff. below). Pronounced with a soft *g*.

131 **This' a** This is a (Abbott 403 comments on the ellipsis of 'is'). Perhaps the apostrophe is Crane's (see Textual Analysis, p. 196 below).

132 **this wretched woman here** Assuming Isabella to be still on stage, these words would probably be accompanied by a gesture towards her; 'here' may however be a demonstrative adjective as in 3.2.91, 'this Angelo': see 139 below, 'this woman', and 158, 'this woman'.

136 **scurvy** bad, offensive.

139 **abused** imposed upon (*OED* Abuse *v* 4).

140 Friar Peter's testimony against Isabella must come as a shock to the audience, and to her also, if she is still on stage.

141 **touch** sexual contact (*OED* sv *sb* lb).

142 **ungot** not begotten.

Not scurvy, nor a temporary meddler,   145
As he's reported by this gentleman;
And on my trust, a man that never yet
Did, as he vouches, misreport your grace.
LUCIO My lord, most villainously, believe it.
FRIAR PETER Well; he in time may come to clear himself;   150
But at this instant he is sick, my lord,
Of a strange fever. Upon his mere request
Being come to knowledge, that there was complaint
Intended 'gainst Lord Angelo, came I hither
To speak as from his mouth what he doth know   155
Is true and false, and what he with his oath
And all probation will make up full clear
Whensoever he's convented. First, for this woman,
To justify this worthy nobleman
So vulgarly and personally accused,   160
Her shall you hear disprovèd to her eyes,
Till she herself confess it.

                              [Exit Isabella, guarded]
DUKE   Good friar, let's hear it.
Do you not smile at this, Lord Angelo?
Oh, heaven, the vanity of wretched fools.
Give us some seats. Come, cousin Angelo,   165
In this I'll be impartial: be you judge
Of your own cause.

                    Enter MARIANA *[veiled]*

              Is this the witness, friar?

162 SD] *As Capell; Lever places it at 125; At a motion of the Duke, the officer and Isabella withdraw to a distance. / NS; not in*
F   167 SD] *As NS; after* Frier? F   167 SD *veiled*] Rowe; *not in* F

145 **temporary meddler** one who meddles in
secular affairs (Johnson).
148 **he** i.e. Lucio, 'this gentleman' of 146.
148 **vouches** alleges.
149 Lucio begins to speak prose here and so
continues to the end.
152 **strange** unknown or exceptionally great
(*OED* sv *adj* 7).
152 **Upon . . . request** Commentators suggest
'solely upon his request' or 'on his personal
request'.
157 **probation** proof.
158 **convented** summoned.
160 **vulgarly** in public (Johnson suggests

'grossly, with such indecency of invective, or by so
mean and inadequate witnesses').
161 **to her eyes** directly, to her face (as in *2H4*
3.1.64). It is not certain whether it is meant
literally. See 5.1.120 n.
163 **smile** Compare Hamlet's remark (1.5.108)
that one 'may smile, and smile, and be a villain'.
166 **impartial** A heavy irony: the Duke repeats
the travesty of justice perpetrated in Jonson's
Sejanus 3.1, where the cruel emperor Tiberius
has his deputy conduct a trial to license judicial
murder, and the brave victim Silius protests 'Is he
my accuser? / And must he be my judge?' See the
discussion at pp. 44–7 above.

First let her show her face, and after speak.
MARIANA Pardon, my lord, I will not show my face
    Until my husband bid me.   170
DUKE What, are you married?
MARIANA No, my lord.
DUKE Are you a maid?
MARIANA No, my lord.
DUKE A widow, then?   175
MARIANA Neither, my lord.
DUKE Why, you are nothing then: neither maid, widow, nor wife?
LUCIO My lord, she may be a punk, for many of them are neither
    maid, widow, nor wife.
DUKE Silence that fellow. I would he had some cause to prattle for   180
    himself.
LUCIO Well, my lord.
MARIANA My lord, I do confess I ne'er was married,
    And I confess besides I am no maid.
    I have known my husband, yet my husband   185
    Knows not that ever he knew me.
LUCIO He was drunk then, my lord, it can be no better.
DUKE For the benefit of silence, would thou wert so too.
LUCIO Well, my lord.
DUKE This is no witness for Lord Angelo.   190
MARIANA Now I come to't, my lord.
    She that accuses him of fornication
    In self-same manner doth accuse my husband,
    And charges him, my lord, with such a time
    When I'll depose I had him in mine arms   195
    With all th'effect of love.
ANGELO Charges she moe than me?
MARIANA   Not that I know.
DUKE No? You say your husband?
MARIANA Why just, my lord, and that is Angelo,
    Who thinks he knows that he ne'er knew my body,   200
    But knows, he thinks, that he knows Isabel's.

168 her face] F2; *your face* F   **185–6**] F; I . . . not / That . . . me. *Pope*   **197–8** *As Cam.; Ang.* Charges . . . me? / *Mar.* Not . . . know. / *Duk.* No? . . . husband. F

177 Thirlby quotes a proverb 'neither wife, widow nor maid' (Tilley M26); the answer to the proverbial riddle is 'a whore', as Lucio knows.
  178 punk prostitute.
  185 known had sexual intercourse with.

188 benefit sake.
196 effect manifestations.
197 moe more, i.e. other persons.
199 just true.

ANGELO This is a strange abuse – let's see thy face.

MARIANA [*Unveiling*] My husband bids me, now I will unmask.
    This is that face, thou cruel Angelo,
    Which once thou swor'st was worth the looking on.   205
    This is the hand which with a vowed contract
    Was fast belocked in thine. This is the body
    That took away the match from Isabel
    And did supply thee at thy garden-house
    In her imagined person.

DUKE   Know you this woman?   210

LUCIO Carnally, she says.

DUKE Sirrah, no more!

LUCIO Enough, my lord.

ANGELO My lord, I must confess I know this woman,
    And five years since there was some speech of marriage   215
    Betwixt myself and her; which was broke off,
    Partly for that her promisèd proportions
    Came short of composition, but in chief
    For that her reputation was disvalued
    In levity. Since which time of five years   220
    I never spake with her, saw her, nor heard from her,
    Upon my faith and honour.

MARIANA   Noble prince,
    As there comes light from heaven, and words from breath,
    As there is sense in truth, and truth in virtue,
    I am affianced this man's wife, as strongly   225
    As words could make up vows. And, my good lord,

203 SD] *Rowe; not in* F

202 **abuse** deception.

207 **belocked** Intensive form of 'locked'. E. Schanzer, 'The marriage-contracts in *Measure for Measure*', *S.Sur.* 13 (1960), 81–9, sets out the difference between *sponsalia per verba de praesenti*, a declaration by both parties that each took the other at the present time as spouse, which was legally binding irrespective of any change in circumstances and whether or not the union was consecrated (in short, a full marriage), and *sponsalia per verba de futuro*, a sworn declaration of intent to marry in the future, but not absolutely binding: in the latter case failure to furnish agreed dowry would justify a unilateral breach, except that 'if a man contract spousals conditionally with a Woman ... and ... in the mean-

time he have access to her, as to his wife, these doubtful spousals do thereby pass into Matrimony' (Swinburne, *A Treatise of Spousals* (1686), written some hundred years earlier; so also William Perkins, *Of Christian Oeconomie*, chapter 4); cited by Lever, pp. liii–liv. See 3.1.204, p. 35 n. 1 and 1.2.129–30 n.

208 **match** appointment, assignation.

209 **supply** satisfy.

217–20 Angelo's reasons (if true) would have justified breaking a *de futuro* contract.

217 **proportions** marriage portion, dowry.

218 **Came ... composition** Proved insufficient for the agreement to be confirmed (Lever).

219–20 **disvalued ... levity** rendered valueless through moral levity.

But Tuesday night last gone, in's garden-house,
He knew me as a wife. As this is true,
Let me in safety raise me from my knees,
Or else for ever be confixèd here   230
A marble monument.

ANGELO   I did but smile till now.
Now, good my lord, give me the scope of justice,
My patience here is touched. I do perceive
These poor informal women are no more
But instruments of some more mightier member   235
That sets them on. Let me have way, my lord,
To find this practice out.

DUKE   Ay, with my heart,
And punish them to your height of pleasure.
Thou foolish friar, and thou pernicious woman
Compact with her that's gone, think'st thou thy oaths, 240
Though they would swear down each particular saint,
Were testimonies against his worth and credit
That's sealed in approbation? You, Lord Escalus,
Sit with my cousin, lend him your kind pains
To find out this abuse, whence 'tis derived.   245
There is another friar that set them on,
Let him be sent for.

FRIAR PETER Would he were here, my lord, for he indeed
Hath set the women on to this complaint.
Your provost knows the place where he abides,   250
And he may fetch him.

DUKE   Go, do it instantly.

[*Exit Provost*]

And you, my noble and well-warranted cousin,

251] *One line, Dyce;* And . . . him. / *Duke.* Goe . . . instantly. F   251 SD] *Capell; not in* F

230 **confixèd** fixed firmly.
231 **smile** See above, 163 and n.
232 **scope** full extent.
233 **touched** injured, hurt (with a resultant stimulus to act).
234 **informal** mentally disordered, deranged (compare 'infirmity' (47), 'frame of sense' (61)).
235 **more mightier member** more (politically) powerful person. Angelo claims to suspect some state intrigue – an intelligent false trail, intended to gain him time and room to manoeuvre; yet he has accidentally hit upon the truth.
237 **practice** plot.

239 **foolish friar** Referring presumably to the absent 'Lodowick', thus condemned on Lucio's word, despite Friar Peter's defence of him at 144 ff.
240 **Compact** In league.
243 **sealed in approbation** proved beyond question (Johnson compares the stamp or seal on silver or gold plate, weights and measures, marking the fact that they have been tested and proved genuine or true).
245 **abuse** deceit or wrongdoing.
252 **well-warranted** approved by good warrant.

Whom it concerns to hear this matter forth,
Do with your injuries as seems you best
In any chastisement. I for a while will leave you;   255
But stir not you till you have well determined
Upon these slanderers.

ESCALUS   My lord, we'll do it throughly.

Exit [Duke]

Signior Lucio, did not you say you knew that Friar Lodowick to
be a dishonest person?

LUCIO *Cucullus non facit monachum*, honest in nothing but in his   260
clothes, and one that hath spoke most villainous speeches of the
Duke.

ESCALUS We shall entreat you to abide here till he come, and
enforce them against him. We shall find this friar a notable
fellow.   265

LUCIO As any in Vienna, on my word.

ESCALUS Call that same Isabel here once again, I would speak with
her.

[Exit an Attendant]

Pray you, my lord, give me leave to question, you shall see how
I'll handle her.   270

LUCIO Not better than he, by her own report.

ESCALUS Say you?

LUCIO Marry, sir, I think if you handled her privately she would
sooner confess, perchance publicly she'll be ashamed.

Enter DUKE *[disguised as a friar]*, PROVOST, ISABELLA, *[guarded]*

ESCALUS I will go darkly to work with her.   275

LUCIO That's the way: for women are light at midnight.

255-7] *As Dyce²; In . . . while / Will . . . haue / Well . . . Slanderers.* F   257 SD] *Capell; Exit.* F *(after* Slanderers*)*
268 SD] *Dyce, after Capell; not in* F

253 **forth** thoroughly, to the end.
254 **with** in the matter of.
256 **determined** reached a judgement.
257 **throughly** thoroughly.
260 **Cucullus . . . monachum** The cowl does
not make the monk. A proverbial phrase; also in
Promos and Cassandra, Part 1 3.6.
260–1 **honest . . . clothes** i.e. only the holy
robes themselves are honourable, not the man
who wears them.
264 **enforce them** urge them strongly.
264 **notable** remarkable (in a bad sense).

270 **handle** Lucio quibbles on the sense
'fondle' (Colman, p. 197).
272 **Say you?** What's that you say? Lucio
weakens a moment under this reproof. Compare
Pompey's hint to Escalus (2.1.106) which earns a
rebuke.
275 **darkly** secretly.
276 **light** Lucio plays on the senses 'bright'
and 'wanton', implicit also in his own name and
nature.
276 **women . . . midnight** Lever notes parallels in Marston, *Antonio and Mellida*, Middleton,

ESCALUS Come on, mistress, here's a gentlewoman denies all that
    you have said.
LUCIO My lord, here comes the rascal I spoke of, here with the
    provost.   280
ESCALUS In very good time: speak not you to him till we call upon
    you.
LUCIO Mum.
ESCALUS Come, sir, did you set these women on to slander Lord
    Angelo? They have confessed you did.   285
DUKE 'Tis false.
ESCALUS How? Know you where you are?
DUKE Respect to your great place: and let the devil
    Be sometime honoured for his burning throne.
    Where is the Duke? 'Tis he should hear me speak.   290
ESCALUS The Duke's in us, and we will hear you speak;
    Look you speak justly.
DUKE Boldly at least. But oh, poor souls,
    Come you to seek the lamb here of the fox?
    Good night to your redress. Is the Duke gone?   295
    Then is your cause gone too: the Duke's unjust,
    Thus to retort your manifest appeal
    And put your trial in the villain's mouth
    Which here you come to accuse.
LUCIO This is the rascal, this is he I spoke of.   300
ESCALUS Why, thou unreverend and unhallowed friar!
    Is't not enough thou hast suborned these women
    To accuse this worthy man, but in foul mouth
    And in the witness of his proper ear
    To call him villain, and then to glance from him   305
    To th'Duke himself, to tax him with injustice?

277–8] *As prose,* F2; Come...Gentlewoman, / Denies...said. F   **279–80**] *As prose, Pope;* My ...of, /
Here...*Prouost.* F

A Mad World My Masters, Webster, *Appius and
Virginia*: if not a proverb, this seems to have been
a catch-phrase.
   288 Malone suspected a line to be missing
but Halliwell argued that the Duke-as-Friar's
abruptness is expressive of indignation; the line
may also be spoken in an even tone and yet
convey sharp irony.
   289 sometime occasionally.
   291 in us i.e. his authority is vested in us.
   294 seek ... fox Proverbial, though the Duke

substitutes 'fox' for the usual 'wolf', presumably
alluding to the craftiness he sees.
   295 Good night Say goodbye.
   297 retort return or refer back (to Angelo).
   297 manifest obvious (in its justice).
   301 unhallowed unholy, impious.
   303–4 in ... ear with foul words and in his
hearing.
   305 glance To hit a first object obliquely and
deflect to another (either of an actual missile, or
of a movement of thought, or sight).

Take him hence; to th'rack with him! We'll touze you
Joint by joint, but we will know his purpose.
What? Unjust?

DUKE   Be not so hot: the Duke
Dare no more stretch this finger of mine than he   310
Dare rack his own. His subject am I not,
Nor here provincial: my business in this state
Made me a looker-on here in Vienna,
Where I have seen corruption boil and bubble
Till it o'errun the stew; laws for all faults,   315
But faults so countenanced that the strong statutes
Stand like the forfeits in a barber's shop,
As much in mock as mark.

ESCALUS   Slander to th'state!
Away with him to prison!

ANGELO What can you vouch against him, Signior Lucio?   320
Is this the man that you did tell us of?

LUCIO 'Tis he, my lord. Come hither, goodman Baldpate, do you
know me?

DUKE I remember you, sir, by the sound of your voice. I met you at
the prison, in the absence of the Duke.   325

LUCIO Oh, did you so? And do you remember what you said of the
Duke?

DUKE Most notedly, sir.

LUCIO Do you so, sir? And was the Duke a fleshmonger, a fool, and
a coward, as you then reported him to be?   330

309–10] *As Knight;* What? vniust? / *Duk.* Be ... dare / No ... he F   318–21] *As Winny;* As ... marke. / *Esc.*
Slander ... State: / Away ... prison. / *Ang.* What ... *Lucio?* / Is ... of? F

307 rack instrument of torture by stretching.
In Peter Brook's production of 1950 a torture
wheel was seen in the prison among other
instruments.

307 touze pull out of joint, rack (*OED sv v* 1b).
The verb is used in Marston, *The Malcontent*, on
three occasions. See p. 18 above.

312 provincial Subject to the ecclesiastical
authorities of this province (Dyce).

314–15 corruption ... stew The metaphor is
of cooking a stew, with a play on the word for
brothels, 'stews', and for a cauldron, 'stew' (*OED*
stew *sb²* 1).

316 countenanced connived at, protected by
'cover-up' (see 5.1.118).

317 forfeits ... shop Jocular lists of graded
penalties were customarily hung in barbers'
shops; Hart (1908) cites Richard Harvey, *Plaine*

Percevall (1590), p. 11: 'Speake a bloody word in
a Barbors shop, you make a forfet.' Barbers also
did minor surgery and dentistry.

318 in mock as mark mocked as feared.
Compare 1.3.28, 'More mocked than feared'.

322 goodman A prefix, often ironical, for
persons below the rank of gentleman.

322 Baldpate Alluding to the customary ton-
sure of friars. This need not be taken as evidence
of the Duke-as-Friar's appearance, though presumably it might be. As Duke he would wear a
distinctive hat of some kind (all actors normally
wore hats on stage). At this moment he will be
hooded, but his head will be uncovered by Lucio
at 348.

328 notedly especially.

329 fleshmonger one who deals in flesh, a
fornicator (see 4.3.151–2).

DUKE You must, sir, change persons with me, ere you make that my
report: you indeed spoke so of him, and much more, much
worse.

LUCIO Oh thou damnable fellow, did not I pluck thee by the nose for
thy speeches?   335

DUKE I protest I love the Duke as I love myself.

ANGELO Hark how the villain would close now, after his treasonable
abuses.

ESCALUS Such a fellow is not to be talked withal: away with him to
prison. Where is the provost? Away with him to prison. Lay bolts   340
enough upon him. Let him speak no more. Away with those
giglets too, and with the other confederate companion.
          [*The Provost lays hands on the Duke*]

DUKE Stay, sir, stay a while.

ANGELO What, resists he? Help him, Lucio!

LUCIO Come, sir, come, sir, come, sir! Foh, sir! Why, you bald-   345
pated, lying rascal, you must be hooded, must you? Show your
knave's visage, with a pox to you! Show your sheep-biting face,
and be hanged an hour! Will't not off?
          [*He pulls off the Friar's hood and discovers the Duke*]

DUKE Thou art the first knave that e'er mad'st a duke!
          First, provost, let me bail these gentle three –   350
          [*To Lucio*] Sneak not away, sir, for the friar and you
          Must have a word anon. – Lay hold on him.

LUCIO This may prove worse than hanging.

DUKE [*To Escalus*] What you have spoke, I pardon. Sit you down.
          We'll borrow place of him. [*To Angelo*] Sir, by your leave: 355
          Hast thou or word or wit or impudence
          That yet can do thee office? If thou hast,
          Rely upon it till my tale be heard,
          And hold no longer out.

ANGELO   Oh, my dread lord,
          I should be guiltier than my guiltiness   360
          To think I can be undiscernible
          When I perceive your grace, like power divine,

---

342 SD] *Johnson; not in* F   348 SD] *Rowe; not in* F   351 SD] *Johnson; not in* F   354 SD] *Rowe; not in* F   355 SD]
Hanmer; not in F

337 **close** come to terms, climb down (Onions),
or make a conclusion.
    348 **an hour** A joke, perhaps; Eccles compares
Mucedorus 3.1.26: 'Euen goe hang thy selfe halfe
an hower.'

356, 357 **Hast** Compare 3.2.31 n.
359 **hold...out** continue no longer.
361 **undiscernible** undiscoverable.
362–3 **power...passes** Eccles compares
Gen. 16.13: 'Thou God lookest on me.'

Hath looked upon my passes. Then, good prince,
No longer session hold upon my shame,
But let my trial be mine own confession: 365
Immediate sentence then, and sequent death,
Is all the grace I beg.

DUKE   Come hither, Mariana. –
Say, wast thou e'er contracted to this woman?

ANGELO I was, my lord.

DUKE Go, take her hence and marry her instantly.   370
Do you the office, friar, which consummate,
Return him here again. Go with him, provost.

      Exeunt [Angelo, Mariana, Friar Peter, Provost]

ESCALUS My lord, I am more amazed at his dishonour,
Than at the strangeness of it.

DUKE   Come hither, Isabel.
Your friar is now your prince: as I was then,   375
Advertising and holy to your business,
Not changing heart with habit, I am still
Attorneyed at your service.

ISABELLA   Oh, give me pardon
That I, your vassal, have employed and pained
Your unknown sovereignty.

DUKE   You are pardoned, Isabel: 380
And now dear maid, be you as free to us.
Your brother's death I know sits at your heart,
And you may marvel why I obscured myself,
Labouring to save his life, and would not rather
Make rash remonstrance of my hidden power   385
Than let him so be lost. Oh, most kind maid,

367–8] *Steevens³*; Is . . . beg. / *Duk.* Come . . . *Mariana*, / Say . . . woman? F   **372** SD] *Pope; Exit.* F

363 passes Commentators offer various suggestions: 'course of action' seems preferred, being associated with the primary sense of 'pass' as 'step' (so Harold Jenkins, cited by Lever).

366 sequent that follows as a result.

371 consummate being completed (*OED* cites this adjective as past participle).

376 Advertising *OED* suggests 'adverting, attentive', but Johnson is surely right to see the main sense as 'guiding', 'active in giving intelligence'.

376 holy NS suggests 'dedicated' (*OED* sv *adj* 3a); Schmidt, 'in the character of a priest'.

378 Attorneyed Johnson suggests 'employed as a proxy' but the simpler meaning 'employed as your attorney' may be right.

379 vassal subject.

379 employed and pained put to labour and trouble.

380 unknown sovereignty i.e. the fact of his sovereignty was unknown to her.

381 free generous.

382 sits at affects deeply.

385 rash remonstrance too hasty a discovery (*OED* Remonstrance *sb*: 'demonstration, proof, evidence').

It was the swift celerity of his death
Which I did think with slower foot came on
That brained my purpose – but peace be with him.
That life is better life, past fearing death,   390
Than that which lives to fear: make it your comfort,
So happy is your brother.

ISABELLA   I do, my lord.

Enter ANGELO, MARIANA, FRIAR PETER [*and*] PROVOST

DUKE For this new-married man approaching here,
Whose salt imagination yet hath wronged
Your well-defended honour, you must pardon   395
For Mariana's sake. But as he adjudged your brother,
Being criminal in double violation
Of sacred chastity and of promise-breach
Thereon dependent for your brother's life,
The very mercy of the law cries out   400
Most audible, even from his proper tongue:
An Angelo for Claudio, death for death;
Haste still pays haste, and leisure answers leisure;
Like doth quit like, and measure still for measure.
Then, Angelo, thy fault's thus manifested   405
Which, though thou wouldst deny, denies thee vantage.
We do condemn thee to the very block
Where Claudio stooped to death, and with like haste.
Away with him.

MARIANA   Oh, my most gracious lord,
I hope you will not mock me with a husband?   410

---

392 SD MARIANA] *Rowe; Maria,* F   404 measure . . . measure] *Measure . . . Measure* F

388 **came** Subjunctive: 'would come'.
389 **brained my purpose** knocked my design on the head (Johnson).
390–1 **That . . . fear** See Tilley D27: 'Better pass a danger once than be always in fear.'
394 **salt** lecherous.
396 **adjudged** condemned.
398–9 **promise-breach . . . life** breach of promise (to save Claudio's life), which promise was dependent on violating your chastity. Hart (1905) notes the confusion resulting from Shakespeare's transposing of adjectives: 'double' refers to the two crimes together; there was no double violation of chastity. Furthermore an unintentional double-negative construction gives

the sense 'violation of *breach* of promise' when 'violation of promise' is meant.
401 **audible** loud.
403 **pays** recompenses (for good or ill).
404 **Like . . . like** proverbial: see Tilley L286; 'quit' = repays.
404 The words 'Measure' and 'Measure' are printed in italic in F. See the discussion of the play's title, pp. 1 and 37.
406 Though you were to deny this, your fault is such as to deny you the right to claim superior treatment (Lever). Angelo has confessed his fault, so it only remains for him (hypothetically) to plead for different treatment from that given to Claudio. Remarkably, Angelo has nothing to say.

DUKE   It is your husband mocked you with a husband;
Consenting to the safeguard of your honour,
I thought your marriage fit: else imputation,
For that he knew you, might reproach your life
And choke your good to come. For his possessions,   415
Although by confiscation they are ours,
We do instate and widow you with all
To buy you a better husband.

MARIANA   Oh, my dear lord,
I crave no other, nor no better man.

DUKE   Never crave him, we are definitive.   420

MARIANA   Gentle my liege – [*Kneeling*]

DUKE   You do but lose your labour.
Away with him to death. [*To Lucio*] Now, sir, to you.

MARIANA   Oh my good lord! Sweet Isabel, take my part,
Lend me your knees, and all my life to come
I'll lend you all my life to do you service.   425

DUKE   Against all sense you do importune her.
Should she kneel down in mercy of this fact,
Her brother's ghost his pavèd bed would break
And take her hence in horror.

MARIANA   Isabel!
Sweet Isabel, do yet but kneel by me,   430
Hold up your hands, say nothing; I'll speak all.
They say best men are moulded out of faults,

---

416 confiscation] F2; confutation F   417 with all] F; withall F2   421 SD] *Johnson; not in* F   422 SD] *Johnson; not in* F

---

414 knew had sexual intercourse with. The Duke's is an odd explanation, since presumably the act sealed the marriage according to *sponsalia per verba de futuro*: see 5.1.207 n. It was earlier on the grounds that Mariana's reputation was 'disvalued in levity' that Angelo broke his promise to her.

416 confiscation F2's reading may make more simple sense than F (which on the principle of *praestat difficilior lectio* should make F preferable) except that in this case what is in question is possession of wealth, for which F2's 'confiscation' is preferable; compare Malone's explanation of F: 'by his being confuted or proved guilty of the fact which he had denied'. What the Duke is surely saying is that Angelo's guilt involves all his possessions reverting to the state, and the Duke having power of disposal of them.

417 widow endow with a widow's right (*OED* sv *v* 3).

420 definitive decisive (*OED* sv *adj* 1b; first use as applied to a person).

426 Against all sense Against what is wise or reasonable; also present is the idea of decent strong feeling.

427 in mercy of in the exercise of mercy for.

428 pavèd bed Presumably alluding to the family vault, but perhaps to the practice of burying families of rank beneath the paved floor in the church. The emphasis is on the degree of outrage provoked, enough to give a ghost strength to break through a massive stone slab.

432 Hudson explains the principle as Nature or Providence using our vices to scourge our pride: Eccles compares *AWW* 4.3.72–3: 'Our virtues would be proud if our faults whipped them not.'

And for the most become much more the better
For being a little bad: so may my husband.
Oh Isabel! Will you not lend a knee?   435
DUKE He dies for Claudio's death.
ISABELLA [*Kneeling*]   Most bounteous sir,
          Look if it please you on this man condemned
          As if my brother lived. I partly think
          A due sincerity governed his deeds
          Till he did look on me. Since it is so,   440
          Let him not die. My brother had but justice,
          In that he did the thing for which he died.
          For Angelo,
          His act did not o'ertake his bad intent,
          And must be buried but as an intent   445
          That perished by the way. Thoughts are no subjects,
          Intents but merely thoughts.
MARIANA   Merely, my lord.
DUKE Your suit's unprofitable. Stand up, I say.
          I have bethought me of another fault:
          Provost, how came it Claudio was beheaded   450
          At an unusual hour?
PROVOST   It was commanded so.
DUKE Had you a special warrant for the deed?
PROVOST No, my good lord: it was by private message.
DUKE For which I do discharge you of your office;
          Give up your keys.
PROVOST   Pardon me, noble lord,   455
          I thought it was a fault, but knew it not,

---

436 SD] *Rowe; not in* F   442 died] dide F; di'd F2   443–4] *As Johnson, conj. Thirlby;* For . . . intent, F

---

433 most most part.
438–40 It is significant that Isabella includes the modifying adverb 'partly' suggesting perhaps reluctance to change her view, or the dawning – but not yet full – realisation of the idea that she unwittingly tempted Angelo. Her phrasing nevertheless implies her passivity in interviews with Angelo.
441–2 My . . . died A feeble contradiction of her previous arguments to Angelo in 2.2 and 2.4. It might be argued from Isabella's weak pleading here that she once again lacks personal, inner strength of conviction, accepts strong pressure from others in cases where an independent moral adult needs no prompting. Alternatively it could be claimed that she confines herself strictly to matters of the letter of the law. Rape is nevertheless not accounted for by Isabella's plea. Johnson cannot approve the Duke's mercy to Angelo and notes 'I believe every reader feels some indignation when he finds [Angelo] spared.' It is significant that Johnson speaks of a 'reader''s reaction; in the theatre, reactions may well be swayed to different effect. See the discussion at pp. 34 and 47–50 above.
446 subjects real existing things, or possibly also 'like the Duke's subjects who on the contrary are liable to be punished or controlled', as Durham suggests.
451 It may be noted that the Provost does not actually say Claudio was beheaded.

> Yet did repent me after more advice;
> For testimony whereof, one in the prison
> That should by private order else have died
> I have reserved alive.

DUKE   What's he?

PROVOST   His name is Barnardine.   460

DUKE I would thou hadst done so by Claudio.
> Go fetch him hither. Let me look upon him.

> > *[Exit Provost]*

ESCALUS I am sorry one so learned and so wise
> As you, Lord Angelo, have still appeared,
> Should slip so grossly, both in the heat of blood   465
> And lack of tempered judgement afterward.

ANGELO I am sorry that such sorrow I procure,
> And so deep sticks it in my penitent heart
> That I crave death more willingly than mercy.
> 'Tis my deserving, and I do entreat it.   470

Enter BARNARDINE, PROVOST, CLAUDIO *[muffled] and* JULIET

DUKE Which is that Barnardine?

PROVOST   This, my lord.

DUKE There was a friar told me of this man.
> Sirrah, thou art said to have a stubborn soul
> That apprehends no further than this world,
> And squar'st thy life according. Thou'rt condemned: 475
> But, for those earthly faults, I quit them all,
> And pray thee take this mercy to provide
> For better times to come. Friar, advise him,
> I leave him to your hand. – What muffled fellow's that?

PROVOST This is another prisoner that I saved,   480
> Who should have died when Claudio lost his head,
> As like almost to Claudio as himself.

> > *[He unmuffles Claudio]*

DUKE *[To Isabella]* If he be like your brother, for his sake

---

460] *One line, Steevens*³; I . . . aliue. / Duk. What's he? / Pro. His . . . Barnardine. F   462 SD] *Hanmer; not in* F   470 SD
muffed] *Dyce, after Capell; not in* F   482 SD] *Hanmer, subst.; not in* F   483 SD] *Theobald; not in* F

457 **advice** deliberation.
467 **procure** cause.
475 **squar'st** regulate, frame.
476 **quit** remit (*OED* sv *v* 4) (rare); Dyce
proposes 'acquit'.

482 Commentators note the surprising absence of a speech from Isabella in response to the revelation that her brother is alive, and usually assume she expresses joyfulness in a silent reunion.

Is he pardoned, and for your lovely sake
Give me your hand, and say you will be mine,   485
He is my brother too. But fitter time for that.
By this Lord Angelo perceives he's safe;
Methinks I see a quick'ning in his eye.
Well, Angelo, your evil quits you well.
Look that you love your wife: her worth, worth yours.   490
I find an apt remission in myself;
And yet here's one in place I cannot pardon,
[*To Lucio*] You, sirrah, that knew me for a fool, a coward,
One all of luxury, an ass, a madman:
Wherein have I so deserved of you   495
That you extol me thus?

LUCIO 'Faith, my lord, I spoke it but according to the trick: if you
    will hang me for it, you may – but I had rather it would please
    you I might be whipped.

DUKE Whipped first, sir, and hanged after.   500
    Proclaim it, provost, round about the city:
    If any woman wronged by this lewd fellow,
    As I have heard him swear himself there's one
    Whom he begot with child, let her appear,
    And he shall marry her. The nuptial finished,   505
    Let him be whipped and hanged.

LUCIO I beseech your highness, do not marry me to a whore. Your
    highness said, even now, I made you a duke: good my
    lord, do not recompense me in making me a cuckold.

DUKE Upon mine honour, thou shalt marry her.   510
    Thy slanders I forgive, and therewithal
    Remit thy other forfeits: take him to prison,
    And see our pleasure herein executed.

---

493 SD] *Rowe; not in* F

485–6 Again Isabella has nothing to say. Some
editors punctuate to imply her silent acceptance: ·
so Lever has a full stop after 485 and a colon after
'too' in 486 giving the sense '(now Isabella has
accepted me) Claudio is my brother-in-law'. See
the discussion at pp. 47–8 above.

491 apt . . . myself inclination in myself to
pardon. The phrase 'in myself' half suggests the
idea of the Duke pardoning himself (for his
deceptions as 'Friar').

492 I cannot pardon In fact, Lucio is
pardoned of the sentence of execution. Schanzer,
The Problem Plays of Shakespeare, 1963, observes:

'The sentence initially imposed on Lucio . . .
comes as a shock . . . It becomes much more
comprehensible in the light of James's notorious
sensitiveness to slander, which led to the passing
of a Scottish Act of Parliament in 1585 that
made slander of the King a treasonable offence,
punishable with death' (p. 125).

494 luxury lechery.

497 trick custom; compare 'the trick of it'
(3.2.51).

513 i.e. see that he is married, as we decree;
'execute' = 'carry out', *not* 'put to death'.

LUCIO Marrying a punk, my lord, is pressing to death, whipping, and
    hanging!   515
DUKE Slandering a prince deserves it.
    She, Claudio, that you wronged, look you restore.
    Joy to you, Mariana! Love her, Angelo!
    I have confessed her, and I know her virtue.
    Thanks, good friend Escalus, for thy much goodness;   520
    There's more behind, that is more gratulate.
    Thanks, provost, for thy care and secrecy,
    We shall employ thee in a worthier place.
    Forgive him, Angelo, that brought you home
    The head of Ragozine for Claudio's;   525
    Th'offence pardons itself. Dear Isabel,
    I have a motion much imports your good,
    Whereto, if you'll a willing ear incline,
    What's mine is yours, and what is yours is mine.
    So bring us to our palace, where we'll show   530
    What's yet behind that's meet you all should know.

                                          [*Exeunt*]

514–15] *As prose, Pope; as verse,* F: Marrying . . . death, / Whipping . . . hanging.   531 that's] thats F2; that F   531 SD]
Rowe; *not in* F

514 pressing to death Punishment for prisoners who refused to plead: weights were placed
on a board laid on their chest, with a sharp stone
under their backs (Halliwell, citing Harrison's
Description of England).

521 behind in reserve, yet to come.
521 more gratulate more gratifying.
527 motion proposal; presumably a formal
offer of marriage, as 529 suggests.
530 bring accompany.

TEXTUAL ANALYSIS

Measure for Measure was first published in the First Folio in 1623, where it appears fourth in the Comedies section after *The Tempest, Two Gentlemen of Verona* and *The Merry Wives of Windsor*, and fills quires F and G. All these four plays were set from transcriptions (not extant) prepared by the professional scrivener Ralph Crane. Eight transcriptions by Crane of other plays performed by the King's Men are extant, and date from 1618 to 1625. Analysis of these reveals much about his habits. Ralph Crane is known to have been 'not reluctant to interfere with his text, consciously or unconsciously, when its meaning was obscure to him'.[1] Thus Shakespeare's play is mediated to us by a transcription that may partly obscure the nature of its copy, and by a process of printing in which the compositors – the men who actually composed the text from pieces of type – may also have made changes, errors, or omissions, when following Crane's transcription.

The nature of the copy

What was the nature of the copy Crane was given to transcribe? The answer cannot be certain and must be sought for by an analysis of the only authoritative text, the First Folio, beginning with the compositors, and then considering other evidence. Throughout it will be well to bear in mind the possibilities for the kind of copy which lies behind Crane's transcription. It is relevant to recall the likely process of Shakespeare's composition and transmission of his work. We may assume he wrote out a draft in ink on separate sheets, not necessarily beginning with the first scenes. During the process of composition cancellations, additions, and other changes would be entered, some interlined, some in the margins. When a sheet became too untidy it might be copied afresh. When completed to his satisfaction, the manuscript might therefore comprise some fair-copy sheets, others with few changes, some with a number. If the author expected to make a fair copy himself, the marks for cancellation or transposition might be less than clear to someone else, and if a scribe was brought in to make a copy, confusion might be possible.

The author's completed draft, before being fair-copied, is often referred to in modern editorial discussion as 'foul papers', a term which unfortunately might seem to suggest intermediate, not completed, manuscript. Once completed, the author's work would be the basis for a fair copy used in the playhouse and called

---

1 T.H. Howard-Hill, *Ralph Crane and Some Shakespeare First Folio Comedies*, 1972, p. 133.

the 'book'.[1] This fair copy would be in charge of the 'bookholder' or 'book-keeper', who was responsible for seeing that properties and stage effects were on cue during performances. He may also have been responsible for prompting. Individual actors did not have the whole script; instead each part with its cues was copied out on a long strip and these were distributed to the cast. The practice with regard to prompt-books in later historical periods, where detailed practical performance notes were recorded, may not be a wholly reliable guide to Elizabethan playhouse 'books'. Evidence is lacking.

Crane, then, may have used as a basis for his transcription: (a) a completed manuscript in Shakespeare's hand, not a fair copy, including changes made in the process of original composition, but also, possibly, other changes made some time later than the first performance; (b) a manuscript fair copy prepared with authorial approval or acquiescence for theatrical use, the playhouse 'book'; (c) a playhouse 'book' with additional changes made after Shakesepare ceased to have any connection with the company, the King's Men.

Both the 'book' and the authorial manuscript might have been extant at the time it was decided to have a transcript made by Ralph Crane. In the long period of time before the transcription was made the manuscripts may have suffered wear and tear, and in places may have been difficult to decipher.

The Folio text of *Measure for Measure* was set by compositors who divided the work between them, as was customary. Attribution of particular sections of text, if it can be ascertained, may be significant for editorial purposes since assumptions about the habits of a given compositor may be relevant when trying to infer what stood in the copy, or in establishing patterns of work in the printing house. Unfortunately, in the case of *Measure for Measure* it remains uncertain which compositor set a number of pages, as the tables of suggestions given below make clear.

THE COMPOSITORS AND CASTING-OFF OF COPY

In his major study *The Printing and Proof-Reading of the First Folio of Shakespeare* (1963) Charlton Hinman exploited two separate methods to establish patterns of setting and distribution by the compositors. He identified individual pieces of type and recorded their recurrence in sequence through the pages of the Folio, and he tabulated and analysed peculiarities of spelling of common words, thereby identifying individual compositors. These two independent tests reveal a great deal of how the Folio was printed. Hinman established that during the printing of quires A to E, those immediately preceding *Measure for Measure*, Jaggard's compositors were engaged with the concurrent printing of another work, Thomas Wilson's *Christian Dictionary*. The setting had ended (if not the machining and distribution) with the beginning of quire F, although from the now suddenly irregular type-recurrence which Hinman traced in quires F and G he found that

[1] As Greg notes in *Elizabethan Dramatic Documents*, 1931, p. 192, and as Florio records in his *World of Wordes* (1598), as cited in the *OED Supplement* under Book *sb* 8b.

'the distribution procedure followed during the printing of most of the Folio was not followed here' (II, 380). As a consequence Hinman was not able to identify compositors from the evidence of type-recurrence, although he did suggest identifications by using analysis of spelling peculiarities. Some of these have subsequently been questioned, first by T.H. Howard-Hill[1] and John O'Connor[2] who have independently offered alternative suggestions of compositor stints for these quires F and G.

Given the sparse evidence, attribution of columns and part-columns to particular compositors has varied from analyst to analyst. Hinman supposed that signature F was set by Compositors A, B, C and D. Howard-Hill discounted A, suggesting B, C and D. O'Connor agreed with Howard-Hill except for F2v, F1va, F1b, F6v. This can be set out as a table. In quire G Hinman's Compositor A was

	F3v	F4	F3	F4v	F2v	F5a	5b	F2a	2b	F5v	F1va	1vb	F6	F1a	1b	F6v
Hinman	A	A	D	A	C	D	D	D	D	B	D	D	B	A	A	D
Howard-Hill	C	C	D	C	C	C	D	C	D	B	D?	C	B	C	D?	D/C
O'Connor	C	C	D	C	D	C	D	C	D	B	C	C	B	C	C	C

again discounted by the others: Howard-Hill supposed B, C, D and F to be at work, but O'Connor saw evidence only of B, C and F; Werstine[3] slightly modified O'Connor: he based his findings on analysis of Hinman's typographical evidence and discerned distribution patterns indicating that the compositors co-operated on distributing the same wrought-off pages. Jeanne Roberts[4] has questioned the existence of Compositor F altogether and Werstine is reported to follow her in this. It is evident that attributions as provisional as this cannot be treated as definitive. Hinman supposed that the order of the formes for quires F and G was

	G3v	G4a	4b	G3	G4va	4vb	G2v	G5	G2a	2b	G5v	G1v	G6a	6b	G1a	1b	G6v
Hinman	B	D?	D	B	D?	D?	B	A	A	A	A	D	A	A	D	D	A?
Howard-Hill	B	C	F	B	F	C	B	C	D	C	F	B	F	C	B	D	C
O'Connor	B	C	F	B	F	C	B	C	F	C	F	B	F	C	B	C	C
Werstine (Roberts)	B	C	FD	B	FD	C	B	C	FD	C	FD	B	FD	C	B	C+B	FD+C

that indicated in the tables above, starting from the inside. This would normally mean that casting-off (that is, the estimation of how much copy might neatly fit each Folio page, made necessary because the pages were not set in the order we read them, but as in the table above, pages 1 recto and 6 verso being composed

1 'The compositors of Shakespeare's Folio Comedies', *SB* 26 (1973), 61–106.
2 'Compositors D and F of the Shakespeare First Folio', *SB* 28 (1975), 81–117.
3 Paul Werstine, 'First Folio Comedies: cases and compositors', *SB* 34 (1981), 206–34.
4 Jeanne Roberts, 'Ralph Crane and the text of *The Tempest*', *S.St.* 13 (1980), 213–33.

simultaneously to make the last forme of the quire) would only be needed for the first half of the quire, and that miscalculations would be most likely to show up in pages 1 recto and 1 verso and 2 recto. Werstine speculated that simultaneous setting of two quires might have been undertaken, requiring more casting-off.

In any case there is no significant problem in either quire F or G associated with casting-off errors. In quire G there are a number of instances where prose is printed as verse (which uses more space and therefore could be a sign of stretching the text to fill out a page): only eleven lines of the last page are taken up by text, half the page being filled by an ornament, below the list of characters. Rather than being a sign of poor casting-off, however, the printing of prose as verse is to be explained by the compositor, B, being influenced by Ralph Crane who 'did not extend lines of prose uniformly to the right-hand margins of his transcripts'.[1] Compositor B was responsible for most of the prose-as-verse settings. The obvious place for a problem to occur, F1v, does indeed show a crowded page, but this has been plausibly explained not as a result of poor casting-off but of the compositor's error in including lines marked for deletion in the manuscript and therefore not taken into account by whoever undertook the casting-off. Whatever stints they are allotted (and this remains a matter of some dispute among analysts), the compositors reproduce a striking number of the peculiarities of their copy, allowing it to be certainly identified as the work of Ralph Crane. Assumptions about the identity of a compositor for any particular passage, given the kinds of problem encountered in the present text, could add little to influence an editor, even if the identity of compositors were more secure than it is.

THE SCRIBE

Ralph Crane's characteristic spellings have been noted from other transcriptions he made from dramatic manuscripts; those appearing in *Measure for Measure* include *ceizes, coheard, confes'd, creadit, encrease, flowre, happely, masques, midle, misterie, sirha*. His preference for the spelling *boldnes, doublenes, fewnes, goodnes, greatnes, newnes, seednes, sweetnes* and *witnes* survives in the text. He habitually preferred colons to semicolons; the Folio *Measure for Measure* has many colons and very few semicolons: one colon for every 34 words (close to Crane's average in his dramatic MSS., which was 1:27), one semi-colon for every 135 words (Crane's average was 1:123). Crane generally preferred question marks to exclamation marks (there are no exclamation marks in *Measure for Measure*, which does on the other hand have one question mark for every 66 words). He liked apostrophes, which are frequent in the present text, and in forms characteristic of Crane such as *I'haue* (3.1.4), *ha'st* (5.1.356, 357), *do'st* (1.2.98), *'Faith* (2.1.229, 5.1.497), *'fore-noone* (2.2.165), *Good'euen* (3.2.183, 4.3.141), *'Saue* (2.2.26, 166), *'blesse* (3.2.10), *'Please* (2.2.29), *'Pray* (2.2.2), *pray'thee* (1.2.51). Crane's liking for hyphens is evident in unusual hyphenated compounds: *en-skied* (1.4.34), *run-by* (1.4.63), *Sister-hood* (2.2.22), *tested-gold* (2.2.154), *all-building-Law* (2.4.94), *vnpre-par'd*

---

1 Howard-Hill, *Ralph Crane*, p. 36, cited by Eccles, p. 298.

(4.3.58). There are 75 parentheses, many more than in the Folio comedies set
from non-Crane copy, though fewer than Crane's norm.

Like the other Folio plays printed from Crane transcripts (except for *The Merry
Wives of Windsor*, where space is lacking), *Measure for Measure* has a list of all the
characters following the end of the play. Crane also apparently added *The Scene
Vienna*. The play is divided into acts and scenes, as are the other Folio comedies
printed from Crane transcripts (only two of the remaining nine comedies in the
Folio have acts and scenes). Howard-Hill observes that act and scene divisions are
correctly marked in all Crane's transcripts. Speech headings are consistent in
form: Mistress Overdone is *Bawde*, Pompey *Clowne*, though both are named in the
text. The stage directions are sparse, but entrances are mostly accounted for.

There are some puzzling, apparently contradictory features in the text, some
seemingly pointing to authorial foul papers, some to theatrical transcription. This
is another feature probably indicating Crane, since Howard-Hill notes that
Crane's scribal procedure resulted in an influence 'so strong that it obscures
evidence of the kind of manuscript which he transcribed' (*Ralph Crane*, p. 138).
Although Crane, in other texts, has been shown to have interfered with the
wording of SDs, he seems to have done so with a reader in mind, and it is not likely
that he would remove important SDs, though he did sometimes move them – for
instance, to make massed entrances. Perhaps he faithfully followed his copy in the
SD *Francisca a Nun* (1.4.0 SD) and *Frier Thomas* (1.3.0 SD) where the wording might
be Shakespeare's, written at the head of a scene 'in case [Shakespeare] should
later decide to use them' (Lever, p. xxv). Crane lists Friar Thomas as well as Friar
Peter in his final list of characters, though they may well be alternative names for
the same character, an indecision on the author's part characteristic of foul papers.
Crane also lists the Duke's name as *Vincentio* although it nowhere appears in the
text. Greg suggests that the opening SD in the manuscript Crane was given to copy
did have the name *Vincentio*.[1] Why it was omitted in the text, given Crane's known
care with the presentation of the beginning of a play, is inexplicable. Nevertheless
these features do seem to indicate access to foul papers. There are several SDs for
indeterminate numbers, *Lords* (1.1.0 SD), *Officers* (1.2.97 SD), *Citizens at seuerall
doors* (5.1.0 SD), which as so-called 'permissive' SDs[2] might indicate an author's
completed draft rather than a playhouse 'book' (not being practical in specifying
how many actors are required because such details were left to the later stage of

---

1 W.W. Greg, *The Shakespeare First Folio*, 1955, p. 355. Greg proffers the weak alternative
   suggestion that Crane invented the name for the list. There are lists after *The Tempest* and *The
   Two Gentlemen*, the first two plays in the First Folio, then comes *The Merry Wives of Windsor*, which
   may have been intended to have a list, but there is clearly no space on the page, then follows
   Measure for Measure which again has a list. (All these were set from Crane transcripts.) Greg notes
   that later on in the First Folio the few plays that have lists appended would otherwise have unused
   and unwelcome bare space on the last page. Crane transcripts of other non-Shakespeare plays
   have such lists.
2 Greg, like Dover Wilson, notes that in general the stage directions in this text are very bare, with
   no direction for noise, even at the beginning of 5.1, where a flourish, or trumpets, might be
   expected.

theatrical production). Crane did efface some features he considered dispensable, but in the cases cited above he seems to have faithfully followed his copy, preserving wording which is familiar from other Shakespearean texts showing traces of an author's draft (though he may have removed the name *Vincentio*, and if so, perhaps he made other interventions). Although these SDs seem to indicate an author's draft, it may be noted that they are relatively few in number.

Since Crane did alter SDs when transcribing other plays, it could be that he omitted minor SDs that stood in his copy for *Measure for Measure*. There are in fact a number of staging problems connected with exits, and taken together these might be seen as pointing to authorial draft, to manuscript not yet prepared for practical use in the theatre. We may begin with two somewhat minor instances where it is possible that no exit SDs would have stood even in a playhouse 'book' but where it is also possible that Crane might have omitted them. The first is in 1.4 concerning the Nun: should she exit or is she intended to stay on stage but in the background? The second concerns the Duke and Provost in 3.1.52. The dialogue indicates that they must find concealment (a situation like that in *Troilus and Cressida* 5.2). Presumably they do not actually exit but retire without leaving the stage. The evidence is inconclusive. In other instances now to be considered, however, it seems unlikely that Crane, assuming him to have been uninterested in stage performance, would have deleted SDs of manifest dramatic importance even to a reader, in such crucial places as 3.1.159, where Isabella must withdraw out of earshot, or 3.1.171, where the Provost must come forward; most probably Crane is here being faithful to his copy, which at this point was not marked with stage directions. At 4.1.55 ff. Crane might have 'normalised' SDs: Isabella and Mariana may be intended by Shakespeare only to walk out of earshot, but F marks exit and entrance for them. These cases can mostly be cleared up by reference to the dialogue, and the alternative stagings seem allowable (although removing Juliet from 1.2 would have to involve cutting some dialogue – and this is discussed in footnote 1 opposite). In the case of 5.1.121 ff., however, it seems an exit SD is missing: at some point Isabella is to leave the stage; the Duke says 'To prison with her!' at 121, after which she has one line, 125, and then nothing until 378; in the intervening time she is ambiguously referred to as if present: 'this woman' (139, 158), then the ambiguous 'Her shall you hear disprovèd to her eyes', (161); but then at 240 the Duke accuses Mariana of being 'Compact with her that's gone', showing that by this point she is supposed to have exited. Escalus calls for her at 267, and the Folio has a SD for the entry of Isabella at 274, and she is addressed three lines later but does not reply, and at 374 the Duke addresses her as if she has been present for some time. It is likely that in this case, as in others, Shakespeare intended the character to be a silent presence on the stage, from 274 to 378, so modifying the meaning of the action.

JULIET IN 1.2

This seems confirmed by the special case of Juliet in 1.2, where the dialogue requires her silent presence, which undoubtedly has an eloquent effect. It is possible that Shakespeare changed his intentions in the act of composition and decided not to bring Juliet on here, then failed to cancel the dialogue or SD, but I believe not, and there is a further reason for thinking that bringing on Juliet rather than removing her is Shakespeare's revised version. This concerns the odd duplication in 1.2.71–7 of information about Claudio's arrest which has already been given. The compositor evidently found himself short of space, printing two SDs on the same line as dialogue (F1va, *Enter Bawde*, and F1vb, *Enter Clowne*). He gives *Scena Tertia* a narrow box followed by the entry squeezed into one line and unleaded. He shortens *Gent.* to *Gen.* to squeeze a line and 'on' to 'o' at the end of another (33, 65). Line 106 is turned over. This represents a saving of seven lines, the space needed for 71–7. The best explanation for this is that whoever cast off this passage realised that 71–7 were redundant (perhaps they were faintly marked for cancellation in the MS.).[1]

Shakespeare's manuscript could by now have been difficult to interpret, with additions perhaps not clearly marked for insertion, and cancellation marks. A transcriber might be daunted and decide for safety's sake to transcribe everything. Crane evidently transcribed carefully; was it the caster-off or some other person with an interest in the text as dramatic literature, who considered that the lines 71–7 were redundant? It seems virtually certain that the caster-off calculated on the assumption that these lines were to be deleted, yet the compositors failed to omit them, thereby giving themselves difficulty with overcrowding the page. Was this because the manuscript was not clearly marked up, or was there some last-minute reversal of the decision? There can be speculation that the dialogue between Lucio, the Gentlemen and Mistress Overdone (1.2.1–66) was written by someone other than Shakespeare, as Dover Wilson supposed,[2] but the apparent allusions to contemporary events of 1604 (discussed at pp. 22–3 above) indicate that the dialogue was written then, and it would seem, therefore, most probably by Shakespeare. When was it marked for cutting? Possibly for a sensitive performance in 1604 (or after censorship, or self-censorship), but since the topical allusions would have lost their point in later years, someone else might have marked them for cutting in preparation for a stage revival or for publication in the First Folio. In

---

1 A conjectural reconstruction might go as follows: Shakespeare could have begun the scene originally with 67 or 70, then gone on with 77–95. He could then have added the passage giving Claudio's offence and fate, 71–7, which he perhaps marked for insertion after 67 or 70, and at the same time added the lines 96–7, where Pompey announces the entry of Claudio, the Provost and Juliet. Since the speech headings for 'Clown' are consistently *Clo.* in 71–7 and 96, whereas they are *Clow.* for 80–96 (noted by Lever, p. xx, n. 1), it may be assumed that 96–7 was written at the same time as 71–8, both passages serving to emphasise the case of Claudio. Shakespeare could then have written a new beginning for the scene (with Lucio, the Gentlemen, and Mistress Overdone). Realising then that this made his previous beginning redundant he could have marked 71–8 for deletion, but left 96–7 because he wanted to preserve the dramatic effect they announced. Thus Shakespeare's final decision would be that Juliet should be present in the scene at this point.

2 e.g. 'It is sheer mud, dreary, dead; not even a maggot stirs. Let the reader consider these 57 lines of prose in isolation, and ask himself if Shakespeare could have written them, at any period of his career' (NS, p. 107).

the theatre, the repetitions of the news about the proclamation and Claudio present no significant problem, serving indeed to emphasise a point about the way the news is received by various characters, and it cannot be certain that this was not Shakespeare's final design.

POSSIBLE TONING-DOWN OF OATHS

It has been suggested[1] that elsewhere material has been deliberately removed from the text, the word 'God' having almost certainly been changed to 'Heaven' at 2.4.4, as the pronoun in the next line indicates:

> Heaven in my mouth
> As if I did but only chew his name . . .

'Heaven' or 'heavens' occurs 44 times in the text, and in some of these instances it is possible to substitute 'God', so that it has been suggested that the text has been deliberately purged of oaths and that this should be connected with the passing of the statute of James I in 1606, the Act to Restrain the Abuses of Players. The word 'God' does not appear at all in the text, nor does it in other comedies in the Folio printed from Crane transcriptions, except for *The Merry Wives of Windsor*, where it occurs four times.[2] This could indicate that Crane was instructed to remove offensive expressions, but it might have already been done in the copy he was given. If so, who might have done it, when and why? Perhaps before performance the play was felt to be in substance already capable of giving offence, so that it was prudent to remove verbal provocation of this kind; such a decision could have been made and entered in the author's papers or the playhouse 'book' before first performance. Perhaps (according to another hypothesis) oaths were toned down in response to the Act of 1606: but this was some two years after the first performance, and it would seem probable that it would be done in the playhouse 'book'. Why should the changes also be entered in Shakespeare's papers? Were they being used as the basis for a new prompt-book, and were all the other revisions and changes therefore made at the same time, after 1606, the date of the Act against blasphemous expressions? Alternatively, did the author's papers remain as Shakespeare left them at the time of original completion, 1604, without some or all of the changes, and were some changes entered into them at the time they were handed to Crane? (In the latter hypothetical case the changes could have been taken over from the playhouse 'book', which may have been felt to be too valuable to be given to the scribe.) It is not possible to be clear, presumably because Crane effaced the tell-tale signs. It may now be appropriate to review other signs of revision, bearing in mind the overall question of whether the manuscript Crane was given was Shakespeare's alone, or whether intervention by others seems probable.

---

1 White made the suggestion in 1854, developing a note by Thirlby, and Lever suggested that Crane may have removed oaths. Howard-Hill considers the question undecidable, Eccles (p. 295) thinks the play was 'carefully purged of oaths'.
2 Eccles, p. 295.

THE JUSTICE IN 2.1

At the end of 2.1, speech headings assign several short speeches to *Iust.* and at the opening of the scene the SD marks the entrance, possibly as an afterthought, of *Iustice*: *Enter Angelo, Escalus, and seruants, Iustice*. Perhaps Shakespeare first assigned these speeches to the Provost, and then changed his mind. The dialogue at the end of the scene concerns Claudio, and the Provost is sent off by Angelo (36) to summon the priest to confess Claudio. This errand could be simple enough to permit a prompt return, certainly by the end of Escalus's interview with Elbow at 235. As it stands this is the only scene in which the Justice appears and he has very little to say. Possibly he was invented when Shakespeare noticed that the Provost begins the next scene, and so could not be on stage at the end of this present scene: hence the apparent afterthought of the entry direction at the beginning of 2.1. It may be noted that no direction for the Provost's exit is given in the Folio (though this is a not uncommon type of lapse throughout the Folio).

THE DUKE'S SPEECH IN 4.1

In 4.1 the Duke's speech at 56–61 was supposed by Warburton to be part of a speech at 3.2.158 moved by the players. Warburton considered the speech to refer to Lucio's scandals and to be 'absolutely foreign' to the context in 4.1. Johnson noted that although the speech has a practical function in filling up the time while the ladies converse, it is really too short; 'they must have quick tongues and ready apprehensions' to understand one another in so brief a time. But Johnson's approach here is one assuming a literal-minded naturalistic treatment of time not consistent with the play's method (see the discussion of the time scheme at pp. 203–4 below). Warburton's hypothesis is open to similar objections. Warburton considers the Duke's grave brooding on scandal an implausibly abrupt change of subject. It might be argued on the other hand that it is psychologically plausible as a soliloquy in which the Duke's darker preoccupations, suppressed during the urgent business of planning, now compulsively surface in his pause (much as the dark brooding of Duke Altofront emerges in soliloquies in *The Malcontent*). Furthermore the lines serve to restate, in advance of the play's complex final movement, the major theme of the trials of the governor. If it is only a question of smooth fitting, these lines – 4.1.56–61 – could, as Warburton says, fit smoothly in at 3.2.158 (though not solely or inevitably there, perhaps), but the objection is that smooth fitting is not characteristic of this play and has a dramatically softer and weaker effect than placing them in 4.1. No doubt the ladies conversing apart in 4.1.56 do need a covering speech from the Duke, but it need not be long. Did Shakespeare write a speech which was for some reason cut? If so, transferring lines from 3.2 seems a curious piece of botching, and it would be surprising if Shakespeare, assuming him to have been present, was unable to compose a fresh speech to replace what was cut. Warburton's idea that the speech was transferred by the players from 3.2 remains a mere hypothesis, devised apparently to support his narrow assumptions about plausibility.

4.3 AND 4.5: LUCIO AND VARRIUS

The next instance concerns 4.3 and 4.5. To begin with the latter. In 4.5 the Duke names several characters new to the audience, none of whom is given subsequent speaking parts and only one of whom is personally addressed, when in 4.5.11 the Duke says 'I thank thee, Varrius' and tells him that the others have been told to meet him at the city's gate (as happens in 5.1). These non-speaking and (apart from Varrius) perhaps 'ghost' characters – though their presence may be implied in the vague SD *Lords* (5.1.0 SD) – appear to have been summoned out of air to serve the local dramatic function of courtly 'background' for the Duke and his reassumed official role (as Greg notes). They have, rather anomalously, Roman names. The brief scene seems as if hastily written, or as if some of the dialogue was cut (possibly in the interest of the overall dramatic rhythm). Shakespeare may have judged just enough was left to create a sense of bustling activity in preparation for his evidently complex but as yet undisclosed scheme at the gate. Clearly Greg's idea[1] that Shakespeare wanted to emphasise the Duke's return to secular public affairs by introducing Varrius and the rest is persuasive. The abruptness with which Varrius is introduced has also led to speculation that a passage earlier in the play introducing these members of the court circle and giving them a more substantial stage presence was cut. Where might such a passage originally have stood? A little earlier there is a scene with anomalies and discrepancies, 4.3, which is possible.

In 4.3 the discrepancies are as follows: the Duke-as-Friar sends the Provost at line 83 to conceal Barnardine and Claudio 'in secret holds' and to send the head of Ragozine to Angelo. The Provost goes, and the Duke explains to the audience that he will write and send letters to Angelo via the Provost telling Angelo to meet the Duke 'a league below the city'. The Provost enters with the severed head only to exit at once. At 122–3 the Duke-as-Friar tells Isabella that the Duke has arranged to meet Escalus and Angelo 'at the gates'. He tells Isabella to give a letter to Friar Peter telling him to go to Mariana's house 'tonight' (132). Then enters not the Provost but Lucio, greeting them with 'Good even' although it has been established that it is morning (see 39, clearly showing that Barnardine's hanging is set for morning, though he will not get up for it; and 69–70, showing that it is near 5 a.m., the hour prefixed for Angelo to receive Claudio's head). Later, in 5.1, Lucio says that this meeting of the Duke-as-Friar with Isabella took place 'yesternight'.

To explain the confusion about time and other discrepancies Lever proposed the following hypothesis:[2] the confusion about the time of day could be due to Lucio having been substituted for the Provost, who in an earlier version (so goes the hypothesis) must have returned at 140. At that point the Duke would have given Isabella her dismissal because the Duke must make sure she does not learn from the Provost that Claudio has not in fact been executed: she must remain for the time being ignorant of this if the Duke's scheme is to succeed. Lucio was thus

1 Greg, *The Shakespeare First Folio*, pp. 354–5.
2 Lever, pp. xxii–xxiv.

substituted for the Provost because Shakespeare had not brought Lucio on stage since Act 3 and now needed to bring him to the audience's attention in preparation for the Act 5 dénouement. The assumption would be that, when writing the Lucio dialogue at a later stage than the first composition of the scene, Shakespeare forgot that 4.3 is supposed to be set early in the morning. The person invited to meet the Duke 'a league below the city' is not Angelo (contradicted by the opening of 5.1) but, in Lever's view, Varrius. The phrase at 4.3.84 should read 'to Varrius' not 'to Angelo': the previous line, which also has the phrase 'to Angelo', misled either scribe or compositor into erroneous repetition. This suggestion has the merit of neatness and could be right. It might be possible to build on Lever's suggestion and to propose that if there was an earlier passage dealing with Varrius it could have been in 4.3 following Isabella's words at 128. The emphasis on the secular and public domain would then have been reintroduced via Varrius here in 4.3 – the Provost, having been so embroiled in the Duke-as-Friar business, could not well serve this purpose. But Shakespeare then saw the need to bring Lucio back. It could be speculated that early experience of the play in performance could have prompted this idea, but this assumes Shakespeare not to be master of his craft in an important area. Shakespeare can be shown to be a trenchant reviser of his own drafts, and in the present case it is plausible that the changes were made during the process of composition, perhaps once the play as a whole was nearing completion and its shape and rhythm – highly wrought as they must be in approaching the tragi-comedy's climax – were given their final form. The plot substance of the cancelled Varrius passage might be partly absorbed into the Duke's speech after 4.3.128 and also into 4.5, which one could speculate was written partly to compensate for the deletion from 4.3. It may be noted that Varrius has no lines in 5.1; perhaps he was originally given some at the opening of the scene but then it was decided that his visual presence would suffice, allowing emphasis to fall on Angelo and thus pointing up the parallel with 1.1.

THE TIME SCHEME

Several minor discrepancies in the play's time scheme are simple slips by the dramatist, and of a kind spectators will not notice in performance; these include Angelo's demand for Isabella's answer 'tomorrow' (2.4.168) contradicted by her telling Claudio in 3.1.100 that 'This night's the time', and the Duke's request to the Provost for 'four days' respite' (4.2.141) when later he promises to return to Vienna 'within these two days' (4.2.172–4). Such minor discrepancies contrast to the much more substantial one of Lucio's greeting to the Duke at 4.3.141. This is noticeably contradictory and seems to be in fact a sign of disturbance in the manuscript. Shakespeare's dramatic handling of time generally in the play disregards exactly consistent narrative time – so that, for instance, on the one hand the proclamation is only two hours old while, on the other, Mistress Overdone and Pompey have apparently re-established themselves by 2.1 in a hot-house in the city; or, again, the Duke's absence seems in one sense a prolonged one consistent with a long journey as far as Russia or Rome, while in another sense the play's action is compressed into a few days. These features are characteristic of Shakespeare's dramaturgy in other plays and do not indicate revision or abridgement in this play, rather being integral to its design and artistry.

Summary: the nature of the copy

The survey of the text allows us to return to the question posed at the outset. There are some possible signs of Shakespeare's working drafts: the naming of the Nun and Friars, the permissive SDs, perhaps the name Vincentio. There are possible signs of revision, most of which seem likely to be authorial, though the removal of 'God' at 2.4.4 looks like rough-and-ready *ad hoc* revision by another hand. The stylistic argument of Dover Wilson[1] about the Lucio–Gentlemen dialogue in 1.2 does not convince, and, given the challenge of the experimental mode and genre Shakespeare was working with in this play, it is very plausible indeed that he would find it necessary to make changes adjusting the role of Lucio, of the Duke reverting to his public role, and adjusting the dramatic rhythm as the tragi-comic climax nears. That Shakespeare at this stage of his maturity could not foresee practical theatrical problems, as is argued by those who think these revisions to have been made as a result of experience of the play in the theatre, seems debatable.

The view that the copy given to Crane was the playhouse 'book'[2] must be squared with the signs of authorial draft (a script not yet prepared for the playhouse). There is the question of the staging of several significant episodes, which is open, not resolved by stage directions. This might be a further sign of authorial draft, though it might be that such exits and entrances, once worked out in rehearsal, did not need to be or were not on this occasion entered in the 'book' by the book-keeper. Still, the absence of these stage directions scarcely strengthens the argument that Crane's copy was the playhouse 'book'.

The hypotheses suggested at the beginning of this Textual Analysis were three. There is no particular evidence for (c), a playhouse 'book' with additional changes made after Shakespeare ceased his connection with the company. Uncertainty about what degree of practical annotation characterised a playhouse 'book' (the so-called 'prompt-book') means that at least access to a playhouse 'book' by Crane

---

1 In fact Dover Wilson developed an elaborate theory of successive revisions of the text. An original text, he suggested, was reduced in length for court performance in 1604: 'Now, if we imagine that the abridgement of 1604 was made from the existing players' parts and not on Shakespeare's MS., that this original unabridged MS. was afterwards lost, and that the prose adapter, therefore, constructed his text from the players' parts of 1604, hastily transcribing them and filling out the play with additions of his own, we are making a not unreasonable guess as to the origin of the actual copy used for the printing of *Measure for Measure* as we have it' (NS, p. 113). E.K. Chambers, *William Shakespeare: A Study of Facts and Problems*, 2 vols., 1930, I, 453–7, examined and refuted this case.

2 Revived by J. Jowett and S.W. Wells in their discussion of *Measure for Measure*, in Stanley Wells and Gary Taylor with John Jowett and William Montgomery, *William Shakespeare, A Textual Companion*, 1987, p. 468.

cannot be ruled out, while there are indications that authorial draft (so-called 'foul papers') lies behind Crane's copy. It is possible that some years after 1604 wear and tear of the playhouse 'book' had led to a fresh copy being commissioned from a scribe, who supplemented this 'book' by consulting the authorial draft; or it is possible that this is what Crane himself did. Such a hypothesis accommodates the features of the Folio text noted above, without giving credence to purely hypo-thetical suggestions. Nevertheless even this hypothesis must remain uncertain. It remains even more uncertain what kind of further interventions Ralph Crane may have made, beyond his certain imposition of spelling and punctuation habits of his own; but the fact that the evidence here surveyed presents some riddles probably does indicate that he did efface telling features of his copy.

Lineation

VERSE AND PROSE

Measure for Measure has a number of irregular lines in the body of otherwise regular passages of verse, and it also has scenes in which verse and prose are mixed. Generally it is clear which is which. 1.2.98 ff. is verse dialogue in which Lucio speaks prose; in 2.1.118 Angelo interrupts in verse after a long passage of prose dialogue; verse changes to prose in the middle of 3.1; in 3.2 the Duke begins with what looks like a half-line of verse, switches to prose in speaking to Elbow, to verse in addressing Pompey, perhaps retains verse for half a line whilst com-menting on Lucio's first speech after his entrance, reverts to prose in his exchange with Lucio, reverts to verse after Lucio's exit, addresses Escalus first in verse, then prose, and ends the scene with a speech in octosyllabic couplets. In the next scene, 4.1, the Duke and Mariana use both prose and verse in their first dialogue; in 4.2 prose changes to verse at Claudio's entrance but even the Duke reverts to prose after 111. A complex alternation between prose and verse is apparent in 4.3, and in the final scene Lucio reverts to prose at 149. Given the fact that the manuscript might well have been untidy, with additions and deletions, and possibly in poor condition due to age and wear, a few of the verse lines may have seemed prose to a copyist. It is known that Crane did not extend prose lines uniformly to the right-hand margin, so that some of the prose may, in his transcript, have looked like verse: the compositors did set some prose as verse. However, we may certainly find reason to think most of these alternations within scenes are deliberately designed by Shakespeare to serve dramatic purposes, and by no means indicate anything other than the author's design; an editor has simply to set out verse and prose with this in mind and as convention requires, although there are one or two places (recorded in the collation) where there has been disagreement about which is which.

SHORT LINES

In modern editions of Shakespeare's plays the layout of verse speeches is not arbitrary and insignificantly conventional, but deliberate, to convey either a break and change in direction or a flowing continuity between speeches. A substantial number of lines in the Folio text which either begin or end speeches are printed as short lines, not linked. In distinguishing between full verse lines divided between speakers and short lines which stand independently, it is possible to notice the distinction at work in cases where a break is made, with a new subject or abrupt change of direction. A clear instance is 2.3.14–16, which is set out thus in F:

> More fit to doe another fuch offence,
> Then dye for this.
> *Duk.* When muft he dye?
> *Pro.* As I do thinke to morrow.

Here the Provost's long speech ends with a short line, monosyllables adding to an emphatic stark conclusion. The Duke begins a fresh direction with his question, and this is linked to the Provost's answer which completes a pentameter. In 2.4.104–5 it is possible to think Angelo's half-line not a link but rather an abrupt, brutal rejoinder to be signalled as an independent short line rather than a divided hexameter:

> That longing haue bin ficke for, ere I'ld yeeld
> My body vp to fhame.
>
>   *Ang.* That   F5^r
> _____
> ——————
> *Ang.* Then muft your brother die,̣
> *Ifa.* And 'twer the cheaper way :
> Better it were a brother dide at once,   F5^v

Here the current of emotion and moral argument is flowing between them so that one half-senses Angelo is waiting for his chance to make the devastating point 'Then must your brother die', which comes in eager (almost victorious) response: therefore I link the two short lines. It remains conjecturally possible that half a line has dropped out of Angelo's response, since the catchword is wrong: but as the text stands, an editor cannot invent half a line on the flimsy evidence of a catchword which may itself be wrong, and given two short lines, I choose to link them. By contrast I preserve as independent short lines the later exchange at 2.4.142–3:

> *Ang.* Plainlie conceiue I loue you.
> *Ifa.* My brother did loue *Iuliet*,
> And you tell me that he fhall die for't.

These two short lines are abruptly contrasted in content and rhythm: the idea in Isabella's is not anticipated by Angelo; it is a shock, and is followed by a second shock in her next line.

A difficult case is 2.2.42. Angelo's speech concludes with a short line, Isabella begins with a short line: should they be linked?

And let goe by the Actor.
Isab. Oh iust, but seuere Law :
I had a brother then ; heauen keepe your honour.

If Isabella's first short line is linked with Angelo's short last line the resulting verse line is a virtual hexameter, and there are a number of such irregular lines in the verse of F. If the link is made it implies that Isabella's response completes Angelo's thought, representing a syntactically balanced figure for Justice's scales. Yet if Isabella's short line is considered independent it would then stand as a new piece of thinking, moving from acceptance – 'oh iust' – to resistance – 'but seuere Law' – so that the next line would urge Angelo to recognise the human feeling involved, and the formula 'heauen keep your honour' would carry a reminder of religious values as well as offer a neutral formality of withdrawal from debate, giving Angelo a chance to reconsider. I think the lines should be linked, because although Isabella's response broaches new matter for her case, she does not at once develop it. She is bewildered; without having lost the argument she is emotionally dejected; and Lucio's intervention to urge her on indicates that he fears she has lost heart. At the same time it remains evident that her short line is also independent in other ways. So much bottled-up emotion in both speakers is about to break out, and actors can give varying degrees of warmth and force, or measured or excitable rhythm to this exchange, according to the larger design of their interpretation.

In his article surveying short lines in Shakespeare,[1] Fredson Bowers notes that statistically Shakespeare preferred three stresses to two stresses before the break in a divided line; Bowers advocates preservation of short lines where a significant rhetorical pause exists or where no sequential link is discernible between the respective short lines. There are difficult cases: Bowers argues for unlinked short lines at 2.2.41–2 on the grounds that Isabella's speech is preceded by 'a marked rhetorical pause' reinforced by her 'exclamation made largely to herself' (as Bowers sees it) which is 'very close to change of address'. I would accept that a change of address in a short line beginning a speech would normally require setting as an unlinked short line, though I cannot agree with Bowers's description of this exchange (see my note in the Commentary for 2.2.42). At 2.2.146 Angelo's short line beginning a speech after a short line ending Isabella's certainly is an aside and a change of address and so I do not link it. Another instance of this criterion's relevance is 5.1.18–19 (see Commentary note), or 4.6.8–9, where a change of direction is abrupt, so that the link between Isabella's ending short line, 'That's bitter to sweet end', and Mariana's 'I would Friar Peter –' is not made; instead Mariana's short line is linked to the line following, giving a regular pentameter, completing the thought. Other instances are discussed in the Commentary at 1.2.137, 1.3.6–7, 1.4.72, 2.1.8.

1 Fredson Bowers, 'Establishing Shakespeare's text: notes on short lines and the problem of verse division', *Studies in Bibliography* 32 (1979), 74–130. Compare also Marvin Spevack's discussion in his edition of *Julius Caesar*, 1988, pp. 152–3.

There are some instances of short lines in F which seem to have no rhetorical significance – for example, 2.4.119 or 5.1.32:

> Or wring redreſſe from you :
> Heare me : oh heare me, heere.

This also applies to 1.2.123, 124 and 5.1.68. Each of these lines seems too long for the column measure but the compositor could simply have run the extra words over to the next line. Instead, apparently influenced by the syntactical break, he has printed the line as two separate halves, marking the break with strong punctuation. There are other instances which on the other hand do seem to have significance in pointing up rhetorical effect – for example, 1.4.72:

> To ſoften *Angelo* : And that's my pith of buſineſſe
> 'Twixt you, and your poore brother.
>   *Iſa.* Doth he ſo,
> Seeke his life ?
>   *Luc.* Has cenſur'd him already,

Another case is 2.2.117 ff. where alternative line arrangements have been proposed (as the collation records), making a full line and a short one, thus:

> Would use his heaven for thunder, nothing but thunder: –
> Merciful heaven

Yet F's arrangement, keeping emphasis on the first phrase's paradox, seems to be rhetorically superior:

> For euery pelting petty Officer
> Would vſe his heauen for thunder ;
> Nothing but thunder : Mercifull heauen ,

At 3.1.54 many editors have not allowed Isabella's first word to stand as an independent short line, though such very short 'interjectional' lines are frequent in Shakespeare, as Abbott (512) shows. F's lineation is rhetorically effective here and must be preserved:

>   *Cla.* Now ſiſter, what's the comfort?
>   *Iſa.* Why,
> As all comforts are : moſt good, moſt good indeede,
> Lord *Angelo* hauing affaires to heauen
> Intends you for his ſwift Ambaſſador,

Textual cruces and editors

When dealing with lineation it is sometimes necessary to take account of grammar and syntax, as these instances show; but *Measure for Measure* is remarkable for the extraordinary fluidity with which grammatical structures are subtly altered as a sentence unfolds, and the ambiguities of feeling and thought frequently express themselves in language which an editor must strive not to over-discipline for the sake of mere conventional correctness or unsuitably limiting clarity. Imposed editorial punctuation can also have the effect of insisting on one meaning where otherwise several possible and interesting alternatives reveal themselves. For instance at the very beginning of the play the Duke's speech has been assumed by many editors to be corrupt at 3–8:

> *Efc.* My Lord.   (fold,
> *Duk.* Of Gouernment, the properties to vp-
> Would feeme in me t'affect fpeech & difcourfe,
> Since I am put to know, that your owne Science
> Exceedes (in that) the lifts of all aduice
> My ftrength can giue you : Then no more remaines
> But that, to your fufficiency, as your worth is able,
> And let them worke : The nature of our People,

The fact that line 8 is excessively long, on the other hand, might indicate that the scribe has preserved a word or two which Shakespeare decided to cancel. If Johnson's emendation ('But that to your sufficiencies your worth is abled') is accepted, it reduces the line to a hexameter. Yet the author need not be assumed to be writing the kind of speech he gives Claudius in the first court scene in *Hamlet*, all obvious and platitudinously public. Shakespeare was able to reveal complex and contorted states of mind through ambiguous and disjointed speech at the period he wrote *Measure for Measure*, and all the suggested emendations to this speech on the ground of its supposed incoherence seem unwise. It cannot be proved that lines have not been cut or omitted in error by scribe or compositor, nor that Crane has not tried to decipher an untidy manuscript and in the process erased the evidence that might yield a fully coherent, grammatical sequence of sentences. Yet, as they stand, the ambiguities and uncertainties in the speech can certainly be successfully interpreted. There are hesitations and false starts, or changes to the grammar. Whether this is supposed to be the result of the Duke's actual state of mind, or deliberately contrived by him to leave his substitutes confused as to his plans and their respective responsibilities, is open to interpretative choice; but given the function of the speech in context – to show the audience a duke hastily bidding farewell, apparently in circumstances of such informality as to seem clandestine – and the function of the scene as a whole – to leave two deputies uncertain as to their respective responsibilities, the whereabouts of the absent Duke, and the duration of his absence – the suggestion of elliptical obscurity clearly must not be erased by editorial intervention.

It is necessary to dwell at some length on these lines, 1.1.3–9, since there are a number of passages later in the play where the same principles are involved. For example Claudio at 1.2.103–5 expresses himself ungrammatically, so that Johnson suspected a line to be missing:

> *Clau.* Thus can the demy-god(Authority)
> Make vs pay downe, for our offence, by waight
> The words of heauen ; on whom it will, it will,
> On whom it will not (foe) yet ſtill 'tis iuſt. (ſtraint.

But the lines may be spoken so as to bring out the changing structure as it evolves: the association of 'weight' shifts from 'pay down' to 'words of heauen' and then from 'heauen' to 'will'. Each added phrase changes the structure or suspends it. Editorial emendations seek to impose a grammatical or rational order: but is that appropriate? When compared to Claudio's later speech on death, the sense of oppression in his speech at 1.2 seems wholly characteristic of him. Submerged connections, disjunctions, mark the way that Claudio's introspective mood makes his delivery of his thought hard to follow. In his later speech on death at 3.1.118 ff., grammar seems to give way to accelerating associative process in Claudio's imagination; image generates image at a hysterical pace:

> To be impriſon'd in the viewleſſe windes
> And blowne with reſtleſſe violence round about
> The pendant world : or to be worſe then worſt
> Of thoſe, that lawieſſe and incertaine thought,
> Imagine howling, 'tis too horrible.

Efforts to impose grammatical regularity and coherent utterance here are not persuasive: 'Of those that lawless and uncertain thoughts / Imagine howling', for instance (Theobald's emendation) is inappropriately collected and rational.

The Duke's speech at 1.3.20 ff. is another case:

> *Duk.* We haue ſtrict Statutes,and moſt biting Laws,
> (The needfull bits and curbes to headſtrong weedes,)
> Which for this fourteene yeares,we haue let ſlip,
> Euen like an ore-growne Lyon in a Caue
> That goes not out to prey: Now,as fond Fathers,
> Hauing bound vp the threatning twigs of birch,
> Onely to ſticke it in their childrens ſight,
> For terror,not to vſe : in time the rod
> More mock'd,then fear'd : ſo our Decrees,
> Dead to infliction, to themſelues are dead,

Here there is the difficult reading 'weeds' which in the interests of reason Theobald emended to 'steeds'; and later on its involved syntax seems to tangle itself up, 'fond Fathers' never arriving at the active verb they require according to the structure with which they are introduced. Here a mimesis of actual spontaneous utterance may be Shakespeare's aim, the contortions indicative of the Duke's evasive and suspenseful schemes and habits of mind. A further instance of this may be apparent in the speech a few moments later, 41 ff.:

> I haue on *Angelo* impos'd the office,
> Who may in th'ambush of my name, strike home,
> And yet, my nature neuer in the fight
> To do in slander : And to behold his sway

This, like the previously cited passage, is discussed in the notes in the present edition.

READING LIST

This list includes most of the books and articles to which reference is made in the Introduction and Commentary to the present edition. It does not include the many excellent books on Shakespeare's comedies in general, nor does it offer a guide to the large and excellent range of studies on the early Jacobean theatrical, social and political contexts of the play.

Bennett, Josephine Waters. *'Measure for Measure' as Royal Entertainment*, 1966
Bentley, Eric. *The Playwright as Thinker*, 1946
Bradbrook, M.C. 'Authority, truth and justice in *Measure for Measure*', *RES* 17 (1941), 385–99
Brook, Peter. *The Empty Space*, 1968
Brown, John Russell. *Shakespeare and his Comedies*, 1957
Coleridge, S.T. *Coleridge's Shakespeare Criticism*, ed. T.M. Raysor, rev. edn, 1960
Eccles, Mark (ed.). *Measure for Measure*, 1980 (New Variorum Shakespeare)
Empson, William. *The Structure of Complex Words*, 1951
Felperin, Howard. *Shakespearean Romance*, 1972
Foakes, R.A. *Shakespeare: The Dark Comedies to the Last Plays: From Satire to Celebration*, 1971
Gibbons, Brian. *Jacobean City Comedy*, second edn, 1980
  ' "Bid them bring the trumpets to the gate": staging questions in *Measure for Measure*', *Huntington Library Quarterly* 45 (1991), forthcoming
Greenblatt, Stephen. *Shakespearean Negotiations*, 1988
Grivelet, Michel (ed.). *Mesure pour Mesure*, 1957
Harris, A.J. '*Measure for Measure*: A Stage History and an Interpretation', Unpublished M.A. thesis, Birmingham, 1959
Hawkins, Harriett. *Measure for Measure*, 1987
Honigmann, Ernst. 'Shakespeare's mingled yarn and *Measure for Measure*', *Proceedings of the British Academy*, 1981
Jamieson, Michael. 'The problem plays, 1920–1970, a retrospect', *S.Sur.* 25 (1972), 1–10
Jowett, J., and Wells, S.W. *Measure for Measure* in Stanley Wells and Gary Taylor with John Jowett and William Montgomery, *William Shakespeare, A Textual Companion*, 1987
Kirsch, Arthur C. *Jacobean Dramatic Perspectives*, 1972
Knight, G. Wilson. *The Wheel of Fire*, 1930
Laroque, François. *Shakespeare et la Fête*, 1986
Lever, J.W. (ed.). *Measure for Measure*, 1965 (Arden Shakespeare)
Lascelles, Mary. *Shakespeare's 'Measure for Measure'*, 1953

McGinn, Donald J. 'The precise Angelo', in J.G. McManaway (ed.), *J. Quincy Adams Memorial Studies*, 1948

Mehl, Dieter. Introduction to L.L. Schücking (ed.), *Mass für Mass*, 1964

Miles, Rosalind. *The Problem of 'Measure for Measure'*, 1976

Powell, Jocelyn. 'Theatrical trompe l'œil and *Measure for Measure*', in *Shakespearean Comedy*, Stratford-on-Avon Studies 14, 1972, pp. 181–209

Pope, Elizabeth M. 'The Renaissance background to *Measure for Measure*', *S.Sur.*2 (1949), 66–82

Rossiter, A.P. *Angel With Horns*, 1961

Salingar, L.G. *Shakespeare and the Traditions of Comedy*, 1974

Schanzer, Ernst. 'The marriage-contracts in *Measure for Measure*', *S.Sur.*13 (1960), 81–9

The Problem Plays of Shakespeare, 1963

Shell, Marc. *The End of Kinship*, 1988

Slights, Camille Wells. *The Casuistical Tradition*, 1981

Stevenson, David L. 'The role of James I in Shakespeare's *Measure for Measure*', *ELH* 26 (1959), 188–208

The Achievement of Shakespeare's 'Measure for Measure', 1966

Williamson, Jane, 'The Duke and Isabella on the modern stage', in Joseph G. Price (ed.), *The Triple Bond*, 1975, pp. 149–69